OUT OF ACTION

Also by Chris Cocks

Fireforce: One Man's War in the Rhodesian Light Infantry (available from Paladin)
Cyclone Blues
The Saints—The Rhodesian Light Infantry (editor and compiler)

Out of Action
by Chris Cocks

ISBN 13: 978-1-58160-707-9
Printed in the United States of America

Published by Paladin Press, a division of
Paladin Enterprises, Inc.
Gunbarrel Tech Center
7077 Winchester Circle
Boulder, Colorado 80301 USA
+1.303.443.7250

Direct inquiries and/or orders to the above address.

Visit our website at www.paladin-press.com

The powerful sequel to *Fireforce*—one
man's war in the Rhodesian Light Infantry

OUT OF ACTION

CHRIS COCKS

PALADIN PRESS • BOULDER, COLORADO

To Guy, Gemma,
Jarrett and Rebecca,
for their unconditional love

Chris Cocks lives in Johannesburg. He is the author of *Fireforce* (now in its fourth edition); a novel, *Cyclone Blues*; and is the editor and compiler of *The Saints—The Rhodesian Light Infantry*. He is currently writing a biography, of his childhood, of growing up in the Federation of Rhodesia and Nyasaland, and the subsequent adjustment to life in the rebel colony of Rhodesia.

Some names have been changed

Too many people learn about war with no inconvenience to themselves. They read about Verdun or Stalingrad without comprehension, sitting in a comfortable armchair, with their feet beside the fire, preparing to go about their business the next day, as usual. One should really read such accounts under compulsion, in discomfort, considering oneself fortunate not to be describing the events in a letter home, writing from a hole in the mud. One should read about war in the worst circumstances, when everything is going badly, remembering that the torments of peace are trivial, and not worth any white hairs. Nothing is really serious in the tranquility of peace; only an idiot could be really disturbed by a question of salary. One should read about war standing up, late at night, when one is tired, as I am writing about it now, at dawn, while my asthma attack wears off. And even now, in my sleepless exhaustion, how gentle and easy peace seems!

Those who read about Verdun or Stalingrad, and expound theories later to friends, over a cup of coffee, haven't understood anything. Those who can read such accounts with a silent smile, smile as they walk, and feel lucky to be alive.

Guy Sayer, *The Forgotten Soldier*
By kind permission of Batsford Brassey, Inc.

Chasm

I have held the deep, dark colours
Of my soul
In my hands
While Madness watched
Waited

His shifting features fled
Firmed again
My Face looked out at me

I drove his incohesive figure back
Fought back
To a room where meaning is

But he waits
He waits out there still
In the dark, deep reaches of my soul

Chas Lotter

PART 1: War 1979–1980

PART 2: Peace 1980–1995

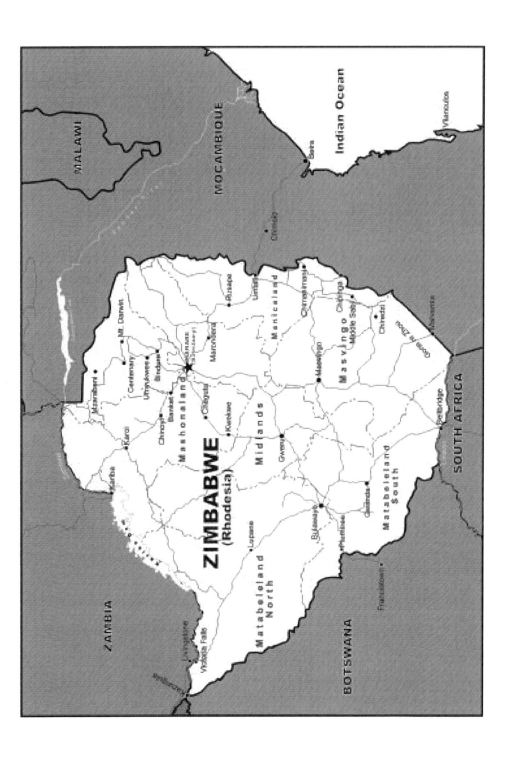

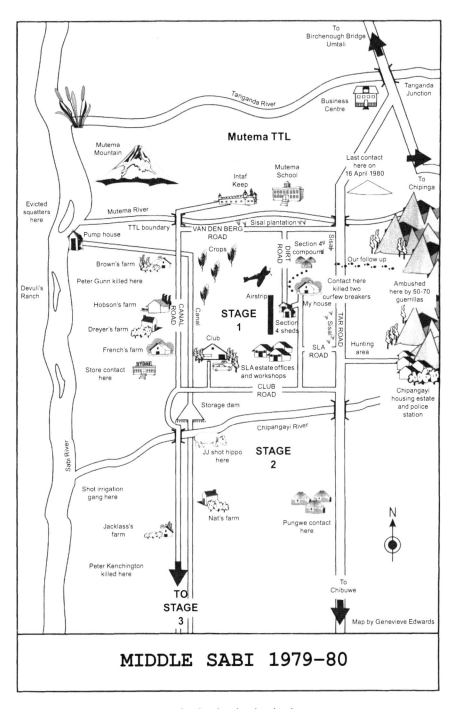

MIDDLE SABI 1979–80

Scale
10 kilometres

part 1

War 1979–1980

We come to the valley

Michael Gelfand Clinic, Harare: Tuesday, 21 February 1995

I have now been here for four days but it feels like a lifetime. Jim is in the bed next to me. He has been here for three days. He's eighty-something and he can't eat solids. He has cancer in his throat and they cut away his vocal chords. So now he has a hole in his throat about one inch in diameter where his Adam's apple used to be. It looks like an anus.

I like Jim and I think he likes me, though he can't say so because he has no vocal chords left. Jim's wife died last week and then Jim's family sold his house and is moving to England. So Jim's in the clinic with me. He's waiting for a bed in an old-age home. I suppose that will be when someone dies.

A woman from the Anglican Church visited Jimmy and me today. It turns out that, like me, Jim is an Anglican, and that a priest is coming tomorrow at ten o'clock in the morning to give us communion. It will be the first time for me in over ten years.

Jimmy has got flu which has gone to his chest, so he is forever bringing up great globs of phlegm. He doesn't always know out of which orifice the phlegm will be emitted so he has a bunch of tissues on hand. Sometimes it comes out of his nose and sometimes out of his mouth but more often than not he catches it at the hole in his throat. He can't eat solids so all his food has to be liquidized beforehand.

Two rooms down the beautifully polished corridor lives Lizzy. Lizzy is a black girl in her twenties. She is wheelchair-bound and a lunatic. Last night she tried to get into our room but failed, because Jim's TV stand had blocked her wheels from getting past the door. Eventually, Jim's night nurse heaved with all her might against the door to block the way. It turned out Lizzy wanted me to ghostwrite a book for her that night. It sounded interesting but we couldn't find a pen. And at any rate the night matron intervened and chased Lizzy back into her hole.

One of the nurses tells me that today Lizzy is being moved to another hospital as all the inmates have been complaining about her trances, her gnashing of teeth and wailing in tongue. I think the nurses will be pleased to see her go.

Middle Sabi: February 1979

It was unbelievably hot, mid-forties I guess, as we pulled into the Chipangayi housing complex. A black police reservist, his shiny SLR rifle leaning uselessly against the fence, swung open the diamond-mesh gates, the one side dragging in the dust as it opened. Unsure where to go, I vaguely pointed the Renault 12 in the direction of the nearest shady tree. Ten to one the cooling system was set to explode again. Goddamn French—always trying to get fancy with their cooling systems. I figure the asshole who designed them never for one minute thought the car would be exposed to mid-to-upper forty-degree-centigrade temperatures in a convoy situation travelling at eighty kays an hour.

"Let the dogs out," my wife snapped, her forehead beaded with sweat. "And let's get that dog crap out the car."

I pulled up under the tree, Bob Marley's *Exodus* still blaring on the tape. I could feel Ish, the Alsatian, clambering up the back seat, panting for the dry, limpid air. Her hot drool dribbled down on to the back of my collar.

"Fucking dog!" I cursed. "Where's her lead?"

We'd already lost Geronimo—the tabby cat—before we'd even got out of Salisbury the previous day. He'd somehow managed to squeeze his fat, furry bulk out of two inches of open window and had fled back down the road in the direction of our now-empty Greendale cottage. We couldn't have stopped otherwise we'd have missed the convoy departure time. My wife, distraught at the loss, had phoned her parents that night from the grubby Umtali motel with a plea to rescue the cat, if at all possible.

She scrambled under the seat for the leash as Jasper, the fox terrier, tried to make a dash into the front-seat area of the car via the handbrake route. My left elbow came back with a jerk and caught the little dog on the snout. It winced and retreated back in to the shit- and vomit-smattered back seat.

My wife glared at me. "There's no need for cruelty!"

She was right. I immediately felt a heel. In due course the dogs were leashed and I let them out. Poor things. They were exhausted—shamed by their own filth. It wasn't their fault. Four hours in the car from Umtali, with no stops. The bowl of water, most of which had been spilt over the upholstery a few minutes after the convoy had started its odyssey, had long been licked dry.

They rushed around, sniffing the strange smells, urinating sporadically and ineffectively, and getting hopelessly tangled up in each other's leash. My wife was cleaning the back seat of the car with a towel. Well, that was the end of that towel. I could almost smell her distaste for the task at hand and noticed her turning her head away, retching and gagging from the foul stink of the steaming dog turds and piss and vomit.

I observed a white man approaching, striding purposefully towards us. By his gait, it appeared he was a man of some importance, though this was perhaps an image he'd worked at. He swept up to the car with Jasper the foxy trying to jump up at him. The man looked angry, but not with the dog. It seemed he was the type who always looked angry or concerned. In his late thirties, he wore a perpetual, worrisome frown. His complexion was florid, probably more from the sun than anything else. He had the kind of skin that behaves like that. Apart from a not-much-used camouflage combat jacket, he was dressed in civilian clothes—standard farming garb of ankle-high *veldskoene* (suede bush shoes), sky-blue stockings half-up and half-down, navy-blue boxer shorts and a white Airtex shirt. Tucked into a trashy Rhodesian-issue holster, sat on his hip, was a 9mm pistol of some sort.

"I've fucking had it, man!" he blurted out dramatically.

In the corner of my eye I saw my wife look up from her dog-shit cleaning exercise. That wouldn't have impressed her.

"Uh ... sorry?" I muttered, unsure of the man's tack.

"Ja! Fucking had it!" he repeated loudly, looking at me for the first time.

"Sorry, had what ...?" I trailed off. I'd almost addressed him as 'sir', instinctively.

His voice rose another pitch, his arms flailing wildly. "That!" He pointed to what looked like a broken-down pick-up truck, fifty or so metres away.

"What happened?" I asked quietly, feeling I should have known about this. Was he angry with me?

"And another. When will it all fucken' end? When we're all fucken' dead?" His voice was cracking with emotion.

"Why ... is someone dead?" I asked tactfully.

It almost looked like he was about to break into tears, his brow creased deeper with troughs of angst. "I ask you! Is someone dead! Another good man ... gone."

"Who?" I pressed.

He looked at me for a second time, like I was some kind of alien for not knowing. "Oh right, you've just come in on the convoy, so you wouldn't have heard."

No, I wouldn't have heard. And anyway, people were being killed every day. So what? What makes this guy special?

"A first-class man. Peter Kenchington. Shot down in cold blood ... by these ... by these ..." words were failing him his description, "by these ANIMALS!"

"Peter who?"

He looked at me again, this time like he despised me. "Kenchington. Water Bailiff."

"Oh."

He grabbed at my arm and Ish the Alsatian made to go for him. I pulled hard on the leash.

"C'mon. Come and see for yourself," he choked for his audience. "Come and see what these animals can do. This whole valley's falling apart at the seams."

I didn't say anything. As far as I knew this was only the second white person killed in the Middle Sabi. The other had been Peter Gunn the previous year. My curiosity got the better of me and I followed the man to have a look at the ambushed vehicle. The driver's door was hanging open, liberally peppered with bullet holes. All the windows were shattered and the tyres flat. Broken glass and dark stains, which could only have been Mr. Kenchington's blood, covered the Rexine upholstery. Ish and Jasper sniffed at it, their tails erect, feathering.

It looked like they'd tried to burn the truck but hadn't been too successful, as testified by the uneven black streaks on the bodywork of the white Peugeot 404. The man was pacing agitatedly around the truck like a confused elephant calf mourning its dead mother after a cull.

"Sorry," he said abruptly. "I've been bloody rude. My name's Rob Hobson."

We shook hands. I told him my name and introduced my wife, Carol. He didn't shake her hand.

"You must be the new people coming to work at SLA?"

SLA—The Sabi-Limpopo Authority, a Ministry of Agriculture initiative, to open up large irrigation projects across the Lowveld, the southeastern area of Rhodesia.

"Ja, I'm going on to Section 4."

"Well, this must be a helluva bloody welcome for you, he said, shaking his head slowly from side to side. "Betcha you're not used to this sort of stuff, hey?"

I was about to say something when I felt my wife prod me in the ribs, like "shut up and let's get out of here".

"I don't want to alarm you unduly, but I think it's only right that you should know ..." he continued.

"Know what?" my wife chipped in, the edge in her voice plain.

Rob Hobson immediately recognized the tinge of her alarm. "Well, I shouldn't be telling you this, but Section 4's got a pretty nasty reputation for being a bit of a terr hotbed. Bad bunch that Section 4 lot. Always feeding the gooks. Y'know ... that sort of stuff. Seems like they pretty well do what they want. Totally rabid."

I couldn't mistake the challenge in his tone. Challenging me to get them under control—and I'd barely arrived.

"Well, anyway," he said abruptly, "I've got work to do, you know. The war's gotta carry on." He said it in such a way, intimating that we were keeping him from his duties. "Gotta sort out this little lot," he patted the Peugeot for effect. "You wouldn't believe the paperwork involved. Poor old Gordy Gandanga's up to his neck in it."

"Gordy who?" I asked. Like I was meant to know him too. I vaguely wondered where the corpse was. Cooking somewhere no doubt—not much chance of a proper morgue here.

"Gordy Allen, the local GC guy. Ground Coverage. Cops. BSAP. They call him Gordy Gandanga 'cause he's so effective in tracking down the bastards. But he doesn't need this bloody nonsense. Poor bugger ... seems to take it personally. And the member-in-charge at Chipinga doesn't help either—like he's almost blaming Gordy."

"Sorry to keep you from your war," I interrupted facetiously, "but how do we get to SLA from here?"

The sarcasm was missed as Rob Hobson gave us directions to the Sabi-Limpopo Authority central estate offices.

He shook hands with me again and said how he was looking forward to seeing us at the club that evening.

We drove out the gate. Carol had surreptitiously dumped the shit-filled towel in an old forty-four-gallon drum.

"Bit of a drama queen," she retorted, as the black police reservist closed the gate behind us.

*

I started my new job as the manager of SLA Section 4 the following day, overseeing 1,200 acres of irrigated cotton and wheat. I had just turned twenty-one, having fought for over three years in 3 Commando, The Rhodesian Light Infantry. A month before I had been Lance-Corporal Cocks. Now I was Police Reservist Cocks, attempting to begin a civilian career in agriculture. I knew nothing about farming, but I'd been offered the job a few months before by Jeff Fredericks, the managing director of SLA. Jeff's son, Paul, had been my machine-gunner in 3 Commando for a while and, I suspect, out of gratitude for 'looking after' his son (who was a more-than-capable soldier anyway), Jeff had offered me a job. I'd been quite touched and more than a little grateful. Jobs weren't easy to find in 1979 war-ravaged Rhodesia.

Ironically, although I'd signed out of the RLI, I was still officially a serving member of the Rhodesian Army and was expected to report to one of the territorial battalions for a six-weekly call-up every six weeks. Six-weeks-on-six-weeks-off, they called it. I'd been faced with a dilemma, as one of the conditions of my employment with SLA was that I attested into the Police Reserve. That way, I could serve my time in situ on the estate—rather than being posted far away to some remote border area for six-week periods. Quite understandable, I suppose.

Apart from the job angle, the thought of actually having to serve in a demoralized, half-baked territorial outfit filled me with dread. I'd used up most of my lives in the RLI and a TF, a Territorial Force, unit would almost certainly have heralded my doom. (Less than four weeks before, I'd taken several AK sounds through my magazine pouches and water bottles, on the webbing on my hips—quite how one didn't hit flesh is nothing short of a miracle.)

I'd approached Army Headquarters in Salisbury where I was told in no uncertain terms that I would most definitely not be released from my Territorial Army obligations. I pleaded my case with some poxy territorial clerk, wearing some meaningless NCO rank, but to no avail. For Christ's sake, my job was on the line here. But he wouldn't budge.

So with a great deal of petulance and anger I'd stormed off to Police General Headquarters, just off Manica Road, where I voluntarily attested into the British South Africa Police as a Field Reservist, no questions asked. I never really got to know the police rank structure, apart from constable and commissioner, but the attesting officer had been delighted to accept such an experienced veteran into the ranks, perhaps cocking a snook at the army.

I was secretly pleased. I'd bucked the system. Though, until independence some fifteen months later, I lived in fear that the Military Police would arrive on my doorstep and haul me away into detention.

A phone call that night from my parents-in-law confirmed that Geronimo had been safely retrieved.

Across the Sabi

Michael Gelfand Clinic, Harare: Wednesday, 22 February 1995
About a dozen times today I thought Jim was dead and I had to go up close and check his breathing. The night nurse says he has lost a lot of weight in the last couple of days. He's quite perky at the moment because he's watching an England vs. Wales rugby match. I don't think he'll last the week. Celia saw him crying yesterday. I think he's pining for his wife.

I found out today that Granny Crozier has two other grannies in her room. I'd always suspected as much while en route to the toilets. But today my suspicions were confirmed as the nurse brought all three of them out on to the verandah for a sit-down session. Granny Crozier is certainly a bit loopy. Her favourite party trick is to take her clothes off in public. Not that she's an exhibitionist or anything like that—just a nutter.

I also discovered a young girl in No. 10 who, according to Celia (Celia is my mole), has just had a silicon job on her tits. She's about eighteen or nineteen and seems quite nice, though Tim down the passage says her tits are still pretty small.

We took communion today but only ate the body of Christ and didn't get to drink his blood. Celia wants me to ask him tomorrow why he skipped the wine bit.

Middle Sabi: March 1979
Following the old army premise of keeping a low profile in and around base camps and, in fact, anywhere where men of rank are

looking to preoccupy 'other ranks' with menial, time-consuming and time-wasting tasks, I did just that during my first few days at Middle Sabi.

No one said anything to me about any kind of military or paramilitary commitment, and I certainly wasn't about to say anything either. Fully engrossed with unloading the Glens Removals truck and setting up our new house, I occasionally presented myself at the SLA offices, more or less central in the Middle Sabi irrigation scheme. I met the general manager, Max du Preez and the field manager, Chris Cloete, in effect Max's number two.

Both were affable, elderly Afrikaners and both with a twinkle in the eye. Max was marginally older than Chris, had more hair and was distinctly less portly. They both seemed to take to me and made us feel very welcome.

The outgoing Section 4 manager, also an Afrikaner, by the name of Jan, spent a few days showing me around the section and introducing me to the senior black section staff. I met Samuel, my mabalani-to-be, on the second day. A *mabalani* (a Shona / Ndebele derivation of the English word 'balance', therefore a person who balances the books) is a very important person on any farm, and is regarded with much awe and respect by the field workers. Firstly, it is accepted that he is literate and numerate—this in itself is worthy of esteem; and secondly, by virtue of the fact that he has more than a significant modicum of control over the wages, always cash, creates an aura of power. He is seen to have the trust and respect of the white man in charge.

Ho hum!

Jan had been effusing over Samuel before I'd even met him. "Get him on sides, Chris. He's a really good guy. The eyes and ears on my section." (Jan's continued usage of '*my* section' did begin to irritate after a while.) Slightly curious about Jan's almost sycophantic attitude to Samuel, I was more than interested when, at long last, I met the icon. Samuel immediately sized me up and I did the same. I saw an overweight black man, probably in his late thirties, with the big gut of a man who lives well and is not involved in physical exertion. His brow was beaded with sweat. But it was the eyes that did it for me. There was the look. Like he was forcing himself to look me in the eye, and seemingly saying, "What's your angle, white man? Are you with me or not?"

It was several months later that I was to catch him out fiddling the books. I guess I knew from the moment I met him that he was crooked. So either he had been extremely efficient in camouflaging his ill-gotten gains or Jan had been just plain dumb. Or ... maybe I was just plain naïve. But for the moment I shook his hand, making a mental note of his nervous grovelling. In retrospect, he was more than likely saying to himself, "Oh no! Not another one to break in!"

Perhaps Jan was right. Perhaps it was prudent to 'cultivate' Samuel. A crooked mabalani who was 'on sides' was infinitely preferable to an honest one who was not—if there were such a phenomenon. The burnt-out wreck of the Agricair crop-sprayer at the end of the airstrip, just the other side of the Section 4 sheds, possibly bore testimony to this. Apparently the gooks had done that a couple of weeks before my arrival. An economic target of opportunity, no doubt, but more likely a warning to the whites of the valley; whites who had become complacent and fat from the profits of the government-subsidized cotton prices.

Every other farmer in Middle Sabi appeared to own his own aircraft. Apart from the obvious prestige of such a status symbol, owning an aircraft immediately qualified the owner for PRAW, or Police Reserve Air Wing, duties. Certainly more attractive than slogging it out on the ground in PATU—the Police Anti-Terrorist Unit, itself a part of the Police Reserve, or possibly worse, in the Police Reserve itself, where, primarily, aging farmers were forced into convoy and guard duties. So PRAW offered a more glamorous, less arduous and a more independent method of 'doing one's bit'.

Added to that was the marginally less attractive bonus of building up one's flying hours on government fuel.

Samuel *tsked-tsked* and shook his head sadly as Jan was pointing out the sorry, charred remains of the Agricair aeroplane.

"That's what did it for me y'know, Chris," Jan stated, lowering his voice to emphasize the apparent tragedy of it all. "I mean, the airstrip's only four hundred metres from my house. The bastards could quite easily have put that RPG rocket through my kids' bedroom window." He studied my face for some sort of reaction. I tried to wrinkle my brow in a gesture of solidarity.

"So that night, I said to the wife, 'That's it, doll! We've got kids to think about ...'"

It was left unsaid that they were moving to South Africa. The 'SA' word was in many cases regarded as tantamount to treason—all the more so in the presence of a black man. After all, what would he think? He had nowhere to run. Bad for morale.

I tried nodding in sympathy, but found I couldn't. Not from any moral high ground, but simply because I'd never given it much thought. Oh well, I shrugged inwardly—good luck to the guy. I was more interested in his departure and leaving *his* section and *his* house to me. He was beginning to cramp my style and I was itching to take control of the section, all 1,200 acres of it, with a permanent labour force of one hundred and twenty people and a casual labour force of around six hundred.

A few days later, the same day in fact when Jan donned his newest safari suit and left the valley and Rhodesia forever, I was summoned to the main SLA offices. Someone called Errol wanted to see me. I clambered onto my bright green Suzuki 90 trail bike that I'd just bought from Frik Maas, the Section 8 manager and Chris Cloete's deputy, and raced off to the offices, my wife hollering at my back that I'd done enough bloody fighting for the bloody country. By now, the man at the gate knew who I was and, without getting up, nonchalantly swung open the red-and-white-striped boom with the deft flick of a toecap.

I vaguely knew that this fellow Errol worked somewhere in the workshops and that he was some sort of authority in the Police Reserve. He wouldn't want to be seeing me on workshop business, now would he? It could only mean 'doing my bit'. I parked the bike in the shade of a tree near the fuel tanks and scanned the vast area of workshops, an undercover shed with open sides, for Errol—he'd be the one in the white coat, working at the lathe, he'd said. There he was, beyond the ranks of the great John Deere tractors and combine harvesters.

Picking my way through the gleaming morass of machinery, I deferentially stopped in front of the biggest lathe I'd ever seen in my life. (I'd always been under the misapprehension that a lathe was a small hand tool, about a foot in length, used for trimming wood.) That must be Errol, religiously cranking away on a shining hand wheel, moving the impressive workings of the lathe along.

He stopped cranking and looked up. "Howdy!" he boomed. "You Chris?"

I nodded. He looked okay. Big and bulky, early forties, thick mop of sandy hair that draped down over his forehead, getting in the way of the solid, fifties-style, black-rimmed spectacles that geeks wear. Beneath the open, white dustcoat, he was wearing the ubiquitous safari suit. Long socks, the even-more-ubiquitous pale blue with double mauve stripes at the fold-down bit, and new *veldskoene*. A true Rhodesian, I thought. Better play it carefully.

He switched off a bunch of switches on the lathe, which was still dribbling water out of a thin stainless-steel pipe over curly bits of metal filings, and moved clumsily, with a distinct limp, to greet me. The lathe intrigued me. What on earth was it doing?

"Hi, I'm Errol." His voice boomed again over the constant roar of the workshop.

I shook his hand, very aware of his ham-like, vice-like grip. "I'm Chris. Pleased to meet you."

"Welcome," he was said, studying me. "RLI, I hear?"

"Ja." Civilians held this strange god-like image of the Rhodesian Light Infantry, so it was never a bad thing to say you'd served in the RLI. It certainly knocked on the head any unasked questions about 'doing one's bit'.

"Regular or NS?" he fired at me again. Setting the playing field, no doubt.

"Regular," I replied. Another big plus in my favour. Regular meant I'd wanted to be there. NS, or National Serviceman, meant I hadn't.

He nodded approvingly and grunted, pointing at his gammy leg, "Me too. Regular in Malaya, Congo and Aden. SAS." The pointing at the leg obviously meant he'd been wounded in one of these exotic places. Nevertheless, I was impressed. He didn't come across as the run-of-the-mill, skiving civilian pretending he wasn't.

"It's good to have you here,' he continued, still clasping my hand. "'Bout time we had a bit of professionalism in this fucking valley. Fucking wankers," he said expansively, waving his arm about, indicating Middle Sabi farmers in general, "all snivel off to PRAW and convoy duties. It's you young fuckers who have to do all the grunge work, and they're the fucking owners with a stake in the place. Cunts!" he finished succinctly.

I rather liked this vitriolic attack on the perception of white solidarity. This man didn't mince his words—a very positive man.

"Have you drawn a weapon yet?" he asked.

"No." I wondered briefly whether I'd done something wrong. Old army habit. "No, I haven't. Should I have?"

Errol was shaking his head. "Fucken' typical. The wankers get an RLI veteran into their midst—a godsend—and what do they do?" he asked rhetorically.

I shrugged foolishly.

"Fuck all!" he spat. "Don't even give him a fucken' weapon." He was still shaking his head. "Tell you what. I've got to go and see the member-in-charge at Chipinga tomorrow, so I'll draw a weapon for you then."

I shrugged again. "Okay, if that's fine by you. What about magazines and ammo?"

"Ja, I'll draw those as well. How many mags you want?"

"Dunno. 'Bout eight, maybe ten."

He whistled, nudging me co-conspiratorially. "Phew! You RLI blokes like your firepower. Dunno if I can get that many, but I'll see what I can do."

I was warming to the subject. If I was being re-armed, I may as well get it done properly. "And what about some grenades? And a shotgun?"

"Okay, okay. Slow down. You don't know what those Chipinga cops are like. They'll fucking demand a commission of inquiry if you carry on like this. Think you might want to try and win the war on your own," he laughed.

"So, I take it that there's going to be some sort of call-up for me?" I added hesitantly, not wanting to force the issue in any way.

Errol looked at me in surprise, "You mean you haven't been briefed?"

"About what?"

Errol slapped his thigh in mock resignation. "Well fuck me dead! I don't fucking believe it. No one's briefed you?"

I shook my head as he continued, "They've made you stick leader for the valley's northern PATU stick."

I wondered who 'they' were, assuming, correctly as it turned out, that this referred to the police up at Chipinga. Evidently we fell under Chipinga's control. It seemed odd that our Lowveld PATU operations were being controlled by policemen eighty kilometres away up in the mountains of the Eastern Highlands. But I shrugged it off. There was a lot that didn't make sense in this war.

I learned from Errol that there were two constituted PATU sticks in the valley, one operating south of the club, the mid-point of the whole irrigation scheme, and the other, 'mine', operating to the north. On paper each stick boasted a strength of between six and eight PATU members, but invariably could only draw on four or five at any one time; for a variety of reasons such as leave, illness and, as I was to discover shortly, just plain didn't feel like it.

"What happened to the north's stick leader?" I asked.

"Oh, that's Manie Dreyer. He's still in the stick, but when he heard you were coming, he decided to step down as stick leader. Reckoned you'd be more experienced and, anyway, he wants to concentrate on his tracking. Brilliant tracker, you know."

I felt a mite flattered.

"Oh, I almost forgot," Errol added. The member-in-charge at Chipinga has asked if you could help out one of the Chipinga PATU sticks."

I could see what was coming. "How do mean, 'help out'?"

"Ja, well," he said, clearing his throat, "you see, the Chipinga mounted stick has been tasked with clearing out the squatters across the river on the Devuli Ranch side ..."

"Mounted?" I asked. "You mean horses!"

"Ja. Horses. Can you ride? They're short of one man and the member-in-charge wants us to supply one body from Middle Sabi. Are you okay with a horse?"

Foolishly I nodded, "Ja, I can ride, but ... what about a horse?"

Errol slapped my back. "Don't worry about that. Paul Brown has loads of horses. He'll lend you one. I'll get it organized."

There! I'd done it—gone and opened my big mouth. Had I learned nothing from three years in the army! As a boy I'd learned to ride on my grandmother's farm in South Africa. But I hadn't ridden for years.

Errol must have sensed my confusion. "Don't worry, Chris. It's only a ten-day patrol—just trotting up and down the river, evicting a few coons. Nothing too strenuous."

Ten days! *Only!* My wife would be livid. She'd just started to get over the absences of the army days ... and now this.

Sensing my discomfort, and before I could object, Errol intervened.

"It's no big deal, Chris. Bit of a cuff, really. I'll get you organized with your weapons, ammo and rations and I'll speak to Paul Brown about a horse. The Chipinga lads arrive tomorrow evening. The member-in-charge wants you across the river by sunset."

He shook my hand again. "The Chipinga guys are a great bunch. You'll enjoy it."

Ja, sure.

*

With my heart in my mouth, the Arab chestnut vaulted the steep sandbank with graceful ease. We were across the Sabi River now, on Devuli Ranch. I grinned inwardly and patted the side of the mare's neck. The riders ahead glanced momentarily over their shoulders, perhaps surprised that the *Engelsman* was still in the saddle.

I'd liked Melody the moment her owner, Paul Brown, handed over the reins. She was a young mare, big and strong, many hands high. Although I like horses and can ride after a fashion, having been formally trained to ride as a boy at an elite riding school in Port Elizabeth, I don't consider myself 'horsey'. But there was an instinctive bond between the horse and me from the outset. She was spirited, she was graceful and she was exceptionally fast—something I discovered a few weeks later—when giving her her rein in the cotton fields, I took a turn too fast and was thrown off at full gallop into the cotton. Apart from a few bumps and grazes, I was uninjured and it appeared that Melody thought none the worse of me.

When handing the horse over to me, Paul pointed out the saddle that was on the horse. Did I mind that it was a McClelland saddle? Of course I didn't mind, but what was so special, or different, about a McClelland saddle anyway? Paul, a man in his mid-forties, smiled that wry, lopsided smile of his and showed me the salient features. A McClelland saddle, apparently, had been developed in America during the days of the Wild West, hence the characteristically high pommel (for fastening a lasso) and the high back. He went to great lengths to point out that it was almost impossible to fall out of, and that the high pommel also doubled as a kind of bollard on which to cling. I was curious about the actual seat, insofar as there appeared not to be one, but rather a gaping, oval-shaped hole, ringed by thinly disguised round iron.

"Erm, ja," he mumbled, "it takes a bit of getting used to and it can be a bit painful to start with."

I looked at him closely.

"But take it from me. Once you've ridden one of these, you'll never go back to the old conventional saddles."

I took it from him and said I'd give it a go, though perhaps a ten-day mounted patrol might not have been the ideal testing ground. Ten days later, I'd confirmed it wasn't.

"Get on," he interrupted my thoughts. "I'll adjust your stirrups for you."

I mounted the horse aware that Paul was studying me closely, no doubt making sure I knew what I was doing. After all, lending someone your horse was like lending your car. He grunted and heaved as he made the adjustments. I like my stirrup length short, not quite as short as a jockey's, but not far off. I hang on better that way and there's less chance of losing a stirrup. For me, a stirrup half an inch too long is like wearing a shoe a size too big.

The rest of the saddlery was standard. Having been a foot soldier for the past three years, I was particularly appreciative of the large leather saddlebags that Paul had provided. A plastic packet of horse cubes filled a corner of the one bag. For a ten-day ride it didn't look like very much, but Paul assured me that it was plenty. One handful every evening was more than enough. He went on to warn me that a handful in the morning would make the horse frisky, skittish and uncontrollable. I made sure to remember this sound advice.

I noticed that there was no rifle scabbard and asked Paul whether this was the norm. It appeared it was. Rifle scabbards are unwieldy and tend to snag in thick bush. Out of choice I had no sling on my FN rifle. Slings also tend to snag (in the RLI slings were forbidden). So there was no option but to ride with one hand on the reins and the other holding the rifle—somehow. Another challenge.

I'd met the three Chipinga PATU men at Paul's farm, where they unloaded their horses off the seven-tonner. Paul knew them and had warned me that they were quite dour. I looked at them as they saddled their mounts. They were very dour and appeared the very epitome of the *dopper* Afrikaner. Jacobs, Jacobs and Jacobs—two brothers and a cousin, sounding like a firm of Bloemfontein attorneys. Danie, Piet and Fanie, all craggy, sunburned, bearded men, descendents of the *trekboers* who had crossed the Limpopo towards the end of the last century in their quest to escape the tyranny of the despised *Engelsman*.

They introduced themselves with guttural grunts and we shook hands.

"Can you ride?" Fanie, the youngest, asked with disarming directness. His piercing blue eyes shone like steel through the black tangle of shoulder-length hair and beard.

"Ja, some," I replied, noncommittally.

Fanie muttered something in Afrikaans, the gist of which I took to mean that I'd better keep up. They were to ignore me for the next two days. Arrogant, hostile bastards, I thought. I'd show them.

So we came to the top of the sandbank that marked the western bank of the great Sabi River. Danie, the eldest and therefore the leader, had led us across the river at a shallow drift, a few hundred metres downstream of the pumphouse. The river is not simply one watercourse with a bank on either side. It meanders and weaves its way downstream, splitting into dozens of channels—some deep, some shallow and some dry sandbeds. The islands that break up the river's journey are, in places, a hundred metres wide, each island a miniature, self-contained ecosystem, with its own majestic *mwanga* trees, palms, vines, creepers and hordes of chattering vervet monkeys. From one side to the other, the river is over a kilometre in width, at places two, and it took us well over an hour to cross. Of course, there was the ever-present threat of enemy guerrillas. It was unlikely but possible. After all, Peter Kenchington had only been dead a week.

Almost naturally, I had assumed the rear position of the patrol. Up front rode Danie, his horse at a gentle walk. He was casually surveying the scenery about him, smoking a pipe, which only ever came out of his mouth for a refill. Behind him rode Piet, the cousin, and in front of me satanic-eyed Fanie.

The sun was setting, a massive red globe over the flatlands of Devuli, as we found our rhythm and distances—twenty to thirty paces apart. I assumed we would carry on 'til just after sunset. That way, any enemy which might be observing, would be unsure of where exactly we had stopped and bivvied up.

The gentle *clip-clop* of the unshod hooves in the dry dust was almost hypnotic. With the adrenaline of the river-crossing behind us, I took the opportunity to study my new comrades. They were a wild and woolly lot, not dissimilar to how I imagined the old Boer commandos of the veld seventy-five years before. Slouched in their worn saddles, their bodies almost molded with the horses. The mounts themselves were scruffy, tired-looking specimens, with low-slung bellies, small of stature like the Basuto ponies of the commandos.

For no apparent reason we broke into a trot. I saw Fanie glance over his shoulder—perhaps to make sure I was still there. I steadied the rifle across the front of the saddle with my right hand, the left loosely and gently holding the reins. Melody needed no guidance. I rose into a post, like I'd been taught at riding school. It was uncomfortable in the unfamiliar saddle and for a moment I thought perhaps I should emulate the three Afrikaners who weren't posting at all. Rather, they just sat, shaking and jarring and bouncing, like ungainly sacks of potatoes. I wanted to burst out laughing. It looked so silly, but with time I came to see that it worked for them rather well. That was their style and that was how their fathers and their fathers' fathers had ridden. Perhaps they were laughing at me—stupid, stuck-up *Engelsman* with his lah-di-dah posting!

We came to a halt. Danie had chosen the bivvy spot for the night. I began to understand a little of mounted tactics. The final trot to the bivvy spot was probably a safety measure to confuse any unwanted, would-be observers with a sudden change of pace, and to put more distance between them and us. It made sense and I could appreciate it to some extent.

I lay awake a long time that night, considering my circumstances. It was bizarre, almost surreal. Here I was on one of the largest cattle ranches in the world. Did those faceless owners, thousands of miles away in England, even know or care that I was on their land, set to expel the evil, black squatters who had so unscrupulously invaded their property? Were they even aware of these people? Christ! Were they even aware that there was a war on in this country? I couldn't grasp it, my confusion tumbling and scrambling in my head. It was not helped by the sense of loneliness—I felt an emptiness and an aloofness from my patrol colleagues. They still had not spoken to me, and barely among themselves. Brooding, sombre men, sulkily resentful that they had been torn from their farms of coffee and dairy cattle, wrenched from their *vrouens* and *kinders*, like me—to protect the interests of uncaring, greedy land barons, those faceless land barons—*Engelsmanne*, like me, or so they thought.

I rolled over in my sleeping bag and reached into the saddlebags by my side for my hip flask. Neat brandy to dull the loneliness. No guards had been posted. Perhaps the horses were our pickets. I watched their dark shapes, rustling contentedly in the light of the moon, sporadically tugging at the tufts of green sweetveld. I'd wondered whether we were going to hitch them to a thorn bush, to prevent them from running away. No, we weren't; not even a hobble. I'd copied Fanie as he'd unsaddled his horse. What about the bridle? No, that stayed.

The faint metallic clink of a bit sounded in the night and a horse snorted gently. It was comforting. There was something special about these animals.

I woke the following dawn to the hissing sounds of Fanie's little gas cooker. He was on his haunches, making coffee. Nodding a perfunctory greeting to me, he turned away, back to his task. I immediately looked for the horses. They were still there, a few paces from where we'd left them the previous night, still grazing unconcernedly.

Without any great sense of urgency, but with methodical practicality, we packed away our gear and saddled the horses. There was a job to do and it must be done. The sun was now over the Chipangayi hills to the east. It was going to be a hot day, well into the forties, I guessed. Already the birds had gone quiet, seeking out the shady refuge of the riverbanks. A Guinea fowl chattered jarringly in the distance. They would be pairing off soon.

We mounted up and at a gentle walk began our trek south. Danie, pipe in mouth and floppy camouflage hat pulled low over his brow, was studying a grubby 1:50,000 map, leaning it creased and awkward on his horse's neck. We were now on a path, wide and well used. I studied the track for spoor, human spoor. It was all over the place, fresh and undisguised. Civilians. Barefoot mainly, but criss-crossed with a scattering of *takkies* (sneakers) and the omnipresent *nyatelas*, the popular home-made sandals the black people wore, cleverly fashioned from old car tyres, with obvious, telltale treads.

An hour or so later we bumped into a young black herdboy. Not yet in his teens, he was wearing an old T-shirt of indeterminate colour and ragged khaki shorts. He had no shoes. We stopped, as did the boy. His cattle, indigenous Mashonas, with long twisted horns, ignored us, meandering through the acacia scrub, the big brass bells around their necks clanging in a subdued and not unpleasant cacophony.

The boy was stopped in front of Danie, his eyes downcast on the path, the stick of his cattle whisk painting nervous patterns in the dust. Clouds of smoke billowed from Danie's fresh pipe. The aroma filled the air. Piet had dismounted and was adjusting the girth under his horse's belly. Fanie had slumped forward on to his horse's neck, his head resting on his folded arms, bored.

Danie was talking to the boy. I caught an occasional phrase. He was speaking chiNdau, the local Shona dialect. Why are you here? Why aren't you in the PVs, the protected villages of the government? The boy had no answer and held silent. He wiped a trailing glob of snot from under his nose and flicked it deftly to the ground.

Danie appeared to be getting impatient and was prodding the boy's chest with the muzzle of his rifle. Prodding and prodding. The boy tried to stay his ground, but took an involuntary step backward. As he did so, Danie, seemingly awoken from his apparent torpor, swung the butt of the rifle around in a violent arc, catching the boy a cracking blow across the side of his head.

The boy fell to the ground, whimpering in pain. Blood oozed from his ear. I watched dispassionately, for a brief second recalling that T-shirt slogan that was doing the rounds in the white bars of Salisbury—'Happiness is red blood on a black skin'.

I could sense the mounting tension and urgency, as Danie's horse skittishly, unconsciously, trampled the boy with its hooves. The more it tried to avoid the formless shape at its feet, the more its hooves milled and stamped.

Danie turned to the rest of us, *"Kom kêrels! Ons ry!"*

I understood the "Come men, let's ride". We were moving out. Digging my *veldskoene* deep into the strirrups, I gripped the horse's flanks with the insides of my thighs. Already the damned saddle was beginning to hurt, but that was of no consequence now. Melody's ears were up, alert in anticipation. We broke into a canter and I found myself tugging gently on the reins as Melody shaped up to take off. She obeyed and kept her distance behind Fanie's horse. The jingling cowbells faded in the distance as I spared a glance at the boy, still prostrate in the dust behind us. We rode like that for several miles and after some time I began to feel an exhilaration I'd never experienced as a foot soldier, except of course when in an Alouette helicopter. But this time I was driving. I was in control. Up ahead, Danie's right hand came up abruptly and we drew to a halt in a cloud of dust, the horses panting and heaving indignantly. I was hard-pressed not to tumble forward over Melody's neck as I heaved vigorously on the reins. I saw Fanie smiling at me, this time a thin trace of approval. I'd kept up.

Danie was pointing at a wisp of smoke in the distance, rising faintly above the haze of the bushveld. He was talking in Afrikaans and I could only understand a bit. That was the squatters' camp. We must drive them out.

Where to, I wondered?

Smoke break. We dismounted and I led my horse off to the sparse shade of a thorn tree, loosening the girth a fraction. The horse was sweating and I briefly wiped her down with my cloth cap. It was a khaki-green cap, probably East German, which I had taken from a dead guerrilla some months before.

Mounting up a few minutes later, I was aware of the sense of purpose that prevailed. There was a job to do. It must be done. Get it over with. I felt a sense of unease. Were we going into action against unarmed civilians? As a soldier, I had never been deliberately, or wilfully, put into action against civilians. Would there be shooting? Would there be killing? I hoped not. I was tired of killing, tired of blood. But if it was to be … so be it.

We soon broke into a canter and in short time we saw the camp through the spindly ranks of *mopane* trees. With only a few brief seconds to take it in, we broke into a full gallop, like a fucking cavalry charge. Danie was shouting and whooping, waving his rifle in the air as we hurtled headlong towards the camp, a pathetic affair of pole and *dagga* huts and lean-to shelters, patched together from yellow fertilizer bags and bark twine. The din intensified. The horses snorted and whinnied in a frenzy, in clouds of avenging dust, as we rode down the women and the children and the old men, desperately scrambling and screaming to escape from the white demons. We were among them, this wretched band of humanity. Rifle butts were swinging, wood and Bakelite meeting bone and flesh with sickening regularity. I jerked on the reins to avoid a screaming fowl, but the hooves caught the bird in mid-gallop, mangling and grinding the bloody flesh and feathers into a single ether. Nor did I see the old ragged crone below. It was too late and the Arab mare trampled the faceless woman into the dust. She lay silent, unmoving. A cur, bony ribs prominent, slunk off behind a chicken coop, its tail gripped tightly between its legs.

I pulled up. This was madness. The other horsemen had turned at the far end of the makeshift village and were coming back for more, to clean up the dregs in a final sweep. Their horsemanship was incredible. I saw them wheeling their mounts, backing them up, twisting and turning, the reins hanging loose, as they went about the business of eviction.

And then it was quiet. The old crone wasn't dead and had dragged herself off to the back of the chicken coop. Leave her be, I thought.

For what?

In the distance I could hear the fading, frightened screams of "*Maiwe!*" and the anguished cries of "*Amai, amai!*"—mother, mother. And then they were gone, the silence broken only by the soft whimpering of a dog and the low, drawn-out squawks of dying fowls.

Danie had dismounted and was filling his pipe. His horse, untethered, was drinking noisily from a clay gourd near the dying embers of a breakfast fire. I too dismounted, loosening the girth off Melody's heaving flanks, sheened in sweat.

"*Verbrand!*" Danie barked. "Burn!"

Fanie and Piet were already about the business of torching the encampment. Very soon a black pall of smoke darkened the sun. I squinted through the flames that licked the dry, thatched roofs and yellow, plastic fertilizer bags. I lit a cigarette, its taste burning in my throat, and led the Arab mare away from the village.

Danie nodded at me. A gesture of acceptance. He was not smiling. There was no joy in his eyes, nor malice. The job had been done. A mechanical acceptance. That was all.

We walked the horses to the river and unsaddled, letting them wallow and drink in the limpid pools. I sat against a tree and read my book, Ayn Rand's *The Fountainhead*. It was another world—a world of altruism and architecture. I could not comprehend, but forced myself to read, desperate for something, some grain of truth to come to me.

The days blurred into each other and we trotted and cantered and galloped. My buttocks were bleeding, but the pain became a part of me. Perhaps that was altruism. We came across more herdboys, we rode down more villages and I trampled more old crones. And always there was *die verbrand*, the burning. We evicted literally hundreds of people, to where I don't know. I can only assume they simply moved farther into the hinterland of Devuli, poaching and rustling to survive. There they would establish other camps, which in time would be destroyed by other soldiers and other paramilitaries. It was a futile exercise in cruelty. Yes, the people were breaking the law. After all, they were not in the protected villages, those havens of sanctuary from the marauding bands of raping, murdering Communist terrorists. Our crusade was right. Cruel, yes—but right. It had to be right … I kept telling myself.

But the message was dulled and in the end I banished it from my mind. My buttocks were of more immediate concern. I had thrown away my underpants, useless, encrusted with my blood and pus. Fanie could see that I was in pain, but said nothing—out of respect. We talked of other things; of farming, of women, of horses. The war was not mentioned. There was no requirement. We were living it.

We shared cigarettes and he spoke English to me.

The tenth day came and we crossed the river at noon. At Paul Brown's farm the Afrikaners loaded their horses on to the Nissan seven-tonner.

Danie, pipe still clenched in his teeth, clambered in to the cab. He looked down at me from the driver's window, nodding slowly, "Ja *meneer*! You ride okay for an *Engelsman*."

The killing of Peter and Elias

Michael Gelfand Clinic, Harare: Thursday, 23 February 1995
Jim is better today but he still doesn't look well. The girl with the bigger tits has been discharged. There is, however, a young dark-haired girl in No. 20. We (Celia, Tim and I) are certain she has anorexia. She's as skinny as a rake and wanders around aimlessly with a scale tucked under her arms. At first, I thought maybe she was doing this for effect.

She tried to do a runner a short while ago. I saw her furtively peer out of her room. She was fully dressed in a maroon dress and had her bags with her. I didn't say anything to anyone—I just watched her go. But a nurse caught her at the foot of the stairs. So she's back.

It is currently the morning visiting time and I have no visitors. I think maybe they will be coming in the afternoon. I sometimes feel very alone. Yesterday I had terrible contractions in my chest (around the sternum area). The attacks lasted for about two hours. Eventually, I put it all down to smoking.

The pills took a long time to kick in last night and I only went to sleep around midnight.

I just passed Granny Crozier. She was going to the toilets as I was returning. She is dressed up in her finest and Celia has done her hair. But she is not going anywhere.

I feel very depressed. Jim is vomiting again. I can feel the tears starting to well and the shakes are coming back. I live in fear of telephones and I'm nervous when people come in the room. I'm scared of the people who will visit me later this afternoon.

Jim had visitors this morning and I told them the night nurse wanted some aqueous cream for him. So they went and bought some. It is for his bedsores.

I am crying at the moment. It all seems so futile. I have no control anymore. Have I really been reduced to this? I am going to have a sleep. I can't let the visitors see me like this.

It is 4.30 p.m. and still no visitors. I have a strong feeling that no one will come.

Junior, the young coloured nurse, is pushing Celia around the wards in a wheelchair. I think Celia is pretending to be a granny. I have re-thought. I think the chest pains are caused by all the orange juice I have been drinking.

It's too late for visitors now. Maybe tomorrow.

Middle Sabi: April 1979

1979 was the year punk peaked and I was missing out. I didn't fully understand that I was missing out. I only knew that there was some very good music around and I wasn't really part of it. Of course, I had choices, but I didn't know that either. I could have left the country—what was it then? Zimbabwe–Rhodesia? What a mouthful. In my short lifetime the country had changed its name three times, from Southern Rhodesia to Rhodesia to Zimbabwe–Rhodesia. A year to go and it would have its fourth name—Zimbabwe.

I was listening to the radio on a Saturday morning when this new song came on. I knew immediately, instinctively, that it was an important song and that the group playing it would undoubtedly go on to great things. I missed the name of the song and the group the first time round and sat glued to the Supersonic hi-fi for the next week, desperately waiting for a re-run. My patience was rewarded as it came eventually. It was an unknown band from Northumberland called Dire Straits, and this song, *Sultans of Swing*, was their first hit. It captivated me—the rhythm, the subtlety of the lead guitar, the words and, above all, the lead singer's voice—rough, course, almost out of tune. But it didn't matter. It set the mood for a year, for a decade. I discovered that the lead singer was also the lead guitarist and his name was Mark Knopfler.

And there were other new bands, exciting and dynamic. Elvis Costello and the Attractions with their hits, *Oliver's Army, Peace, love and understanding* and *Accidents will happen*. Elvis Costello—a bizarre mixture of names—a weedy Irish boy with nerdish glasses, hitting the big time. And Blondie, Fleetwood Mac, the Darts ... and Abba still going strong. But one still didn't mention the name Abba too loudly. After all they supported the terrorists.

I identified with these bands, with these singers. They filled a void in my life that I wasn't aware of at the time. They couldn't have been that much older than me, I guess, but it made no difference. I knew of them in their pulsating, thrilling world of rock and punk. But they did not know of me, their biggest fan, stuck in the heat of the dry African bush, fighting a grubby, little, vicious war. It made no sense. Oh, how I pined to be of them, so much so that I went out and bought an old PA system with cumbersome hundred-watt speakers and an old Scarab amplifier. And then a microphone and an electric guitar of no-name brand from the second-hand shop in Rezende Street in Salisbury.

And still the war went on relentlessly.

I met Gordy Gandanga. He came to my house one lunchtime in his beat-up Land Rover. My wife squinted suspiciously through the fly-screen door of the verandah.

"It's that policeman Errol was talking about," she said. "He's come to tell you about a call-up. Don't listen to him."

I ignored her and went out on to the lawn to meet him. He clambered out of the camouflaged Land Rover and slammed the door behind him. A little sandy-coloured mongrel inside the cab bounced up at the lip of the door, yapping frustratedly.

"Watch the bloody dogs," my wife screamed from the verandah. "They'll kill it."

Gordy Gandanga smiled sheepishly as Ish and Jasper came tearing round from the back of the house. The little mongrel yapped more angrily at the sight of the bigger dogs.

"Gondy! Shut up!" Gordy Gandanga yelled. The little dog slid down into the confines of the cab, as Ish and Jasper circled it, sniffing the tyres, ears erect, hackles up.

I shooed the dogs inside and Carol slammed the screen door behind them.

"Sorry about that, Chris," Gordy Gandanga smiled, his hand outstretched. "Gordy Allen's the name." He had a husky voice. It was weary.

I shook his hand, liking him immediately. He was about the same age as me, but he looked tired. He was very suntanned, exacerbating an already swarthy complexion. He took off his floppy camo hat and I noticed he was balding. A few ungainly strands of sweaty black hair hung over his forehead. He wore a camouflage combat jacket over black boxer shorts, with the inevitable *veldskoene* on his feet. An FN rifle poked out from the cab.

"Howzit Gordy. I've heard about you. You're the Special Branch guy?"

"No, I'm GC. Ground Coverage."

"Oh," I said lamely, not really knowing the difference. "You run the show down here, hey?"

"I try to, ja. I'm the only regular cop in the valley. All the rest are Police Reserve or PATU. But it's an ongoing fucking nightmare."

"What is?"

"Ag! Trying to motivate these assholes down here. They're always trying to snivel out of their commitments—especially those PATU okes from the south stick. Dunno why they just don't emigrate. No interest whatsoever."

"You mean Nat Pirsons and Jacklass and those guys?" I'd met them quite recently at the club and I liked them all.

"Ja, them. The member-in-charge at Chipinga hates their guts. Always cuffing it, claiming pay for days not worked, snivelling extra rations and all that kinda bullshit. At least your okes are pretty conscientious, which pisses me off because look at your okes. I mean, Paul Brown is asthmatic, over forty and has a gammy eye. He doesn't even have to be in PATU, for shit's sake."

I'd already met a couple of my stick members; Paul Brown when I'd taken charge of Melody, and a young Yorkshireman who looked like Jesus but was called Tim Anderson. I was still to meet the other two members, Manie Dreyer, the former stick leader and Ant Field, the Bren gunner. I'd gone apoplectic when I'd heard we had a Bren gun in the stick. What about an MAG for Christ's sake? Bren guns—they went out with the goddamn rinderpest! Jesus, what kind of a war was this?

Gordy told me that he had called an 'O Group', an orders group, for the northern stick at 1700 hours. The briefing was to be held at the police station at Chipangayi. It was to be a one-night 'scene'—that night—tonight. Yes, ambush. Yes, I'd be issued a radio at the briefing.

I told my wife and she was angry. How dared he intrude in our home like that! Who did he think he was?

I shrugged. He was the authority.

I climbed on my green Suzuki and puttered off to Chipangayi at five o'clock. Chipangayi was simply a paltry collection of estate houses, barely a suburb. The others were there already, sitting untidily on the verandah of the converted house. I recognized Tim with his long flowing hair and Jesus beard. His twinkling blue eyes sparkled at me. He looked every inch a veteran, though he'd told me he'd never undergone any formal military training. He'd learned his shooting skills from poaching on the Yorkshire moors. He'd come to this country because of his Rhodesian wife, Trish, whom he'd met on a kibbutz in Israel.

Paul Brown smiled at me—that quiet, dry, lopsided smile of his. He had some sort of facial disfigurement, the cause of the gammy eye. I admired the man. Fighting at his age. My respect increased further with time. Never once did he complain, never once did he lag behind, in spite of his age and his asthma.

I met Manie Dreyer. I'd been a bit unsure of this; after all Manie had been the previous stick leader and it couldn't have been easy making way for a young upstart like me. In his thirties, his boyish looks belied a canny soldier and a tracker unequalled. He'd served time in the territorials in one of their more elite tracking units—4th Battalion Sparrows in fact. But there was no hint of petulance. He greeted me warmly and welcomed me to the stick.

And finally I met Anthony. Gentle Ant Field—or 'Munda' as he was known. *Munda*, I learned, is chiShona for 'field'. Well over six feet tall, he had sandy-blond hair and the biggest feet I'd ever seen on anyone, enhanced by a big, booming voice and the laugh of a drunken hyena. He was fondly cradling the Bren gun like a toy and I found this gratifying. A gunner who cared for his gun was invaluable. Anthony was to prove no exception.

So this was my team. In the main, old and untrained, but bubbling with enthusiasm. It made me feel good and I had no reason to feel nervous with them. They had accepted me unreservedly and, I don't believe I exaggerate when I say, with a measure of respect, if not awe. After all, I was a rough, tough, mean killing machine from the RLI.

Gordy Gandanga, his voice hoarser than when I'd met him at lunchtime, called us into the 'Ops Room', previously the dining room. Sparsely furnished with one government-issue trestle table and a few hardback school chairs, I peered through the gloom. A single light bulb, forty watt no doubt, hung from the middle of the ceiling. The one wall was pasted from top to bottom with joined-together 1:50,000 maps of the area. I studied the patchwork and barely recognized the snaking blue ribbon of the Sabi River winding through the valley. Pins with coloured plastic heads were stuck all over. Incidents, I assumed.

Gondy, the mongrel, came trotting into the room as if he owned the place. Anthony called the dog, making funny, dog-like squeaks as he did so. Gondy stopped and wagged his ratty little tail, his little pink tongue darting in and out like a chameleon's. Gondy's coat was coarse and wire-like; his tail looked like it had been rammed up his ass by some kind of canine pervert. Yet, apparently, this mongrel was approaching institution status.

A black constable, informally dressed in a green T-shirt and boxer shorts, came into the room. This was Garikayi, Gordy's right-hand man. He was a confident-looking man, strongly built and handsome. On his hip hung a 9 mill Star pistol.

Gordy cleared his throat, but it was futile. He was hoarser than ever. What was it with his voice? I never did find out. "Garikayi's got some interesting int, gentlemen. I'll let him fill you in."

Garikayi sat casually perched on the end of the table. He spoke with a Shona accent, but his voice was clear and strong. "My informers tell me that we can expect the enemy in Section 4 compound tonight. They are having a big meeting there."

He stopped as everyone turned and looked at me. Section 4 was my compound, they seemed to be saying. Why wasn't I keeping it in order?

"Section 4 has always been a problem for us," Garikayi continued. "It's the largest compound in the valley and is not very close to any other compound. So it is convenient for the enemy. They can come across the main road from the mountains at night with too much ease. They can have the meetings, they can take some beer and take some women. And they can go back across the tar road to the *gomos* before the sun comes up. Too easy."

"Ja, gentlemen," Gordy Gandanga interrupted. "These fuckers are getting too cocky by half and we've gotta put a stop to it. The problem is though, knowing which side to approach the compound from. Garikayi says it's bloody difficult to know which end of the compound they'll be at. I mean, it's a helluva way across from end to end, maybe seven or eight hundred metres."

Garikayi was nodding his agreement as Manie Dreyer spoke. "How many gooks are we talking about here, Gordy?"

Gordy Gandanga smiled sheepishly as he wiped an irritating strand of hair from his brow. "Garikayi?"

Garikayi shrugged. "They say maybe fifty, maybe seventy."

I gulped inwardly. What! Fifty to seventy gooks! Were they serious? And Mr. Bloody Gandanga here wanted the five of us to take them on? "Will we have any kind of back-up?" I asked.

Manie smiled knowingly as Gordy replied, "Oh, ja. You've got Pirsons' stick on stand-by. But that means fuck all. They'll all be pissed as crickets at the club."

My question had evidently sunk home, the gravity of the odds, that is.

"Sorry, Gordy," Anthony blustered, "But if there are so many gooks, why can't we get Pirsons' stick to come along with us?"

"Ja, why not?" Paul Brown supported, nodding sagely.

Gordy Gandanga smiled wearily. "I asked Nat Pirsons today and he told me to fuck off. Said his stick had done its days' quota for the month. I can't force him when he's up to date with his duties."

I could see that Manie was grumbling.

"So, how do you want us to play it, Gordy?" I asked.

Gordy shrugged, resignedly. "Any way Chris. There's a major path leading from the Section 4 sheds to the compound. Y'know the one? It goes right past your housing site."

I knew the path. It was the one the Section 4 workers took every day, to and from work.

"I reckon you should go in on that path," he continued. "It's as good as any and at least you'll be able to approach quietly without bumbling through the bush. Remember, there's not going to be much of a moon tonight. And when you get to the compound, fan out on either side of the path and wait it out. Not much else I can suggest."

"What about curfew breakers?" Tim asked.

There was a dusk-to-dawn curfew in the valley. Only night-shift irrigation workers in the lands were exempt. (Five yards off the edge of the land and technically they could be shot.) Also exempt were motor cars—after all, how was one expected to get to the club after nightfall?

"Shoot the fuckers, I say," Manie added. "'Bout time we taught some of these fuckers a lesson. It's getting totally out of hand. They just ignore the damned curfew and wander from one compound beerhall to the next. I know that they're always visiting the Section 5 beerhall. My workers also go there, but I've actually given up warning them. What's the point when we don't act?" Manie was a settler farmer on the western side of the canal. Settler farmers were private, individual farmers who owned or leased their own farms—as opposed to the quasi-government SLA estate.

Garikayi was nodding his agreement, but Gordy Gandanga wasn't. A frown had creased his brow and the look of concern was apparent. Strange, I made a mental note, that Gordy appeared not to condone shooting curfew breakers. Was he soft? Or what?

Manie's assault was relentless. "No curfew breakers have been shot in this valley for over two years. It's a fucking farce. I dunno why we bother ..."

"Okay, Manie, okay," Gordy Gandanga interrupted, a trace of annoyance in his voice. "You've made your point. But curfew breakers aren't the enemy here. The gooks are."

I could see that Manie was angry, but he held his tongue. They'd obviously had this argument before. Manie was vociferous about it. Gordy wasn't.

The briefing came to a close and Gordy issued me with a crappy A76 radio and a few spare batteries. I stuffed the radio into a kidney pouch on my webbing and hooked up the handset with some old para chord to the D-ring on the left shoulder strap, as near to my ear as possible.

"We'll wait here 'til dark and I'll drop you off on the path. We can go in the Landy. Shouldn't compromise you. My Landy is often out driving at night, so it's nothing unusual."

Manie huffed and walked out into the cooling air of sundown. The midgies were starting up, as he swatted a bunch away from his face. "Ag, let's have a fucking beer before we go. Gordy, you think the cops can stretch to a few beers?"

"Sure. Garikayi!" he called. "Bring some fucking cold *chibulis* here."

The peace was made again.

*

I glanced at my watch, squinting with what little moonlight there was. One of those half-lights in which the flourescent dials on your watch don't work too well. So I cupped my hand over the face. It looked about eight. We'd been here for an hour or so since Gordy Gandanga had dropped us off at the start of the path near the Section 4 sheds. The walk-in had been short and uneventful, but it gave me a brief opportunity to set the order of the stick. Anthony, the Bren gunner behind me, Manie next, followed by Paul, with Tim bringing up the rear. I don't know why I'd chosen that order. I only knew I needed the gunner and the tracker close to me, and, well, Tim at the rear because he was younger than Paul and would presumably have keener senses.

Even in the gloom of nightfall I couldn't fail to notice the litter that lined the path—plastic bags, cigarette packets, old Chibuku beer cartons, tin cans and other debris. I saw the compound lights from about a hundred metres out and signalled the stick to a halt, pleased at the way they all turned outwards, crouching, slightly off the path, alert, weapons at the ready. Even Tim at the back had turned and was facing the rear. Important basics.

"Manie!" I hissed.

Manie came scuttling forward.

"Any ideas?" I whispered.

He shrugged. "Dunno, Chris. I reckon two on each side of the path facing the compound, and old Bogbrush facing the way we've just come in. Also need to watch our tail."

I grinned. "Bogbrush? Who's that?"

I sensed Manie's smile. "That's Tim. They call him Bogbrush because his beard looks like it can get around any S-bend."

Stifling a laugh, I *tsked* the stick for my attention. "Okay, Manie. You and Paul on that side and me and Anthony on this side. Pass word back to Tim that he must stay on this side with Ant and me, but he has to face the rear."

Manie nodded and we positioned ourselves, cautiously. I'd understood from Garikayi that the most dangerous time in approaching a compound was the last twenty or thirty metres. Apparently, the gooks posted pickets on the edge of the compound limit, a few metres in to the bush. The compounds weren't fenced, effectively giving the enemy a 360-degree escape route—similarly creating for intruders the very real possibility of stumbling onto a picket.

It was about half eight. I was longing for a smoke, but instead pulled the hip flask from my camo jacket and took a slug of the brandy. It burned down my throat, filling me with a warm glow inside. I'd long since stopped retching and choking over neat brandy. It had become part of my constitution. I nudged Anthony, lying down flat, hunched over his Bren, and proffered the hip flask. Turning his great bulk towards me, he took the flask and had a sip, nodding his thanks as he returned it.

I was satisfied with our position, four or five metres inside the bush from the edge of the compound. The nearest dwellings, mainly concrete-block structures with corrugated-iron roofs, were about forty or fifty metres from us. Occasionally, the shadowy figure of a woman would drift across our front, but it was, for all appearances, just another uneventful night in the Section 4 compound. The figures of two men could be seen wandering off in the direction of the latrines, laughing loudly and slapping each other on the back. And sounds of voices, fading and then intensifying, could be heard from the inner heart of the compound. Something was going on, but it didn't appear out of the ordinary. I wasn't sure.

I took another slug of brandy and tapped the top of my head with the tips of my bunched fingers—the 'come to me', or 'group on me', signal. Manie saw it and came, lithely scampering across the path, which happened to be three or four metres across at that point.

"Have a sip, Manie," I said softly. Manie grinned and took the hip flask, which was fast becoming a stick ritual. "What d'you reckon, Manie? Do we sit here and wait for something to happen? Or do we snivel into the compound and have a recce?"

Manie was shaking his head. "Uh-uh. We go in there and we'll be compromised in a minute. They're still wide awake. Something's going on in the middle. Maybe gooks, maybe not. I dunno. I reckon we wait a bit and see what develops. We don't want to spook them unnecessarily. If there are gooks here, let's wait for confirmation. One of them's bound to show himself inadvertently."

Some figures, obviously men, were fleetingly visible between a row of huts, about a hundred metres off. I only saw it for a second, but there was something about their stance, the way they were ambling between the buildings.

"Okay, Manie. Let's give it another hour and see what happens."

Manie nodded and went back across the path, melting into the bushes. A rustle at my side—Anthony was shifting his position, getting comfortable. I was impressed. They were all still very alert and we'd been here for nearly two hours.

I was rubbing my eyes, from the strain of concentrating my vision into the glare of the compound lights when I sensed Tim at my side.

"Chris, Chris," he was whispering urgently. "Someone's coming down the path towards us. I think there are two of them. Maybe three."

I listened, ears straining. It was unmistakable—the voices of two men, young men, talking loudly, drunkenly. No doubt returning from the Section 5 beerhall. My mind raced. What to do? Lay low and hope they passed by? But if they happened to stumble on us? Then what? Shoot them in cold blood? I had to hurry. The others were looking at me for direction. And if we did run and hide, perhaps the movement would be picked out from the compound and we'd be compromised anyway.

Something snapped in my mind. They must be shot. Finish and *klaar*. Perhaps it had been Manie's challenge to Gordy Gandanga earlier—about shooting curfew breakers. I rationalized it in a split second. They were curfew breakers. They were breaking the law and must be shot. Made an example of. Fuck them! Arrogant bastards—openly flaunting, openly violating the law of the land. We'd fucking teach them!

"About face!" I hissed. "Do NOT shoot until I do. Understand!"

The men nodded, nervously licking their lips, as they crouched low, fingers caressing the triggers.

We could hear them very clearly. They were still out of sight as the path took a bend ten metres or so from our position. Once round the bend they would only have to take a few paces before stumbling onto our position. I knew we would have to be quick. But then, the decision made, we could not afford to let them get away, wounded or not. Allowing them to escape would cause a loss of face for us. And wounded men can still talk. It was all or nothing.

For a brief moment I was sure I recognized the voices—young men who were my irrigation 'boys'. Maybe Peter and Elias, I don't know. I didn't want to know.

My finger tightened on the trigger of my FN. I peered over the sights at the bush on the bend. There would be no need to take aim at such range. Open-sighted would be fine. They came round the corner, talking very loudly, deafeningly so, or so it seemed in the quiet of that confined little killing ground in the bush.

I could sense the other men, not looking at me, but asking, asking, urging, "Christ, when is he going to open fire? Jesus, they're nearly on us!"

Still kneeling, I felt my body quivering, not with fear but with something else. It was an old familiar feeling. I was going to kill two young men. Dared I think it was anticipation? Adrenaline?

One step closer, two steps.

They were laughing now, lightly holding hands, as is the custom among male Shonas who are good friends.

Three steps, four steps.

For a millisecond I thought of my wife, sound asleep in bed at our home, not four hundred metres away. Well this would wake her up. That was for sure.

Five steps. I could smell them. They were less than four paces from us. I could see the whites of their eyes, their fine teeth flashing in the darkness, their clothing awry from the drinking session. One more step and they'd fall over Tim, literally.

Now!

My rifle was pointed at the man on the left. At his chest. I squeezed the trigger and the detonation roared in my ear, the rifle kicking with old familiarity, comfortable. One shot. That was all that was needed. The others would do the rest.

I saw the man drop like a crumpled rag doll as the Bren gun boomed into life at my side. Manie and Paul were firing furiously from across the path. It was point-blank. There could be no mistake. I lowered my rifle. The other man had fallen without a sound across his dead friend. Both bodies were still, not even a twitch. Dead, dead, dead, I knew from experience. It was that feeling of just knowing.

"Cease fire!" I barked, still trying to keep my voice low. The others had already stopped. It had probably only taken three or four seconds. A strange silence of anticlimax came over. I could sense the other men looking at me, perhaps waiting for the next instruction, perhaps wondering what we'd just done.

I knew quite clearly what we'd just done. We had killed two drunken curfew breakers. That was all. There was no room for self-doubt, no place for the faintest hint of remorse.

I flicked my safety catch on to 'safe' and was about to get up to inspect the bodies at our feet, when the strangest sound erupted at our backs, from the compound.

Shooting ... someone was fucking shooting! I glanced around, incredulous. Was it my men? No. Then who the fuck?

The shooting intensified and the all-too-familiar *thuk-thuk* of Communist weaponry was among us. For a few stupid, dazed seconds, I stared in disbelief at the compound. There was no movement, yet loud, vicious, unmistakable fire being directed ... at us.

"Take cover!" I yelled. "The gooks are in the compound."

The men needed no urging and, in a crash of bodies and weapons, the two corpses ignored on the path, they turned, diving headlong into the long grass and the bushes.

"There they are!" Manie was shouting, his rifle kicking and kicking, firing shot after shot after shot, rapid fire, into the compound. "They thought we were firing at them!"

Anthony was lying prone, hammering away on the Bren. Tim had scurried up the path and was lying prone at my side, firing deliberately, picking potential targets. A cool one, I thought irrationally, as I brought my rifle into the shoulder.

And all around came the enemy fire, seeking us out, getting ever closer and closer. Tracers buzzed and arced through the trees over our heads, zinging whip-like, tearing branches and leaves. I wanted to crawl into the earth. I wanted to stand up and shoot down our enemy. It was becoming a barrage and our fire was deafened, dulled by the intensity of the enemy fire.

I changed magazines, and in a second was again pumping round after round in the general direction of the compound. An occasional figure flashed across our front through the shadows. Where were they firing from? It wasn't that close, surely? Surely we would see them?

My mind was now concentrated, focused. Think logically, Chris. Think about it. What will they do next? Either they'll gap it ... or they'll soon enough find the range. Or worse ... a frontal assault? Not totally unknown. I was shooting all the while and changed another magazine. Anthony was changing magazines on the Bren, those antiquated, upright mags. Paul was changing mags. Manie was shooting.

Christ! I hadn't thought of it! What about mortars? What about rockets? RPGs? Surely it could only be a matter of time before they brought them into play? Gooks always had the fucking things—and a big group like this would have several—RPG-2s *and* RPG-7s.

The intensity of the firing gave no indication that they were likely to withdraw. I made a decision. We would withdraw. It was suicide to stay here.

"Pull back, you okes!" I shouted. They didn't hear me. "PULL BACK!" I repeated, shaking Tim and Anthony on the shoulder. "We're moving back a couple of hundred metres. LET'S GO!"

Within seconds we were on our feet, running down the path, over the two corpses, away from the mayhem.

And then as soon as it had started, it stopped. We were panting, heaving from the adrenaline. I signalled to the men to lie up. We stumbled into the bush and collapsed, dragging at our water canteens.

"Stay alert," I puffed. "Face out and keep your fucking eyes and ears peeled." I was listening, my every sense straining, for that dull *boof* of a mortar bomb leaving its tube. "And not a fucking sound. Keep dead still."

I considered radioing for back-up, but was too afraid the crackle of the A76 would compromise our position. In a few minutes we would know whether the gooks were serious or not about taking it further.

We waited, our hearts in our mouths, pounding into our brains. Surely the gooks would hear, surely? The compound, about two hundred metres away, was silent, an ethereal glow rising above the trees.

We waited. Dead still. Thirty minutes, forty. I don't know.

I made a decision. We would not go back in tonight. That was madness. Tomorrow, when the sun was up, when the sun was in the sky, the enemy's enemy, we would sweep back in. But not tonight.

"Fuck it!" I said loudly, sitting up. "Let's have a smoke."

The others, startled, looked at me like I was mad.

"It's over. They're not coming." I pulled out a pack of Madison and lit up, ignorant of the flame. I inhaled deeply, savouring the first drag as it sucked deep into my lungs. Shit, it was good.

Tim lit up. The others were non-smokers.

"Let's regroup at my house," I said. I was calm, my sweat now cold against my skin. The cigarette was hot in my fingers. "Make sure you've got a full mag on your weapon and keep your distance."

*

My wife was waiting anxiously behind the screen door in her pink candlewick dressing gown. There was a marked spring in our step as we tramped noisily on to the verandah, discarding webbing and weapons. We were alive. We were 'home'. We were the victors.

"Shit, what happened?" my wife asked fearfully. "Are you alright? I've had Gordy Allen on the phone every five minutes. Chris, you better phone him now."

I phoned Gordy through the SLA switchboard, no doubt publicizing the whole affair, as my wife went into the kitchen to make coffee. He was much relieved and said it had sounded like World War Two from up there at Chipangayi. How many gooks did I reckon there were? Thirty, fifty, a hundred—lots. Garikayi had been right—fifty to seventy was about right.

Carol brought through the coffee, which we laced with brandy, while the men relaxed in the easy chairs. They would sleep here tonight and tomorrow morning we would go back in and sweep through the area. Manie said the gooks would be long gone by now, back over the tar road and into the hills of the Chipangayi hunting area.

I thought of the two bodies—Peter and Elias, I was sure of it—dead on the path. And then I thought of my men. They had done well. Our PATU baptism of fire. We were comrades now.

Rocket and mortar attack

Michael Gelfand Clinic, Harare: Friday, 24 February 1995

Jim is dying but he won't let go. I keep praying that he will die quickly. He can't drink on his own anymore. I have even thought about putting him out of his misery. I had Jacky visiting me this morning, so she won't be seeing me this afternoon. I am going on an outing tomorrow. Celia went home today but Tim is still here.

Middle Sabi: April 1979

I was woken at dawn by the sound of a rough-tuned motorbike. Rubbing the tiredness from my eyes, I vaguely recognized the sound of Zack Prinsloo's clapped-out Honda. Zack was our neighbour, and in a short space of time we'd become quite friendly with him and Les, his demure wife.

Stumbling through to the living room, I saw Tim draped over the settee, snoring softly. Manie was on the carpet, rolled up in his sleeping bag like a cocoon. I picked my way around the prostrate bodies to the kitchen door, flicking the kettle switch en route, and pulling out a new pack of cigarettes from the cupboard. An empty brandy bottle and a nearly empty whisky bottle on the sideboard bore testimony to the 'de-brief' of the previous night. My head throbbed dully as I swung open the kitchen screen door. I insipidly knew I had to cut down on the drinking, but that could wait. More important things were at hand.

Zack was waiting under the paw paw trees, near the corrugated-iron lean-to. His faithful, emerald-green pork-pie hat with the little Guinea fowl feather in the hatband was, naturally, on his head, squashed down from the short bike ride. I sometimes wondered if he slept in that hat. The inevitable, barely smouldering butt of a cigarette hung from the side of his mouth. Zack, in his thirties, and recently driven from his family farm in Mtoko in the northeast of the country, was the Section 7 manager.

He'd come over to find out what had happened the night before. He was one of those people who is always happy, always vibrant, and ever optimistic. I suppose, with his kind of background, there wasn't much else to cling to. As a teenager growing up in Mtoko, he and his brother, Hennie, had been involved in a bizarre shooting accident. One of them was fiddling with their father's .22 rifle when a shot accidentally went off. The bullet zipped around the room and entered Zack's right temple, before exiting above his right eye. Ricocheting off a wall the bullet then lodged firmly in Hennie's left temple. Zack ended up partially paralyzed in his left arm and left leg, which caused him to limp slightly. Hennie, with the mirror image of his brother's wounds, suffered paralysis in his right arm and leg, with more of a pronounced limp than Zack and a modicum of brain damage.

"So, what the fuck are you war heroes up to?" Zack laughed. "You must have slotted a bunch, *ne*?"

"Nah. Just a couple of curfew breakers."

"So, what was all the shooting for?" he continued. "Waking us up with all that *kak*, just for two lousy curfew breakers?"

It did seem excessive, but then we hadn't bargained on the guerrilla counter-attack. I told him as much.

Zack invited himself in for a cup of tea, before getting on the near-immobile Honda and heading off to work at Section 7. As the motorbike spluttered out the gate and I was finishing my coffee and whisky, the phone rang. It was Gordy Gandanga. He would meet us at the Section 4 compound in half an hour, to begin a follow-up.

My wife was flabbergasted that we were still needed. Hadn't we done enough? What about our jobs? What about the cotton picking?

Must that grind to a halt because of the war?

Yes, it must.

We walked back along the same path to the compound. Gordy Gandanga and Garikayi were already there, questioning the people. No one had been allowed out. No one had gone to work. The people waited, sullenly huddled in small groups outside their huts. Garikayi was speaking to a young teenage boy, and by the boy's body language I could tell that Garikayi's interview had already got physical. Another slap across the head and the boy went spinning over the clean-swept dust of the compound, holding his hands to his head, futilely shielding himself from the boots and the fists. The people stood sullenly by.

Gordy noticed my stick coming in to the compound and, with the dog, Gondy, trotting happily at his heels, he came to us. A black look crossed his face as he greeted us. I could see he was holding something back. Perhaps it was the dead curfew breakers. Perhaps he really was soft. I said nothing on it.

"Howzit Chris," he said, coldly. "Bit of a *hondo* last night, huh?"

Yes, there had been a bit of a 'war' last night, as he put it. What of it? I nodded silently, wondering whether he would bring up the dead curfew breakers. A chicken squawked in alarm as Gondy yapped at it, lunging and snapping ineffectually.

Gordy glanced down briefly at the dog. I could see he was agonizing over the subject, desperately willing himself to broach it. His confusion was plain, but I wasn't about to help him out. Two curfew breakers who had brazenly broken the law now lay dead on the path. Nothing more. Nothing less. It was finished. Fill in the damned dockets if you must, but move on. Two more corpses meant nothing.

He heaved a sigh. I studied him directly. It appeared he had made a decision. "Chris, I'm going to stick around here and continue our interrogations with Garikayi." No mention of the curfew breakers.

I nodded.

Anthony, squatting on his haunches next to his Bren, was making those silly little squeaking noises to Gondy. But Gondy would have none of it. There were other chickens to chase.

"I want you to do a three-sixty around the compound and see where the gooks were laid up. Then I want you to try and pick up spoor and get going on a follow-up. Okay?"

I nodded. It was as I thought. "Roger that, Gordy."

Deep down I was hoping we wouldn't pick up spoor. Spoor meant follow-up, and follow-ups could drag on for days. From my army days I'd learned that follow-ups, a much-loved tactic of the Rhodesian security forces, invariably came to naught. As soon as the pursuers got within striking range, or got too close, the enemy would simply 'bomb-shell', or split up into pairs or individually, and meet up several days later at a pre-arranged rendezvous point. One tactic we had developed in the military was to leap-frog in helicopters, ahead of the guerrillas, hoping to cut their path. Quick, same-day service and, if it didn't work, well, so what? There were plenty more where they came from.

I fanned the stick out into an extended line and began the sweep around the perimeter of the compound. Almost immediately we came across the first picket positions on the edge of the bush line. Freshly flattened patches of grass, still wet with the morning dew, indicated the bivouac positions. AK-47 and SKS carbine 7.62mm intermediate *doppies*, empty cartridge cases, were liberally scattered over the thirty- to forty-odd sleeping positions that we found on the eastern edge of the compound. Assuming each position slept two 'comrades', Garikayi's estimate of up to seventy guerrillas had not been far off the mark. The positions were well laid out, evenly spaced about twenty to thirty metres apart. Fortunately the line of emplacements had extended away from us, so only those guerrillas at the nearest end of the line had effectively been able to fire on us. It might have been a lot more devastating to us had we faced the line of fire square on.

There were signs of a hurried departure. Several sleeping mats, those ubiquitous reed mats that serve the local peoples so well, were still in place. Unfinished packets of cigarettes; a half-eaten pot of *sadza*, the local maize meal; empty and spilled Coke bottles and various other bits and pieces that ordinarily would not have been discarded so. In the one position I discovered a grenade that had been inadvertently dropped. Quickly checking that it wasn't booby-trapped and that the pin was secure, I slipped it into my kidney pouch. If the BSAP wouldn't supply me, then I'd source my own armaments.

Manie, having detached himself from the rest of us, as is the want of trackers, was searching the ground for spoor some distance off. I'd long learned with trackers that it was best to give them their rein. Keep a benevolent eye on them, for any danger, but let them get on with it. Restraining a tracker was counter-productive and only frustrated him.

The sun was peeping over the hills of the hunting area to the east as we finished the sweep. It was already hot and I noticed I was sweating lightly. I pulled the stick up in the shade of some trees and waited for Manie to finish his business. The fastest way to piss off a tracker is to go bumbling in on his turf, possibly obliterating important tracks.

Dragging on a cigarette, I casually observed Manie. It certainly looked like he knew what he was doing. After twenty minutes or so, he seemed to make up his mind and came to the stick.

"So, what's the verdict, Manie?" I asked, still vainly hoping that he wouldn't have picked up anything.

"Ja," he answered studiously. "They've certainly gapped it east. That's obviously why their sleeping positions were on the eastern edge of the compound."

"When and where?"

"I reckon they gapped it soon after the contact, but there's such a mess of spoor all over the place, it's bloody difficult to tell the difference between civvy and gook."

Gordy Allen had wandered over, listening to Manie's prognosis. His dog had finally succumbed to Anthony's cooing, puppy sounds and was climbing all over his face, licking and pawing the big man. "Ja, that ties in with what the workers say. The gooks've fucked off into the hunting area," Gordy added.

I tried to appear interested. I could see what was coming next.

"The next thing to do," Manie said, "is to establish where their crash RV is—this side of the road, or the other side. I suggest we sweep up and down the other side of the tar road and see if we can cut spoor. My guess is that they've not gone too far. They can't afford to—they have to get their resupplies from the compounds. Also, they'd have to be quite close to water."

Gordy was nodding his agreement. "I don't reckon they would have gone much further than into the foothills."

"Okay, Manie," I sighed, resignedly, "Lead the way." I had a sleeping bag, two water bottles and a can of tinned pilchards. That was the sum total of my preparation for a night out. I felt resentful. I was trying to be a civvy, and they just wouldn't let go. So here I was—neither soldier nor civilian, not Arthur or Martha. I should have stayed in the army, I thought petulantly. At least then it would have been cut and dried.

Gordy Gandanga smiled a wry little smile. Bastard—he knew what I was thinking.

Manie, like all trackers, was anxious to get on tracks, and energetically led us towards the main Middle Sabi–Tanganda Junction road. At Tanganda there is a T-junction. You turn left towards Birchenough Bridge and Umtali, and right up towards the mountains of Chipinga and Melsetter … and the Mozambican border.

We negotiated the sisal plantation, about two hundred metres across. In the early days of the irrigation scheme, eager crop managers had ringed the entire estate with hectares and hectares of sisal plants, but low world prices and sanctions had made the crop sub-economic. As a result, the unharvested sisal had grown wild, its spear-like arms closing ranks to create an almost hedge-like, barbed-wire effect. Chris Cloete had told me that this had been done deliberately, to create a barrier against the guerrillas. I'd nodded at this apparent cunning, but dismissed it as bullshit.

Clambering through a tatty four-strand barbed-wire fence, we arrived at the main road, the asphalt already shimmering in the heat.

Approaching vehicles in the distance heralded the daily Middle Sabi–Tanganda convoy. Just after eight, regular as clockwork.

We waited for the convoy to pass. The lead vehicle, a mine-proofed Mazda pick-up, drove past. I recognized Errol as the driver. Zack, pork-pie hat pulled low over his head, was in the back, slouched nonchalantly over the mounted Browning machine-gun. I wondered if he'd ever fired the thing. Cigarette butt in his mouth, he gaily shouted greetings at us, waving wildly as the vehicle sped towards Tanganda. This was Police Reserve duty. The Mazda was followed by three or four civilian cars, mainly farmers' wives going up to Chipinga for their weekly shopping, or to collect children from school. They looked tense, gripping the steering wheels, concentrating intently on the road ahead. Bringing up the rear of the convoy was a strange, almost prehistoric-looking machine. It was a 'Hyena', a mine-proofed Land Rover, I suspect. From the side of the road, I could hear the poor engine screaming, battling to keep up with the cars in front, under the weight of tons of steel plate and bulletproof glass. Through the little blue-tinted pane of the driver's window, I thought I recognized Frik Maas with his distinctive *bok baart*, a dapper little 'buck beard'.

And then the convoy was past, a dissipating roar in the distance. Normally, they'd be back in about an hour, having handed over their charges to the convening Chipinga or Birchenough convoys.

Striding across the road, Manie was soon at it, nose to the ground in his quest for spoor, like a retriever. Please God, don't let him find any. But I knew he would—he was too good. I went through the motions of fanning the stick out on each side and a few paces back of him.

An hour later, a sudden gesture and a low whoop from Manie suggested he had cut spoor.

"Shit!" I cursed.

"Goddit, Chris," he called to me triumphantly, stopping by a large storm drain that ran under the road. "They crawled through this culvert and RV'd here. Perfect place—hidden from the road and easy to find."

I was grudgingly pleased for him. He knew his job and had done well in a relatively short space of time.

"Okay, Manie," I said. "You're the man. Show me the way."

Anthony started humming a Peter Frampton song. "I want yoo ... ooo ... ooo ... ooh ... ooh, to show me tha way ... every daaaay."

I smiled. Anthony couldn't sing in tune. But he was always in good spirits. Which reminded me—maybe I could sneak a slug of brandy. Why'n the hell not? The hip flask was again full. It had been the first thing I'd done when we got home the night before—and, of course, slipped a couple of ready-rolled joints into one of my magazine pouches. Yes, I'd certainly hit one of those if this dumb follow-up dragged on too long.

As we left the road behind us, progressing slowly towards the kopjes, the low hills of the hunting area, Anthony was singing Bachmann–Turner Overdrive's *You ain't seen nothing yet* behind me. I laughed out loud, warmed by the brandy. He had the stuttering down pat, though a mite slow.

"I met a gennle wormin ... she took my heart away. She said I had it cummin' ... but I wanned it that way."

I tried to march in time to his irregular beat.

"B ... b ... b ... b ... baby, you ain't seen nuthin' yet. BOWM BOWM. N ... n ... n ... no, ya ain't seen nuthin' yet. BOWM BOWM."

He ran out of words, laughing, guffawing, that drunken hyena laugh. I could see that even Manie in front, normally serious and conscientious, was laughing, his back shaking, his head moving slowly from side to side in astonishment.

The bush was getting thicker as we gradually climbed. Still savannah, but becoming increasingly wooded, with regular rocky outcrops popping up from time to time. Good cover, I thought vaguely. But the gooks would be long gone. We were wasting our time.

We were still in single file, picking our way through a pleasantly treed glade, when we came to a large grassy plain to our front. It was a good kay across, maybe more. Manie stopped and crouched, waiting for my instructions. I signalled the stick to stop, noting they'd automatically gone into some sort of all-round defence, in effect facing outwards and covering 360 degrees. I went forward to Manie, studying the lie of the land. On the far side of the plain was an almost wall-like ridge of kopjes, some sort of geophysical fault. Possibly a lopolith, I thought irrationally, suddenly remembering my old geography lessons. The ridge was rocky and well treed, a couple of hundred feet in height. A tall candelabra tree dominated the skyline, like a totem in a sacrificial temple.

"What d'you reckon, Chris?" Manie asked. I could sense his unease. Rightly so. Crossing that plain with no cover available was a great risk.

"Are we still on spoor?" I asked.

Manie nodded. "Ja," he was pointing at the ground to his front. "No question. Like a herd of *mombes* have gone through."

"Which direction d'you scheme, Manie?" I asked, knowing very well there was only one direction they could go. The ridge. The candelabra.

Manie pointed to the ridge. "Just hope the fuckers aren't waiting for us," he muttered ominously.

"Well, we gotta do what we gotta do, Manie," I said glibly. "We'll cross in extended line, well spread out. Single file'd be crazy."

"Okay," Manie grinned at me. "You're the boss."

Stubbing out my cigarette, I gave instructions to the men. Fan out into extended line. Minimum twenty metres apart and look to me at all times. Keep your dressing at all times. The men nodded acknowledgement and got themselves into position.

It was mid morning and, although very hot, the shimmering midday heat haze was still not upon us. Vision was clear and I could almost make out individual rocks on the ridge. I pulled out my binoculars, a crappy police-issue pair, and attempted to scan the objective. But I'd never quite got the hang of using binoculars; I couldn't get the two lenses to blend exactly. So I'd taken to using them with only the one eye and of course I never got the distance I wanted. In the army I'd sometimes used my great-grandfather's old naval telescope. Old but reliable—and user-friendly. I made a mental note to dig it out when I got home.

I signalled the advance and we stepped out, cautiously, feigning confidence. Manie was still on spoor, his head burrowed in the long grass. I steered the sweep line to fit his path and the men molded in easily. It was a good feeling to take, and successfully maintain, control of a sweep line. There was a certain art to it. I revelled in it. That was why I was there.

We'd only gone about two or three hundred metres when they opened up on us from the ridge. I suppose it was inevitable. We were still six or seven hundred metres from the ridge, so perhaps the enemy attack was somewhat premature at that distance. Possibly one of the newer cadres had panicked, or was over-eager to engage us.

Still, we were taken completely by surprise. The first we knew was the sound of a slithering, whooshing sound, followed immediately by a violent detonation not forty or fifty metres to our front. The ground rumbled furiously as the shock waves snaked forward to engulf us. Bits of earth and roots came flying towards us, showering us with dirt and debris.

For a moment I was nonplussed. It looked just like one of those explosions in those kids' war comics. It was all in slow motion, as if I were an observer.

Then I registered. "HIT THE DECK!" I yelled. "RPG-7! FROM THE RIDGE!"

The men needed no urging and fell to ground, seeking out whatever paltry cover they could in the grass.

My backside was still painful and scarred from the horse patrol, and I winced as I crumpled to the earth. The radio was digging into my hips. I'd have to sort that out when I got back. Nothing worse than ill-fitting webbing.

Time stood still for a few moments. Silence. Then another rocket, another furious explosion, this time behind us. I squirmed deeper into the earth, burying my head face-down in the dirt. They were finding the range. The rocket launcher knew what he was doing. I perversely admired him for it. I wasn't afraid, though my heart was pounding in my chest. I was thinking rationally. What could we do?

I peeped through the strands of grass to my front. Little figurines could be seen, swarming among the rocks on the ridge. The angry *pop-pop* of automatic fire from the kopjes could be clearly heard. This was of no concern. I was not worried about the AKs at that range. Too far, even for an expert. But the RPGs. That was different. Another explosion, this time perhaps a mere twenty metres or so behind us, testified to that. And mortars? My dread. Mortars would be infinitely more devastating than the rockets in this terrain.

What to do, what to do? My mind raced. We could turn tail and run. But the rocket man had that range pretty well sussed, and it might prove more dangerous than staying put. And dare I say, it would be cowardly, would it not? I still had something to prove and I could picture Manie's silent censure.

"Anthony!" I yelled, to the unseen figure I knew to be somewhere to my left. "Can you get your Bren into range?"

"Yo! No problem," a voice boomed through the grass. "You ain't seen nuthin' yet!"

"Well, what are you waiting for? Get a bunch of rounds onto that ridge ASAP!"

The reply was the comforting bark of the Bren. At least that would show them we weren't about to turn tail and flee. I squinted through the grass, looking for any of the Bren strikes in the rocks. I saw nothing, but still the little figurines scurried about the ridge.

I noticed Manie. He was firing slowly, single-shot, taking deliberate aim.

"Tim! Paul!" I yelled. "Get some return fire going." Another rocket crashed nearby and our firing stopped for a moment as the men shrank to earth again.

And then, an unmistakable *click-boof.* Jesus, sweet Jesus—fucking mortars. A high-pitched, whistling, screeching sound as the bomb plunged earthwards. Oh sweet Jesus! Mother Mary, mother of God—we were going to be fucked over good!

I cringed again into the ground as the earth shook and heaved. The explosion engulfed us, overtaking our every sense. Whiteness and blackness as one. The air was sucked from my lungs and my gut churned and I wanted to vomit.

And then the waves rolled away, the *pop-pop, crack-crack* still audible.

We had to move. There was no question. Before the next mortar came in on us. *Boof!* Too late. This time it was less accurate and, as the explosion tore across the plain, I grabbed the handset of the radio and called Gordy Gandanga. Pray God, he was at the Chipangayi base set. I'd never get him on his mobile Land Rover set.

The set crackled. "Gordy, Gordy. D'you read, over?"

Silence.

"Gordy, Gordy. Do you read?"

The handset crackled. A distorted voice came on. "Read you threes, Chris. What's happening? We can hear major contact from here."

"That's affirmative. Taking heavy flak from Charlie Tangos. Mortars. Romeo-Papa-Golf Sevens. Can you get Fireforce support?"

Another mortar explosion erupted, this time to our front. Thank shit the mortar man wasn't as consistent as the rocket man.

"Negative," the crackly voice of Gordy came back. "Fireforce not available. I repeat ... not available."

My hand was gripping the handset, the knuckles showing white under the skin. "Can't you get a PRAW up? Anything?"

"Negative. Did not copy. Say again."

"PRAW," I was shouting. "Fixed wing. Papa. Romeo. Alpha. Whisky. PRAW."

"Roger, copied that. I'll see what I can do. Out to you."

Out to me! Like, come back next week and see how your application's gone!

The barrage hadn't lessened in intensity. I had no idea whether the others were okay. Anthony was—I could hear the Bren still hammering away. We had to move. There was only one thing for it. To the front. Maybe we could bluff our way out with a show of aggression. Maybe. Not macho, gung-ho stuff—just a logical solution to the predicament. It'd take them awhile to re-adjust their range.

I dragged myself to my knees. "Extended line!" I bellowed, waving my arms to get their attention. "FORWARD. Let's take that fucking ridge!"

They'd seen me, staring wide-eyed at me, like I was some sort of deranged apparition, but I didn't care anymore. I was standing, weapon in the shoulder.

"LET'S GO!"

They rose obediently. My knees felt like water, my gut was empty, hollow. We trotted, a fast trot, waiting at every step for that hammer-like blow that would knock us down and kill us. We kept on trotting, getting ever closer. Steady. Keep it steady. The small-arms fire from the ridge crackled louder, like angry bees. I glanced at the men. The dressing was good. I could see Anthony was heaving, out of breath, struggling to control the Bren and keep up at the same time. Manie, to my right, had his rifle in his shoulder and was firing steadily as he ran. Good man. Tim was firing on the flank. Paul was firing at the other end. Good men.

Four hundred metres to go. I could now hear the AK rounds around us, above us. Horrible, cracking, buzzing. The white trail of an RPG rocket snaked towards us, but swerved off course and crashed harmlessly behind us.

Steady trotting. Keep on going. Keep on firing.

Two hundred metres, one fifty, one hundred. The ground getting rockier. Some cover. That was something. Trotting, trotting, trotting. Firing, firing, firing. Keep it mechanical.

Fifty metres to go to the foot of the ridge. And then the air was filled with the roaring sound of an aeroplane, droning, lumbering at our backs towards the ridge. I gasped, breathless, looking up, as the cumbersome beast swooped low over our heads and climbed angrily, almost vertically to the summit. And then he was gone, in a tight turn into the sun, coming back for another run.

The PRAW pilot was on his radio to me. "Chris, Chris," he was gabbling excitedly. "Charlie Tangos are gapping it. Down the other side. Like fucking rabbits. Jesus! They're all over the place."

The plane swarmed low for another run. That Cessna sound had to be the most comforting feeling in the world. I stood tall, urging the men up the ridge, to the summit. Like *dassies*, rock rabbits, we scrambled and clawed our way up, tripping over rocks, but uncaring. The summit of the ridge had become our life purpose. The enemy had long since stopped firing, fleeing east into the mountains. And breathless, exhausted, we came to the top.

Firing a few desultory shots at fast-vanishing figures in the distance, we collapsed on the rocks—a few minutes before the enemy's sanctuary—now ours.

It was done.

"Chris, d'you read?" It was the PRAW pilot, circling overhead.

I wondered who the pilot was. "Go."

"Roger, I'm returning to base. You okay to get back from there? Need any more help?"

"Negative, thanks for your help."

"Roger that. We'll see you at the pub tonight. Cheers and out."

Old fossils

Michael Gelfand Clinic, Harare: Saturday, 25 February 1995

I am very excited as today I am going home for the day. I am being collected at 11 a.m. I was up at dawn and had a bath and a shave. I am determined to show Jacky that I am 'normal' and that I have things under control.

Jim is still alive—just. He can no longer drink as the liquid just pours out from the hole in his throat. I asked the night nurse if this means that he has to go on to a drip and she said, "No, there is nothing anyone can do for him now."

Middle Sabi: May 1979

Life took a turn towards some sort of normality, though normality was an unknown for me. I was guessing what it was like to be a civilian, what it was like to be a farmer. I went through the motions of appearing for work at the section every day. It became routine— allocating the *gwazas,* the piecework, for the day. So many hundreds of metres weeding per man, and, if he was done by ten, then good luck to him—he could knock off. Many of the workers would recruit their wives and children to assist.

The day after our contact in the hills, the follow-up after the killing of the curfew breakers, I had arrived at work on my green Suzuki. Samuel opened up the section gates and let me in. Not a word was said on the subject. It was as if it had never happened. I kept waiting for the recriminations, the accusations, the look in the eyes that screamed 'murderer'. But nothing. It was as if Peter and Elias had never existed.

In a way I was grateful that I didn't have to face their anger and their pain. But in a way the silence was worse. They knew I was involved. They knew, they just knew.

I tried to broach the subject, perhaps a modern-day Macbeth. "Samuel, did you hear all that shooting at the compound that night?"

Samuel, his eyes downcast, glanced at me for a split second, checking whether he had heard right. "Yes, sah. Everyone was hearing the shooting. Very, very terrible."

"Yes, awful. I heard they were curfew breakers?"

Samuel looked at me again, this time longer. His brow was perspiring lightly. He knew that I knew. The one eye squinted a fraction, the tiniest flicker of disapproval, of censure. It was as if he were saying, "Why did you do that, white man? What for? The *vakomwana,* the 'boys', were in the compound. But what of it? They weren't causing trouble. They weren't attacking you whites. Why did you have to do it? Why?" But instead he said, "They had been drinking beer at Section 5. They were drunk. They did not know."

I nodded. It was his way of saying, curfew breakers or not, they were innocent civilians who had inadvertently broken the law. A warning perhaps or a fine. Even gaol. But death?

I smiled thinly at him. "Well, it is finished now. Have the cotton scouts come in yet?"

He handed me the results. It was a daily ritual and something that intrigued me. Cotton scouting is a crucial aspect of growing cotton. Every day, the cotton scouts, generally workers who'd shown some ambition and intelligence and who'd attended various agronomic courses, would go into the vast, flat cotton lands and literally scout for cotton pests—the myriad of bugs and worms that could destroy a crop within days.

It was a whole new world to me. Here was an enemy, in some cases, micro-millimetres in size and almost invisible to the naked eye, that needed constant monitoring, constant surveillance and continual chemical control. The list seemed endless, with each variety of pest having a peculiar modus operandus. Red bollworms and American bollworms—great caterpillars that bored into the developing cotton boll and rendered it unusable; loopers and semi-loopers that ate the leaves; aphids and red spider mites that attacked the underside of the leaves, dessicating and killing. On and on and on. For a time, I actually wondered why we grew the crop at all, so vulnerable was it to the vagaries of nature. And then the strategies and the tactics of chemical spraying—for when the pest levels reached a certain threshold there was no option but to spray. There were dozens of different insecticides, acaricides and fungicides with dozens of permutations for mixing into cocktails, to kill as wide a cross-section of pests as possible. Agricair was back in business—a new crop-sprayer had been dispatched to the valley as a replacement for the charred wreck that still sat on the runway. The aeroplane was busy each and every day, spraying hundreds and hundreds of hectares.

I enjoyed the science of it and soon found myself co-ordinating the crop-spraying programme for the entire estate and not just my own section. It was tangible. Here was an enemy—deal with him.

But in reality, we section managers had very little control as to how the crop was grown. We were told which tractors and which implements would be used for the land preparation. (Anthony was in overall charge of the estate land prep.) We were told which variety of seed to plant. We were told what fertilizers to use and what rates to apply. We were told what irrigation cycles to use.

We were effectively administrative managers, weighing in the cotton and paying the wages. There was little incentive offered and little initiative required.

The settler farmers, on the other hand, were very different. In the main ambitious, innovative and eager to reap large yields, they ran their farms efficiently and productively.

I became friendly with several of the young settler-farm managers, most of whom were in the south PATU stick. Nat Pirsons, the blond stick leader, was a year or two older than me. Unlike me he had a qualification—he'd attended Gwebi Agricultural College near Salisbury where he'd gained his agricultural diploma. With deadly straight, peroxide-type hair, an indication of his northern European heritage, he was a cocky, jovial type with an acerbic wit and not too much respect for our parents' generation, let alone blacks. Both our elders and 'our blacks' were obviously the cause of this stupid war, this futile waste-of-time war that got in the way of the proper issues at hand—like making money.

'Jacklass' van Deventer was Nat's perfect foil, with an equally passionate dislike of the war and everything it stood for. Not as vitriolic as Nat, Jacklass expressed his dissatisfaction with an unco-operative and work-to-rule approach to military commitments. He was nicknamed 'Jacklass', an Anglicized derivative of the chiShona for 'jackal', because of his dark, angular features.

Another south stick member was Nev Paterson, a witty land surveyor, seconded to SLA to open up new lands in the bush south of the estate. With eyes like a spaniel and a droopy Zapata moustache, he was a happy-go-lucky fellow, who fell in with Pirsons and van Deventer without hitch. Jimmy Dawson, a good few years older than the rest of us, was the one stick member who had a passion for military work, though this was never allowed to override the general lethargic climate in the stick.

The last member was a complete enigma. Pim Erlank, or 'Lank', a Dutch Reformed Church stalwart, was a *dominee*-in-waiting, a gentle giant who wore a perpetual grin on his face. Swarthy and built like a lock forward, he handled the stick's heavy-barrelled FN with consummate ease. He fitted in easily and, although an excellent soldier, he was very amenable to the avoidance of military excesses as espoused by his stick leader.

We would meet at the club every evening and drink the night away, playing darts, snooker and cards. The wives of the valley would organize the club dinners and for two dollars, the meal was a giveaway.

Invariably Nat and Jacklass would get involved in an argument with some of the 'old fossils', as they were referred to, (or alternatively 'borrowers' or 'oxygen thieves'). Don Hounslow was usually the target. Don could best be described as 'a man of Africa'. Gnarled and sunburned, with bushy, blond eyebrows and the inevitable khaki safari suit, he was everything that epitomized our parents' generation. Old-fashioned, conservative, staunchly pro-establishment, he would brook no truck from young upstarts like Nat and Jacklass. Unfortunately for Nat and Jacklass, Don held some sort of senior position in the Police Reserve, with a certain amount of authority over our PATU sticks. I also found this extremely galling. Simply because he was a solid and enthusiastic supporter of the war and because of his age, he could call the shots.

"So you old fossil," Nat would say, cane and Coke in hand at the bar counter. "What fucken' wild goose chase are you Napoleons going to send us on next? More ambushes in the middle of nowhere? Just hoping that maybe some gook stupid enough will happen to stumble on our cunningly laid ambush?"

"Hey!" Don grunted, eyes bleary in the glass of whisky. "Wotcha fucken' language. There's women here."

Jacklass, at Nat's side, baited some more. "Ja, what do you okes do? Stick a map on the dartboard and where the dart lands, that's where the ambush'll be?"

Nat laughed aggressively. "Tactics, Jacklass, tactics. The gooks are bound to fall into the trap. I mean, with fifty thousand square miles to choose from, they just *have* to fall into our trap. Amazing odds."

"We have to keep a presence at all times," Don grunted, still trying to maintain a semblance of authority, the youngsters' sarcasm lost on him.

"Hah!" Nat snorted. "Is that how come we're winning the war?"

Don shook his head slowly, like addressing a recalcitrant schoolboy. "Lissen, sonny! It's a question of containing the war until the politicians can reach a settlement with the terrorists. Politics, my boy, politics. You wouldn't understand."

"Wellington!" Jacklass shouted to the black barman. "More *doro*! Now! Same again. You better give the old man one more. Then he must go home. He's had enough."

Wellington, ever eager, grinned and reached for the cane and whisky bottles.

"Hey! Pup!" Don turned to Jacklass, trying to focus. "Who rattled your fucken' cage? Less of the fucken' 'old', huh!"

"Steady, Don. There're women present," Nat mimicked.

Don was quite drunk now. "Agh! Fuck the women!" he slurred.

"Wouldn't you wish?" Nat quipped.

Wellington lined up the fresh glasses on the counter, wary of the build-up of tension on the other side. The young white men would not let up and the old man would not leave. It could only come to one thing.

The older man was now prodding the one youngster in the chest with his finger. "Lissen here, Nat. Any more of your shit and I'm going to get you thrown out of PATU, y'hear!"

Nat and Jacklass collapsed in hysterical laughter. "Shit, Don. Where do we sign? Discharge us now. Dishonourably! Please, please, anything," they implored.

Don missed it. "I can you know. I can get you fucken' thrown out," he continued earnestly.

"Well, you old fossil. Don't just boast about it. DO IT!" Nat challenged.

This was the last straw for Don. He staggered to his feet, the barstool clattering on to the quarry-tiled floor. "I'm gonna teach you young whippersnappers a fucken' lesson, y'hear!" He swung a fist at Nat, wild and inaccurate. Nat grabbed the outstretched arm and locked it in a vice-like grip, patting Don's cheek at the same time. This infuriated the older man and he struggled like a wounded buffalo, heaving and cussing, vainly trying to escape the grip. And the more he struggled, the more Nat and Jacklass laughed. Another bar stool went tumbling, glasses smashed to the floor and the women left the bar, haughtily shaking their heads and muttering that, honestly, these were supposed to be grown men. It was pretty well like this every night. In some respects, I actually think Don enjoyed it. Perhaps not, but he kept coming back for more.

Through all this brouhaha, Zack and I would carry on with our darts. We were becoming a formidable team, and only Tim and Jimmy Dawson would occasionally get the better of us. Tim, also a precise shottist, driven during his Yorkshire youth by hunger and the resultant poaching, was arguably the best darts player in the valley. He was also English and all Englishmen were good darts players. So he said.

It was in May 1979 that Carol broke the news to me that she was pregnant. She was twenty and I still only twenty-one, but I took it all in my stride, possibly because I had no idea of what was entailed. I vaguely knew that having children was a cumbersome and burdensome responsibility. But was I not a man? Had I not endured more than three years of bloody warfare? Surely, a child was easily manageable after that? Surely?

My parents in Salisbury were suitably mortified. I had not been the model child during the past five years. Aged sixteen, I had prematurely and under unpleasant circumstances left the exclusive private school I'd been attending. I'd continued with my education at Commercial Careers College in Salisbury, where no one seemed to give a damn whether you grew long, unwashed hair, wore filthy jeans and smoked dope. As a result, there was nothing to rebel against, so I'd knuckled down to my A' Level studies, between frenetic bouts of pinball, and surprisingly, passed four.

Then came the army. That dreaded little manila envelope arrived one day at my parents' house. My call-up papers for my national service. Romantically, I considered myself a 'Communist' and a pacifist (anything—as long as it rebelled agsinst the system), so, 'for the cause', naturally made plans to desert. I'd been accepted to the Sorbonne to study law, but the question of desertion was more pressing, as was the lure of a Panamanian cargo ship perhaps waiting for me in the Lourenço Marques harbour.

In the end, I got cold feet, succumbing to a fear of the system and my parents more than anything else, and had duly presented myself at Cranborne Barracks in Salisbury on 6 January 1976. It was to change the course of my life—irrevocably. Midway through my term of the one-year national-service period, the Minister of Manpower, Roger Hawkins, another of the out-of-touch, Ian-Smith-lackey, Rhodesian Front dinosaurs, increased the period to eighteen months. I shrugged—the Sorbonne was put on hold and I perversely signed on as a regular for a three-year term.

Was this done for some sort of masochistic shock effect to piss off my parents? Possibly not, but it certainly had the effect of driving them into an insane rage of futile frustration.

Not content with this *coup de main,* a year later aged nineteen, I proudly announced to my parents my engagement to Carol. They screamed, they shouted, they cajoled, they cried. Couldn't I see I was ruining my life? Couldn't I see that I was throwing it all away on this young nobody-farm-girl? That just made it worse and I adamantly dug in. Damn them! I was in control. I was a blooded veteran. I would do it *my* way. Let them see.

But they never did see, and although they came to the wedding a year later it was under sufferance. A grudging acceptance because they'd run out of words.

By the time of my discharge from the army, the Sorbonne now a long-forgotten dream, they'd more or less given up. Okay, if you want to become a farmer, go and do it. We won't stop you. We can't. Do what you want to do. You always have.

So although this was the prevailing familial attitude at the time, the body blow of a child on the way was just too much to swallow. If anything this was for them the final *coup de grâce* in the career of young

Christopher. A career that was doomed before it had even started.

I'd allowed the war to dominate my psyche. I lived it, I breathed it—not because I wanted to, not because I was some crazed psycho-killer who got off murdering babies—simply because it was all-pervading and I was there. I was in it. It had become an instinctive matter of survival and that overshadowed everything. There was no place for questioning, no place to actually consider that there were choices.

And as the war ground on from one day to the next, without the faintest sign of abating, so I turned more to myself, in a perverted effort to escape from myself and the reality of my circumstances, which I barely understood anyway. I only knew that I wasn't where my karma said I should be. Where that was, God alone knew.

I found the answers in alcohol and drugs, which had become such a part of my life in the army. And as I escaped from my current being in search of the real me, the ideal persona, I became more and more confused. And so I was forced to resort to the drugs again in a never-ending cycle of highs and lows, the latter characterized by self-recrimination, self-loathing and guilt.

The tedium of the section manager's job didn't provide much in the way of stimulation. The routine spliff at nine o'clock in the middle of the cotton lands, ostensibly checking the irrigation, became the routine spliff at eight o'clock. And then another at midday, which was time for a beer anyway. By then, the workers would have completed their *gwazas*, so what point was there in going back to work?

I'd started on slimming tablets by then. Little yellow pills known as 'Lemslim', this was an insidious beast that replaced the valium and morphine of the army days. The first few times you only needed three or four to get buzzing, effectively 'speeding'. But as the usage increased so did the dosage requirement, so much so, that towards the end of my addiction period of some three or four years, I needed to take more than twenty a time to get the same effect. Supremely fit, my body was able to withstand the withering side effects—continual diarrhoea, vomitting and severe impotence.

Yet throughout this period of my life these were my own dark secrets. No one knew what I was doing in the middle of the lands; no one would have guessed that the small plastic phial in my pocket was the bearer of so many of those little yellow pills; no one would have thought that my anorak pocket held the faithful hip flask. Not even my wife. Oh, it was very cool to boast to my friends of the roof-high marijuana plant that I was growing outside the bedroom window, the *dagga* cookies that I would take along to the parties, to the club; and it was cool to buzz, cool to get high and laugh.

The club became my *raison d'être*. It was at the club that I could let go, get drunk, get high. It was a sensory assault and a sensory escape. There was nothing else.

Like any young man, I'd had the world at my feet. But it was slipping away from me and the more it slipped away the more I convinced myself that it was still within my grasp. Maybe not right at that particular moment, but never far away—certainly within easy reach as and when I wanted it.

But right now, I didn't want it. I didn't know what I wanted.

Zen and the Matchless

Michael Gelfand Clinic, Harare: Sunday, 26 February 1995

I went on another outing today. It was fine but I had to draw on all my strength to stop myself from shaking and bursting into tears. The depressions have been very black and I feel so alone. The future seems empty.

My friend Martyn went back to England today. I envy his happiness. He just seems so together.

Jim is refusing to die. He smiled at me today. I will miss him if I get out tomorrow. He must be very strong inside.

Middle Sabi: June 1979

Another distraction arrived—in the form of an old Matchless 500cc motorbike I'd recently bought from my brother-in-law. It was a wonderful old thumper—a big, black beast that leaked oil everywhere, but the *aficionados* assured me that a Matchless that didn't leak oil wasn't a true Matchless. This satisfied me.

Carol helped me unload it off Nat's Peugeot 404 pick-up and nearly got squashed in the process, as the beast lumbered clumsily down the flimsy wooden ramp. I shooed her away and she scowled at me. Pregnant women shouldn't be doing that sort of thing, I chided.

I prepared for the maiden Middle Sabi voyage. I'd ridden it before in Salisbury where Carol's brother had showed me how to get it started and how to control it. Dressed in boxer shorts and a T-shirt, I flicked out the kick-start with my foot. Helmets weren't compulsory then, so naturally I didn't wear one. Now the tricky bit. Firmly holding the handlebars, the bike upright off the stand, I put my left foot on the kick-start and gingerly pumped at it, taking up the slack and getting a grip on the compression. With an almighty leap I came down with all my weight on my left foot. The machine, out of sorts from idleness, grumbled ineffectively.

"Go on, 'Easy Rider'!" my wife laughed from under the thorn tree that dominated the front lawn. "Where's your power?"

"Humph!" I grunted, taunted into a determination to get the beast going. A bit like a horse, I suppose. Got to let them know who's boss.

I jumped on the kick-start again, but this time, with the accumulation of compression, the lever flew back with incredible speed and violence, like a metallic whip, and caught my exposed left calf a stinging blow. I fell to the ground, clutching at my leg, cursing and moaning in pain. The bike slowly tumbled on to the lawn, soft and friable from the irrigation sprinkler that went twenty-four hours a day.

Carol was laughing as I forced myself to my feet and hauled the monster upwards again.

"Hey! Mind the lawn. I don't want that filthy oil all over the place," she cried out. "You'll never get that thing started anyway. Why don't you take it down to the workshops and get Errol to have a look at it? Dunno why we bought the damned thing in the first place. We've got a baby on the way, y'know? Should be buying prams and baby tenders, and things like that. Not motorbikes and PA systems."

Here we go again. Never going to let up on that PA system. I squinted at her, the evening sun at her back, behind the elongated shadows of the thorn tree. Her long, brown hair blew gently in the breeze. She was a good woman. Barely twenty years old, but a woman nonetheless. Put up with a lot. Maybe that was her farming-stock background.

"What's a bloody baby tender, anyway?" I shouted back. I was panting from the exertions, but it had now become a matter of pride. "Sounds like some sort of fucking tugboat?"

"Mind your language. You're gonna have to learn to control your tongue when the baby comes, y'know. You're not in the army now with all those scummy mates of yours!"

Nukka, nukka, nukka, I mimicked under my breath, positioning the evil kick-start lever in place. My calf was still smarting. There'd be a massive bruise in a while.

"I heard that," she shouted.

Ensuring that the throttle was fully closed, I jumped on the lever again. This time, I timed it right and, as the engine belched angrily, I tapped open the throttle with my right hand. It caught and roared into life, great billows of old blue smoke engulfing the lawn. I revved the throttle until the machine was screaming—well, the nearest a Matchless could ever come to a scream—and then tapped off slowly until the engine was purring contentedly in the idle.

Carol was waving the smoke away from her, coughing and spluttering. "Where you gonna go?" she shouted.

"I thought I'd take it for a burn up to Tanganda and then maybe back via the club. Nice to show the okes."

"Tanganda Junction? That's miles!" she said, the alarm plain in her voice. "What about the terrs? It's getting dark too, y'know."

"Agh! This monster will outrun them anyday."

"What about your rifle? You want your child to grow up an orphan, huh? Have some bloody consideration!"

"Okay, okay. Will you get it for me? It's in the lounge. And you better bring the sling. Oh ... and can you bring my smokes as well?"

Shaking her head with a 'boys-will-be-boys' attitude, she went inside the house and came back a few moments later with the FN. She was holding it tentatively. It was heavy for her. Slinging the weapon over my back, I slipped on my teardrop Polaroids and saddled the bike. It was a great feeling, I thought, the black leather fabric cool and comfortable under my backside. Remember to keep your legs away from the exhaust. It'd burn like a bitch.

I tapped the throttle and kicked the machine into first gear, wheeling her round the thorn tree. "Seeya later, babe!" I shouted in my best Peter Fonda voice. She waved as I gently guided the bike through the gates. I kicked it into second gear, cruising steadily down the dirt road, out of the housing site.

Which way? Go right, north from the sheds, away from the SLA offices. Away from any form of civilization.

I turned the bike north and gathered speed on the dusty road that went past the Section 4 compound. Elias and Peter's compound. Into fourth gear now, ducking the Section 3 irrigation sprinklers on the edge of the cotton lands. Be careful of stones. A tennis-ball-sized stone at this speed would flip you.

Black workers in faded red overalls stared at me curiously from the roadside. Children with oversized yellow fertilizer bags, crammed full of freshly picked cotton, scattered in all directions, laughing and screeching at the same time. And mothers, babies towelled in on their backs, panicked, gathering up the snot-faced, pantsless toddlers and scurried onto the verges.

Past Section 2 which had recently been amalgamated with Stan Mastak's Section 1. Any farther and I'd hit the Section 1 sheds. Stan, the ramrod-straight Polish officer, the grand veteran of Monte Cassino, would have knocked off by now. I slowed down as I noticed the Van den Berg Road turn-off approaching, the last access road to the main tar road before Section 1. And beyond Section 1… the Mutema River and the Mutema Tribal Trust Lands.

TTLs—the black 'homelands', the communal lands—those perceived—and real—hotbeds of Communist guerrillas, those vast areas I'd never even dreamed had existed until I joined the army. A people and a way of life so different, so alien, from anything I'd ever known as a boy. I remember my first visit into one of these TTLs. It had been up near Mount Darwin and we'd gone in by helicopter. I remember my confused sense of betrayal, of anger. Why had no one ever told me that such places existed? Why hadn't we been taught about the masses, the *povo*—the people of this country? I knew about Richard the Lionheart. I knew about the Great Fire of London, the War of the Roses, the Western Front, the Somme, Delville Wood, the Magna

Carta and Sir Walter Raleigh. But I knew nothing of the country of my birth. Not necessarily my country. There was a difference.

I stopped the bike at the corner of the Van den Berg Road, letting it gurgle away at the idle, and pulled out a ready-rolled joint tucked away in the thirty-pack of Madisons. One final spliff before the burn. One final slug of brandy. I inhaled with anticipation, sucking hard and fast to hasten the effects of the marijuana. The sweetness, the gentle dullness that came over, and the faintest, faintest hint of a headache, indicated it was working.

With a sense of gentle abandon, I spat into the palm of my hand and extinguished the hot little roach in the spittle. Then, rolling the butt-end into a tight black ball, I prepared a 'nosey', a 'snifter', inserting the roach-ball between two match heads. I lit the matches and watched, mesmerized, as the flames flared in the evening light. Rapidly pasting the base of the matches with saliva, to prevent the matchsticks from burning away, I studied the operation closely. The trick was to burn the roach to a certain point, and not the matchsticks. Inhaling burnt wood was no fucking good—might clear out the sinuses but that was about all. The roach flared briefly and I sensed it was ready. A thick spiral of blue smoke was streaming upwards as I cupped my hands around the burning ball and took a deep sniff. Sniff again, this time harder; get it in before it burns out. Get a gulp of smoke down the mouth. Don't waste it. The smoke, sweet and acrid, stabbed into my nostrils and down my throat. Shit, it was good. The cherry on the cake.

And then it was done. I flicked the burnt matchsticks away and swallowed the frazzled roach. Waste not, want not. My eyes were stinging, red and watery.

I engaged first gear, tentatively opening up the throttle. It was fine. I had it under control. Through the sisal fields towards the main tar road, away from the infernal cotton lands. A dip in the road indicated an approaching flood bund, those river-like storm drains that had been built to handle the occasional flash floods that afflicted the valley from time to time. Normally the bases of the flood bunds were lined with concrete, laid angularly and awkwardly for a car travelling at speed.

I whooped and dropped into second, ramping the bottom of the bund with a thud, squashing the front forks down flat—and then up and away, vaulting the lip of the bund. The evening midgies were starting up, splattering against my Polaroids. Speed through them, I thought, as I opened up the throttle. The main road was in sight and with a brief glance to my right, swung left on to the tar. The surface sounds beneath the engine, from gravel to asphalt, shifted perceptibly—smoother, slicker, easier. Dropping a gear, I opened her up, my scraggly hair streaming in the wind. The speedo wasn't working, but I must have been doing around 70mph, maybe eighty.

I whooped again as I crossed the Mutema River, sandy and shallow. The evening smells of dampness filled my senses. The sombre phalanxes of fever trees, the pale green bark glowing eerily in the gloom … and that strange smell of potatoes, so peculiar to the Lowveld. I learned later that it came from some sort of creeper that thrived in riverine areas. Vervet monkeys chattered and screeched in alarm in the bush on the side of the road, before dashing maniacally across to the other side, mere yards from the roaring machine.

I let go the handlebars and stretched my arms out like I was flying. Perhaps this was the art of *Zen and the art of motorcycle maintenance?* I'd read the book a couple of years before and hadn't understood a thing, apart from the buzz of riding on a motorbike. Maybe now I was getting it?

Low kopjes, covered with mimosa thorn trees and *mopanes,* sped by, as the bike attained its maximum. I couldn't open the throttle further. It had reached its zenith, its crescendo and now it was simply a case of maintaining the orgasmic effect for as long as possible. And then, too soon, the long sweeping bend towards Tanganda Junction came into view.

I tapped back on the throttle, rather too rapidly, and the bike backfired like a rifle shot. I started and did it again. It backfired again and I jumped again. Wow! I pulled up at the T-junction, innocuous and inconsequential. Bare, dusty verges where the convoys turned around—that was it—and a directional sign, indicating Middle Sabi and Chibuwe southward, Umtali and Birchenough Bridge northward, and Chipinga and Melsetter eastward, up in the mountains. Tanganda Junction—it sounded so romantic.

The sun was setting and the Mutema Mountains loomed ominously in the west. Adjusting the rifle on my back, I turned the bike around and went home. Zen would have to wait for another time.

A hippo had got stuck in the main canal near J.J. Fourie's farm, just south of the main night-storage dam near the club. It meant one thing.

There was great excitement as crowds of farm workers swarmed at the edge of the concrete-lined canal, pangas flashing in the sunlight. The beast, tightly wedged in its concrete prison, bellowed with fear and rage, desperate to get back to the safety of the storage dam, its home for the coming winter. Her babies, eyes and snouts peeking curiously from the water of the dam, regarded the activity with an element of uncertainty, unaware that their mother was about to die, a mere fifty metres away.

The blacks were babbling with anticipation, the men laughing and joking, making hacking gestures with the pangas. The women, with ubiquitous babies bouncing unconcernedly on their backs, were laying the torn-open plastic fertilizer bags on the green kikuyu grass that lined the canal.

A hush came over the crowd, a path parting, as the tall, imposing figure of J.J. Fourie strode forward. He cocked the FN rifle he was holding.

"*Kom, kom, jou focken nyamazans!* Get out the way!"

The *nyamazans*, the 'creatures', shrank to the verges, blocking their ears with their hands. J.J. was *the* big *bwana* of the valley. His presence automatically commanded respect, even among the whites. Still astride the Matchless, I watched curiously from the other side of the canal.

J.J. brought the rifle to his shoulder. With deliberate aim, he fired. The shot boomed out, the blacks shrinking further into the verge. The hippo thrashed about in the shallow water, groaning in her death throes. An eerie, woeful scream filled the air and I turned away, unable to watch. I wanted to vomit.

Then silence, as the throng waited for the nod from the big *bwana*. I noticed the hippo calves had vanished, submerged at the bottom of the dam.

Imperceptibly, the big *bwana* nodded and with a loud roar the crowd swarmed down the concrete walls into the water, now running pink and red. Laughter and cheers as pangas flashed again and again and again, with dull, hollow thuds. J.J. gave a final glance at the mass, then turned abruptly, FN over his shoulder, and strode off back to his homestead.

I kicked the Matchless into life and slung the automatic FN shotgun over my back. It was time to go duck-shooting with Tim.

Sugar in a jenny

Intensive Coronary Unit, Parirenyatwa Hospital, Harare:
13 March 1995

I am awake and I wonder where I am. Everything is white and stainless steel. There is a bright light shining above me and I blink, unaccustomed to the sterile glare. I am in a bed. Am I dead? There is no one here. It is all very silent. There is a pain in my left arm and I glance down at it. There is a drip inserted. I turn and study the bag of saline solution, suspended on a metal stand next to the bed. It is about three-quarters empty. I assume someone will be coming to change it.

But what for? Why on earth am I in this room, alone, on a drip? What's happened? I panic momentarily. Was I involved in a car accident? Or worse, have I been abducted by some anonymous government department for sinister, mind-altering, experimental purposes? I quickly lift the brown government-issue blankets and inspect underneath. I am wearing a white hospital robe, the kind that ties up at the back. It feels rough against my skin. My legs seem fragile and palid against the starched sheets. No blood, no plaster cast, no bandages. I move, first the one leg, and then the other. They are stiff, but otherwise okay.

There is a noise at the swing door, and through the porthole-type window I see the face of a black woman. She sees that I am awake and comes in. She is a nurse.

"Well, well, my dear!" she says, in that matronly, matter-of-fact voice so universal, so comforting of nurses. "Look who's awake then! Hello Mister Lazy Bones!"

I ask where I am, as she fusses round the bed. I am in the Parirenyatwa ICU. That's the Intensive Coronary Unit—not to be confused with the Intensive Care Unit, I'm told.

"What's the difference?" I ask, my voice slurring.

"Coronary means 'heart', my dear," she explains patiently, her fingers lightly on my wrist, taking my pulse. "The doctor was very worried about your heart."

"How long have I been here?"

"In a second, dearie," she says, as she finishes with my wrist. She goes to the chart at the foot of the bed. "You have been here for six days."

Middle Sabi: July 1979

The valley is a patchwork of colours—white cotton lint, brown cotton plants and green wheat shoots peeking through wet, freshly tilled soil. It is one of the very busy times of the year—taking the last of the cotton off and planting the wheat. Already it is getting late for wheat planting. Any later and the tail-end of the crop will face the risk of the early summer storms, rotting the drying ears.

Anthony's banks of blue 100-horsepower Ford tractors are in one of the Section 4 lands, slashing the senesced cotton stalks, chopping and hacking with the draught mowers behind. The drivers, bandanas covering their faces, narrow their eyes and turn in unison at the headlands for another cut. Great clouds of dust billow around the machines, clogging eyes and mouths. The drivers, their black tousled hair now white from dripping cotton lint, their faces masked in dust, must hurry. Already, the great John Deeres, like knights of old, are lined up, engines roaring, waiting to come in behind with the steel-tined rippers. And behind them more tractors wait their turn, with trailed twenty-four-disc Rome harrows at their backs, to desecrate and pulverize the rock-hard, boulder-sized clods thrown up by the rippers.

And then, with the land preparation complete, the blue Fords will return, this time with yellow Vicon fertilizer spreaders that broadcast the lime and compound fertilizers. And after this, the John Deeres will come back with even larger Vicons, this time throwing out the wheat seed.

I follow behind with my gangs of irrigation 'boys', frantically laying pipes and risers and sprinklers, in order to get the first four-hour cycle of water onto the lands. But it is hurried and great gushers flood the lands from burst pipes. I cover many, many miles on my green Suzuki, rushing from one crisis spot to the next. And, all the while, Chris Cloete, the Field Manager, sits quietly at the headland in his Peugeot 404 pick-up, observing and tut-tutting.

But I ignore him. The RMS, the Railways Motor Service, lorry has arrived at the sheds to collect another load of cotton bales for delivery to Umtali. I have given instructions to Samuel as to how many bales to load, but it needs checking.

The truck is abreast of the *mopane*-log ramp, the shirtless workers heaving and sweating to get the massive hessian bales up the incline and dropped into the trailers. Adroitly grappling the one-ton bales with hand-held claw hooks, they manoeuvre the inert beasts with a skill that I never ceased to admire.

And all the while, the women and children, sacks and fertilizer bags of cotton on their heads, trickle into the yard to weigh the day's picking. The cotton is nearly over and the daily weights have dropped. A few more days and there'll be none.

Satisfied that the loading is in hand, I make my way to the office to start weighing. I sit at a desk under an open window, inside the office. Outside the window, Samuel stands by the large platform scale, ready to call out the name of the cotton picker and her weight of cotton. Already the queue reaches to the section gates. But I scan the line of women and children and see that their bags are not full.

"Okay, Samuel. Let's make a start. Is the scale zeroed?"

He nods and, in Shona, instructs the first woman to place her bag on the scale. He calls out the weight, having deducted one kilogram for the weight of the sack. I mark the weight down next to the woman's name on the ledger. She will be paid at the end of the week, when her week's pickings are added up.

The next woman has trash in her cotton. Samuel is angry and chides her. She is turned away, to go and clean out the dead leaves and twigs that are littering the lint. Dirty cotton would either be downgraded by the Cotton Marketing Board in Umtali, hence commanding a lower price—or worse, rejected and sent back. This would almost certainly result in a severe tut-tutting session from Chris Cloete, with dire threats of a bonus cut.

The next woman places her bag on the scale, as the black-Bakelite, crank-handle phone on the desk rings. I snatch at it. It is Gordy Gandanga. He wants to see me at Chipangayi—urgent briefing.

I instruct Samuel to take over and resignedly climb on my motorbike. What now, for God's sake?

Now, for God's sake, was an ambush at the Mutema School.

"Mutema?" I whined to Gordy Gandanga. "But that's out of our area."

"No it isn't," Gordy smirked. "Your area stretches all the way to the Mozambican border ... and you know it."

Mutema Tribal Trust Land was an old, well-established TTL, its southern boundary the Mutema River, which demarcated the start of the 'commercial' (read 'white') Middle Sabi scheme. Mutema, at least until the commencement of hostilities, had been a model TTL, or more correctly an APA—an African Purchase Area—with a flourishing irrigation scheme, established in the fifties by the old Federal government's Native Department. The black farmers were what were known as 'master farmers' in that they had achieved consistently high yields and had been granted tenure of their small properties by the Rhodesian government. With rich alluvial soils and an abundance of water, their crops of maize, beans, cotton, sunflowers and mangoes flourished.

And with agricultural prosperity grew the schools and business

Marandellas, now Marondera, circa 1979. A dusty little town on the Salisbury–Umtali road. The first stop for the convoy out of Salisbury. *Photo by Tom Argyle*

The eastern border town of Umtali, 1979, seen over the wing of a Dakota. *Photo by Tom Argyle*

Birchenough Bridge in the winter of 1979. The Sabi River is flowing strongly, considering the season. Today, the river is fast silting up. Note the sandbagged fortifications. *Photo by Tom Argyle*

Left: Two Rhodesian Defence Unit (RDU) private soldiers, resident guards on Birchenough Bridge, pose studiously for the camera, 1979. *Photo by Tom Argyle*

Below: A magnificent Lowveld baobab. *Photo by Tom Argyle*

Top: A Middle Sabi cotton land. *Photo from the author's collection*

Above: A soldier relaxes at a deserted store, Tanganda Halt Business Centre, near Middle Sabi, 1979. *Photo by Tom Argyle*

Left: An unplanted Middle Sabi field, with the main irrigation canal on the left. *Photo from the author's collection*

Artist Craig Bone's impression of a Rhodesian stick leader.

Top: An RLI machine gunner cleans his MAG, while based up at the Middle Sabi club. *Photo by Tom Argyle*

Above: RLI troops drying their laundry, while based at the Middle Sabi club. The buildings in the background are aircraft hangars belonging to the more affluent Middle Sabi farmers. *Photo by Tom Argyle*

Opposite page:

Top: A desolate Tanganda Halt, 1979. Nothing but deserted, empty stores, pillaged by ZANLA guerrillas. *Photo by Tom Argyle*

Middle: A view of the Chipangayi Hunting Area, east of Middle Sabi, 1979. *Photo by Tom Argyle*

Bottom: Looking west from the Chipangayi Hunting Area across the Sabi River, with Devuli Ranch in the distance. *Photo by Tom Argyle*

Top: The author's PATU stick relaxes outside a Mutema shebeen, 1979. The author is on the extreme left.

Above: A mine-proofed 'Hyena' troop-transport vehicle—slow, prehistoric and cumbersome. *Photo authorship unknown*

Opposite page:

Top: Mutema Tribal Trust Land in the dry season. *Photo by Tom Argyle*

Middle: A rather depressing rural scene near Birchenough Bridge, 1979. *Photo by Tom Argyle*

Bottom: Mutema Tribal Trust Land, with Mutema Mountain looming in the distance. *Photo by Tom Argyle*

A Craig Bone impression.

Craig Bone's impression of the *pungwe* contact,
Middle Sabi, January 1980.

Top: Although in black and white, this excellent photo highlights the effectiveness of Rhodesian camouflage in Lowveld terrain. Although the camouflage pattern was outstanding, Rhodesian-made kit was of inferior quality. *Photo by Dennis Croukamp*

Above: The artistic graphic effects of the photo lend an almost serene aura to this slain ZANLA guerrilla. *Photo by Dennis Croukamp*

Above: Craig Bone's impression of the last contact, 16 April 1980.

Left: The author, aged 21, holds the brand-new baby Guy, October 1979. *Photo from the author's collection*

Opposite page:

Top left: There's little in the way of serenity in this image. A dead ZANLA cadre lies with his AK-47 rifle and an RPG-7 rocket launcher by his mutilated corpse. *Photo by Tony Young*

Top right: The author with his father, Salisbury 1979. *Photo from the author's collection*

Middle: Sunset over Mutema. *Photo by Tom Argyle*

Bottom: A view of Salisbury over Cecil Square, 1980. The Anglican cathedral is central beyond the trees. *Photo by Tony Young*

Above: Unusually well-dressed ZANLA guerrillas pose for the camera, shortly before Zimbabwean independence, April 1980. *Photos by Dennis Croukamp*

Left: Fletcher, Charlie Norris' 'tame gook', a ZANLA combatant integrated into the Zimbabwean army, views war memorabilia in the author's lounge at Viewfield Farm, Centenary, 1982. *Photo by Charlie Norris*

Opposite page:

Top: Rhodesian troops patrolling the black township of Highfields in Salisbury, April 1980. *Photo by Dennis Croukamp*

Middle: RLI soldiers patrol through the Salisbury city centre, April 1980. *Photo by Dennis Croukamp*

Bottom: A futile show of force. RLI paratroopers in armoured troop transports on Jameson Avenue, downtown Salisbury, April 1980. *Photo by Dennis Croukamp*

Top: A typical northern Mashonaland country scene. *Photo by Tom Argyle*

Centre and left: These beautiful images of the *povo*, the peasants, vividly capture Shona kraal life in the Tribal Trust Lands, circa 1980. *Photos by Tony Young*

centres and beerhalls—natural targets for the guerrillas in that they were capitalist, economically successful and offered a never-ending source of supplies of food, women and recruits. By 1979, Mutema had, to all intents and purposes, become a guerrilla stronghold. Strangely, the guerrillas had allowed Mutema School to stay open, in contrast to their normal tactics of destroying anything that smacked of Rhodesian authority.

The reason for this, Garikayi explained, was that the school was used as a logistical and operations centre by the enemy. The local populace had been successfully 'turned' by the guerrillas. So why destroy a convenient source of recruits? Why destroy pupils, potential guerrillas, who could be indoctrinated into the benefits of 'the struggle' during their normal Rhodesian curriculum, and paid for by the Rhodesian government to boot?

Garikayi had received word that the guerrillas were holding a meeting at the school, either tonight or tomorrow night—undoubtedly the same group of guerrillas that had ambushed us from the ridge in the Chipangayi hunting area.

I shook my head. An ongoing and futile game of cat and mouse. But here, the cat was weary and decrepit. Occasionally, he might catch the tip of the mouse's tail with a lucky swipe from a blunt claw, but he would never destroy the mouse. Never.

"Okay," I sighed. "How do we get in?"

Gordy smiled, secretively. "Chris, I have a present for you. A generous donation from the member-in-charge, Chipinga."

"I can't wait. What are you talking about?"

"Look what's parked outside."

I looked. Apart from Gordy's beaten-up Land Rover, there was nothing ... except the hideous, cumbersome Police Reserve 'Hyena'— that lumbering mine-proofed beast used for convoy duties.

"Dud-duh-duh-daaaa!" Gordy announced with a flourish. "May I present the new troop transport for the PATU north stick."

"Huh! The Hyena?"

"Yup. Can you sign for it before you leave, please?" Gordy was smirking again.

"C'mon Gordy," I whined for the second time. "That thing's totally fucked. Can't we just carry on using our personal vehicles?"

"Nope! The member-in-charge has put a stop to the use of personal vehicles. Says that Pirsons's stick has been tearing the ring out of their mileage claims."

I inspected the machine. The mine-proofing steel plate was shaped upwards in a 'V', to deflect the blast. Entry was through a small, brutally heavy plate door at the rear. I'd never been inside a tank before, but sitting in the cab, was not, I imagined, too dissimilar. Behind the driver's cab were two benches on either side, with thin firing slits in the steelwork. The vehicle appeared to seat six to eight men. The horsepower could probably comfortably cope with two or three.

My misgivings were founded. As I manoeuvered the lumbering machine through the Chipangayi gates, I slammed my foot down on the accelerator pedal. A feeble whine of engine. No power whatsoever. I got up a good run downhill towards the main road and within three to four hundred metres reached top speed of forty kays an hour. Well, at least it *felt* safe. Even an RPG rocket would have trouble penetrating that thick, angled skin.

I picked up the other stick members from their respective houses. First, I stopped off at Tim's house, where his wife, Trish, greeted me with her customary, "Oh, hello Chris Cocks. What can we do for you today?" In other words, "Why do you keep taking my husband away from me, you asshole?"

Manie Dreyer collapsed in hysterics when he saw the Hyena. "Fucking pathetic!" was his succinct comment. "With crap like this, do they really believe we have any chance whatsoever of winning this damned war? Un-fucking-believable!"

The last man to be collected was Paul Brown at Farm 1, on the western side of the canal opposite Section 1. Mutema was about a twenty-minute drive from his farm, so we waited for the sun to set before heading off into darkest Africa.

We'd hardly got out of Paul's gates when the accelerator cable snapped. The Hyena, revs still screaming, glided to a gentle halt by the banks of the canal.

"Un-fucking-believable!" Manie repeated. "Now what?"

We all clambered out and, after much to-do, worked out how to open the bonnet. Sure enough, the throttle cable had snapped near the pedal. Well at least it hadn't broken off near the carburettor.

"Easy, man," said Tim, who was more mechanically inclined than the rest of us. "You just have to bend down below the steering wheel and control it manually."

"Yeah," guffawed Anthony. "Like a wank—do it manually."

"Okay. Let's try," I concluded.

We climbed back in and I manoeuvered my body under the steering wheel. My right hand fumbled for the pedals, and sure enough, found the ragged cable end. I managed to grasp it behind the floppy, useless pedal with my fingers and the engine responded. The problem was, however, that I was unable to manage the cable-pulling and steering at the same time. Tim, ever practical, came forward and, virtually sitting on my lap, took control of the wheel.

And that's how we drove the Hyena for the next nine months. I can't remember why, but we never got round to getting that accelerator repaired. I vaguely recall putting in a requisition order for a replacement cable with the CMED, the Central Mechanical and Equipment Department, at Chipinga. But nothing ever came of it. Perhaps the war really wasn't that urgent.

Within a few kilometres, Tim and I had synchronized our separate driving activities. He steered and changed gear and I controlled the cable. However, I soon found that with my head buried in the bowels of the beast, I became nauseous, exacerbated by the fuel fumes floating around. We therefore had to switch roles every fifteen minutes or so.

It was dark when we arrived at the Internal Affairs keep just across the drift over the Mutema River. The keep commander, a lonely white man in his fifties, came out to meet us. He agreed to keep an eye on the Hyena for us, as we kitted up in our webbing. I pulled out my 1:50 000 map of the area and confirmed with him the location of the school. It was only four or five kays upstream, a gentle, easy walk.

The bush here had been tamed by the rural civilization. Not here the treacherous *wag 'n bietjie* thorn bushes that tore at your clothing. Not here the deadly buffalo beans with the minute, invisible hairs that could drive a man insane and cause him to scratch himself half to death.

In single file, well spread out, we meandered through the pastoral, riverine terrain. Large mango trees, fifty-feet-high, graced the river's edge. The Mutema River, clean and sparkling, glinted refreshingly in the moonlight. This was not the harsh, forbidding bush we were accustomed to.

The school, set a hundred metres or so from the river, was in darkness when we arrived. It was a substantial-looking institution. Large, well-built classroom blocks, neatly arranged in rows, exuded an aura of prosperity. A gravel path, lined by whitewashed rocks, so typical of rural schools, ran up to a quadrangle in front of what I took to be the administrative offices. A crooked *mopane* flagpole took pride of place in the middle of the quad. The flag, if there was one, had been struck for the night. A lovingly constructed stone plinth, with 'A Hearty Welcome to Mutema School' crookedly painted on the face, greeted visitors at the entrance.

The staff and pupils were obviously proud of their school.

The place was deserted. Not a sign of life. With little enthusiasm, I took the stick on a three-sixty of the school, to make doubly sure. Nothing. What now?

Away from the river, the land swept up a gentle incline. I decided to take the high ground and sit it out for a while, going through the motions of doing our duty. I very much doubted that the guerrillas would hold a meeting much later than midnight. That's what we'd do—stick around 'til midnight, do a final three-sixty and then head back to the Intaf keep. I settled the stick in to a good ambush position among some rocks, with a reasonably commanding view of the school grounds. I placed Tim at the rear, facing up the slope in case the gooks happened to come in that way. Short of leopard-crawling in, the gooks simply could not get into the school without alerting us, let alone hoping to conduct any sort of public meeting.

I looked at my watch, clearly visible in the bright moonlight. Nine o'clock. Three hours to go. I worked it out—three or four sips per hour from the hip flask—but this time without sharing.

Time dragged. The men were restless and, although they maintained strict silence, I could tell they were fidgety. They knew this was a 'lemon', a waste of time. The gooks would not come tonight. I thought it through. According to Garikayi's intelligence, the guerrillas were due either tonight or tomorrow night. And although, in the main, Garikayi's intelligence was normally very reliable, we were also aware that on many occasions his informers deliberately fed him wrong information, so that the enemy could hold their meetings, uninterrupted, at another location.

A dilemma. I knew what would happen. If nothing transpired tonight, we would go back and Gordy Gandanga would make us return tomorrow—for possibly another 'lemon'.

I sensed Manie at my side. He was getting impatient. "These ambushes are real hit and miss things, aren't they?" he whispered loudly, almost deliberately.

I nodded, knowing what was coming next. "I reckon we should handle our own int-gathering. I mean, we know our own compounds. Put one tame *munt* in on the inside, pay him a bundle of money for each sighting, and then give him a bonus for each dead gook. I'm bloody sure I'd get results chop-chop from my own compound."

I nodded again. He was right. Bill and Ben—Gordy Gandanga and Garikayi—handling the entire valley's intelligence. It was bound to be a hit and miss affair. GC—Ground Coverage—a lot of ground, sparse coverage.

Manie, with not much respect for the police, or any authority, at the best of times, read my thoughts. "They can call it what they want," he continued, now talking softly, "but it's pretty straightforward. GC, SB, RIC—whatever they call it—it's just about finding the damned gooks and we should be allowed to do it ourselves. Fucking one-off ambushes are an absolute waste of fucking time."

His voice had risen, but I didn't hush him. He was right.

"Y'know, Chris. If the gooks don't come tonight, we'll have to come back tomorrow. And if they don't come tomorrow, what's the bet we'll have to come back the night after? And the night after that!"

"I know," I agreed.

"Well," he said slyly, "if we compromise this position, then we won't have to come back, will we?"

"How d'you mean?"

"We fuck the place over."

"Huh?" I was curious.

"Ja. For starters we can fuck up the school generator. We walked past it when we did the three-sixty. I checked it out in that little shed by the river. Brand-new jenny—probably a donation from some fucken' Swedes. I reckon the jenny supplies all the school's water and electricity requirements. Think about it—no jenny ... no school." He finished with a flourish.

I was listening. "Okay. How?"

"Easy. Just pour sugar in the fuel tank. The sugar acts like a grinding agent. Gets into the pistons and bingo! One fucked jenny." He smiled, triumphantly. "I'll send the hat round and ask for sugar donations from the lads. C'mon, Chris. Why the fuck not? I mean, everyone fucking knows this school is a gook paradise. Fuck them! 'Bout time we showed a bit of aggro!"

I nodded slowly, which Manie took as my acceptance. Scurrying off to the other stick members, he sidled back to me a few minutes later with his dixie-mug more than half full of brown sugar. He showed me the mug. "Plenty. This'll stop their farting in church!"

I'd warmed to the idea. This was cunning stuff. Super-sleuth stuff. Fighting the guerrillas with their own tactics. Sneaky, insidious, clever … and eminently destructive.

We hitched up and made our way down towards the generator shed. The wooden door was unlocked and we shoved our way in. There stood the shining, gleaming Scandinavian generator—a gift from the People of Sweden to the oppressed *povo* of Zimbabwe—or words to that effect on a little metal plaque rivetted to the engine block.

Manie unscrewed the chromium fuel cap with ease, and in a minute he'd decanted the pound or so of brown sugar into the fuel.

It was done. But what an anti-climax! How would we ever know whether it would work, whether the jenny would destroy itself?

"Believe me, it will," assured Manie. "I've seen it before. Starts making all sorts of horrible grinding sounds and then totally fucks out and dies."

I trusted him. But the men were still restless, frustrated. We needed to do something tangible. To vent our feelings.

So we did. With military precision we smashed every single window in the place, neatly ramming our rifle barrels through the glass panes. We ripped doors off hinges, we overturned the desks, smashing the legs; we ripped up exercise books, we laid waste. For a moment I toyed with the idea of taking it further and burning the place down, but in spite of temptation, desisted. The flames would surely attract unwanted attention—namely from the police and the Internal Affairs.

Then, satisfied with our handiwork, we withdrew. Back to the Intaf keep. A sleepy vedette guard let us in. The white man was asleep, he said. We clambered into the Hyena and started it up.

The following day, Gordy Gandanga came to see me at the Section 4 sheds. He'd received an official complaint from Internal Affairs that our PATU stick had destroyed Mutema School. He was very angry and was shouting.

I simply shrugged. My men would never stoop to that sort of wanton destruction of government property. Yes, we'd gone to the school, but had left at midnight after an uneventful evening. Why on earth would we want to destroy the place? For what insane reason? It must have been the gooks. It could only have been the gooks. Obviously they had come to the school after we'd left. So obvious. And they'd vandalized the school as a warning to Intaf. Nothing was sacred, Gordy. Don't you know that? C'mon, man!

Gordy Allen knew I was lying. He knew it. I could see the vein in his neck pumping, his lips dry and bloodless.

Without another word, he turned and stomped off to his Land Rover, the little dog, Gondy, panting at his heels.

What monster had he created? What monster?

Under the Five Roses sign

Intensive Coronary Unit, Parirenyatwa Hospital, Harare: 14 March 1995

The doctor's just been to see me. For a second I had the feeling that he was judging me—like he was wasting his time on someone who'd tried to take his own life and hadn't done a very good job of it. I could tell by his manner—offish and demeaning.

I almost tried to tell him the whole story, to justify it all and rationalize it, possibly more for myself than him. I wanted to tell him that I hadn't wanted to die, that I'd only wanted to escape from the screaming world inside my head that had closed in on me. Just a temporary escape, that's all. Nothing more. I didn't tell him that if I'd really wanted to do myself I would have pulled the trigger of the illegally-smuggled-from-Mozambique Mokarev pistol that I'd shoved in my mouth. "Believe me, buddy. I would have done it, man," I wanted to tell him, like I needed to prove that I had the courage. But I didn't say anything.

But a hundred or so sleeping tablets? Sheesh! All that's going to do is put you to sleep for several days. Might put some undue pressure on the old ticker—that's why you're in the ICU. But really, old chap. Sleeping pills? Almost laughable.

He left and the guilt was back. Not even the bustling matron trying to cheer me up with her clucking and her 'dearies' had any effect.

I close my eyes, the glare of the overhead stainless steel light still burning white behind my eyelids.

I will sleep for another two days. How dare he judge me!

Middle Sabi: August 1979

The shotgun exploded in my ears, the comforting kick bucking into my shoulder. The Guinea fowl, running the gauntlet of the sandy riverbed between the tall rows of *mwanga* trees, fifty-feet-high, spun and tumbled in mid-air and then plummeted to the ground with a dull *thuck*. A flurry of alarm from the Sabi verdure as more birds, screeching and chattering, took flight in a desperate attempt to cross the dry riverbed to the safety of the bush on the other side.

"To your left, Tim!" I shouted. "A whole bunch of them!"

The air was filled with the low, sucking, *whoo-whoo-whoo* sounds of wings beating, flapping anxiously against hard-yielding air, vainly trying to build up purchase and air velocity.

The twin roar, almost simultaneous, of Tim's double-barrelled 12-bore shotgun resounded in my ears and another bird tumbled like a stricken bomber, speckled black and white downy feathers exploding skywards.

And then a whole covey, this time, low and heavy across the sand in the fading light. I still had four cartridges of Number 4 shot in the automatic shotgun. Tim had his gun broken and was desperately reloading as I lowered my barrel, leading the front bird a few paces. Slowly does it, slowly. Make the first shot count. The second would be anybody's guess with the following birds likely to weave and bob off course.

I squeezed the trigger and for the briefest of seconds registered that the front bird had nose-dived into the sand, tumbling and rolling with its deadweight momentum. And then, hardly seeing the other birds, just flashes of movement, I swung the gun and blasted off the remaining three shots in to the mass, one after the other.

My shoulder was aching as I lowered the gun and peered through the smoke and the dust. A good, satisfying ache. The black flashes of two birds crashed in to the trees on the other side, alive and well … to face the guns another day.

"Good one, Chris," said Tim, at my side. "Got a few there, I reckon."

His Yorkshire accent seemed stronger in this sort of environment. Perhaps the fowl shooting took him back to his youth.

I reloaded from the loose stash in my camo combat jacket pocket. It was pleasant to be able to carry a weapon, unencumbered by webbing and pack. We walked up the riverbed and collected the dead Guinea fowl, five in all. Not a bad bag for the evening. They were cunning these birds and would normally sense our approach, before leap-frogging at treetop level to the next island. And normally, we'd have to weave our way around the stagnant pools of water, avoiding the sodden, marshy areas, to the next sandy river course. And the birds, ever vigilant, would see us coming round the island headland and fly tauntingly to the next.

But today, we had caught them off guard by walking across the islands, instead of around them. It had taken a lot longer, what with plunging through the vines and the reeds and the clawing *lantana camara* bush, but the effort had paid dividends. We'd arrived on the lee of the island amidships, directly opposite the flock, way up there in the trees. The sentry had panicked and had flown directly into our sights.

Slinging our guns, we carried the still-warm birds by the feet, their bluey-purple heads swinging and flopping against our bare legs. Occasional drops of congealing blood plopped unnoticed on the sand. Number 4s were about right, we'd figured. Even Number 5s was okay. The size of the shot was small enough not to damage the meat and big enough to give the bird a fair chance with a poor gunman, yet at the same time prove lethal with a hit. We'd tried Number 7s and 8s before. Just too small and, although there was a greater chance of hitting the birds, there was also more chance of simply wounding them. And the Number 1s and 2s? Well, they'd blow a hole the size of a fist through a fowl—if you ever got to hit one.

"Fancy a grog, Chris?" Tim asked, as he casually tossed the dead birds on to the metal floorboards of the pick-up truck. He unzipped a cooler bag.

"Sure do." I carefully leaned my gun against the cab door and tossed in my birds. "What've you got?"

"Bitterly cold Castles," he smiled, passing me a frosted beer bottle. He pronounced it 'Cassill'.

The sun was setting over the river as we drank contentedly, surveying the drying wheat lands to the east, still tinged with green.

"Well," slurped Tim with satisfaction, "that's five less bastards that's gonna eat my wheat." Traces of white beer froth hung like diamonds from his reddish beard. "Jest look at the damage the fuckers do to the edges of the lands. That's a good few bags, y'know?"

I smiled. Tim was like that—a fastidious farmer.

It was dark as we climbed in to the *bakkie* and made our way across the wheat lands, bouncing and sliding through the mud patches of the relentless irrigation. I opened two more beers, the headlights dipping and swaying drunkenly across the never-ending acres.

I felt good. It was good to go shooting with Tim.

Arriving at Tim's little thatched cottage near the main canal, we saw Trish silhouetted in the doorway, her long, slightly frizzy hair haloed against the light from inside.

"Hello, Chris Cocks," she greeted with some warmth. "Got the dinner?"

I smiled and climbed onto the Matchless, slinging the dead birds over the handlebars, having tied the feet together with string. "Ja, we did okay. Your husband's a pretty mean shot."

She put her arms around Tim, dwarfed against his height, as we said goodnight.

I hung the three birds from the rafters of the corrugated-iron lean-to outside the kitchen when I got home. Carol's father had always taught me that birds and game had to 'hang' for several days, until almost green, until the smell was barely bearable. I'd go through the motions and hang them for perhaps a day. That was enough.

The following day, I pulled down the birds and gutted them. I wanted to make a casserole, which is about all Guinea fowl are good for, as tough as they are. But two of the birds were riddled with intestinal worms and I had to burn them on the rubbish heap round the back of the house, by the citrus trees near the security fence.

"What a waste," I muttered, as the flames licked up the line of petrol towards the carcasses.

✳

Jean le Jeune's farm was one down from French's, toward the southern end of Stage 1. Stage 1, the northern portion of the scheme, began at the Mutema River and Brown's farm, and ended at the club. Tim was Brian French's manager. I'd been told that Brian French, a huge, affable man, was German and had changed his name—something that often puzzled me. Perhaps he had a sense of humour; perhaps he had been one of the Waffen SS stormtroopers who had sought shade under the trees of the Champs Elysées in the summer of 1940. Jean le Jeune, on the other hand was a short, dapper French Mauritian, who apparently hadn't changed his name but, like Brian French, was always smoking a pipe. With typical Gallic looks, swarthy and with dark bushy eyebrows, he was a leading light in the community, though I do believe he tended to take himself rather too seriously.

The Lowveld was riddled with French Mauritians, originally sugar farmers who'd been imported into the country during the fifties and sixties to assist in the development of the vast sugar estates opening up at Hippo Valley and Triangle. Most were industrious and successful and, although they integrated well into what were predominantly Anglo-Saxon communities, they retained their own distinctive identities.

"More spaghetti, Chris?" Trish asked, ladle in hand.

I shook my head and took the plate through to the kitchen. Trish was a great cook, never one to complain when the north stick converged on the warmth of their little thatched cottage by the canal. We were on 'stand-by', a peculiar institution that required us to get together in uniform at one pre-arranged spot and wait for something to happen. I'd received word that morning from Gordy Gandanga that he'd received intelligence that possibly one of the farm stores "north of the club" was going to be taken out by the gooks. There were several stores north of the club, but Manie Dreyer, as shrewd as ever, deduced that the most likely target would be either French's or le Jeune's.

So, with Tim's agreement, we decided that the ideal stand-by house would be his. And as usual, unprompted, Trish had cooked supper for us. I'd made sure to park the Hyena behind the house, out of sight from the nine-foot-mat tar road that ran parallel to the canal. If the gooks were going to come, we wouldn't want to spook them with any signs of security forces in the immediate vicinity.

It was about nine o'clock and we were enjoying the evening. Stand-by was not too arduous and invariably ended up as a drunken social event. Trish had some Mozart playing on the stereo. I had one ear listening out for the A76 radio, hissing softly at my feet by the settee; the other listening to the new man, Argyle, filling us in on his background.

Gordy Gandanga was doing a one-man stakeout at le Jeune's store and Garikayi was doing the same at French's. Gordy had felt that one-man OPs were more secure than the whole stick bumbling in and possibly compromising the operation. I hadn't disagreed. It was cold out there. Both were in radio contact. The plan was that, as and when the gooks made an appearance at whichever store, either Gordy or Garikayi would radio through and the stand-by stick would hotfoot it the few hundred meters to the store in question and engage the gooks, having hopefully taken them by surprise. Gordy and Garikayi would have withdrawn by this time, to obviate the danger of getting caught in any crossfire. Manie had laughed at this and told Gordy that this was just an excuse to avoid getting involved in a fire fight. Gordy hadn't thought that particularly funny.

I studied the new man of the stick. Jan Pieter Casper Argyle. An Afrikaner with an obvious amount of Scottish blood, he'd recently come to work as one of the SLA section managers. At the same time, he'd promptly volunteered for PATU duty. This had impressed me no end, as Jan was well into his fifties. He was a craggy, well-worn Charles Bronson lookalike, but with a strong Afrikaans accent. Like Zack Prinsloo, it seemed Jan had also been driven off his family farm and had been forced to find employment elsewhere.

There were several section managers in this position, though I often wondered about the veracity of their claims. I sometimes suspected that perhaps these people were simply poor, derelict farmers who would have gone bust anyway, with or without the war. Genuine Rhodesian *bywoners*, squatter farmers. Certainly that new manager in Hennie's housing site was poor white trash. I'd been round there once for some reason or the other and had been invited in for tea. The furniture was poor-white-trash furniture, but the pièce de résistance was the dining-room table, which was crudely fashioned out of four creosoted gum poles with a sheet of galvanized corrugated iron as the tabletop. And the *bywoner* hadn't even bothered to flatten the corrugations. I discussed this amazing fact with Pirsons and Jacklass at the club one night. We all cruelly agreed that perhaps he couldn't afford a gravy dish, and his *vrou* simply ladled the gravy at the top of the table and let it run down the corrugations to the barefooted *kinders* at the other end.

Jan Pieter Casper wasn't, I believe, a *bywoner*. He was too much like Charles Bronson. He had too much integrity. And besides, he bit the filters off his cigarettes and spat them out before lighting up.

Trish had turned Mozart's volume up. Tim was passing around glass goblets of warm Napoleon brandy and a box of King Edward cigars. I relaxed lazily in the sumptuous draylon settee, a contented glow coming over me. What style, I thought, though marred somewhat by the grubby camouflage fatigues we were wearing. It didn't quite gel—brandy, cigars and Mozart on the one hand—grenades, rifles and uniforms on the other.

My reverie was rudely interrupted by rasping sounds spluttering out from the sub-standard A76 radio. I snatched at the handset. "Ssh!" I snapped at the others. "Someone's trying to get through."

Trish padded across the Persian carpet and turned down the volume on the stereo. The others were silent, the air filled with expectation.

A voice, whispering, came over the radio. Immediately I recognized the husky tones of Gordy Gandanga. "Chris, Chris do you read?"

"Roger, Gordy. I have you fives." I was speaking softly, deliberately so. If Gordy had the enemy in his vicinity and hadn't turned down the volume on his radio, my voice would have come across as loud as a megaphone in the stillness of the night. Even across the airwaves, we could sense the tension in his voice, the adrenaline. I knew he was on to something—like when you hook a big fish and you just know it's a big one.

He was mumbling, trying to soften his voice to almost nothing. "Chris. I have the Charlie Tangos visual in the store. Figures twenty, maybe thirty. Looks like they're cleaning it out. D'you copy?"

I double-clicked the pressle switch on my handset as an acknowledgement. Words were not necessary from my side.

"Chris, I'm going to pull out now. Can you get mobile ASAP?"

I double-clicked again.

"Roger, Chris. Out to you. Good luck."

I double-clicked for the last time.

Already the men were strapping on their webbing, grabbing at weapons. I drained the goblet of Napoleon's, the brandy hot and sensual in my throat. Trish was hugging Tim, her body language showing her fear.

I put on my green gook cap and cocked my rifle as I walked out in to the cold night air. It was nearly midnight. Cheeky bastards, I thought. Taking out a store on the road. Well, we'd see soon enough. I felt that old familiar rush of nerves, my throat now dry, exacerbated by the harshness of the Kind Edward cigar. Tim was at my side, his keys jangling as he opened up the big security gates.

I gathered the men around me. Here was the plan. I knew le Jeune's store. It was set right on the road, facing the canal. I seemed to remember there was a brick pump-house by the canal, more or less directly opposite the store, perhaps thirty or forty metres from the door of the store.

"Tim," I whispered. "Has le Jeune's store got a door at the back?" I was thinking about escape routes.

"No, only the front entrance."

"Good. If they're still inside when we get there, then we've got them fucked. No escape." I could sense Manie straining at the bit, eager to get to the store. I refused to let him rush me. The men must know of the plan, as vague as it might be. Deliberately vague—to allow for flexibility. No plan ever went according to design, I'd long since learned. And the more rigid and convoluted a plan, the greater the chance of a mess. The art was being able to formulate a plan there and then, during the heat of the action.

"We move to the store in single file on the right-hand side of the road. Less chance of being seen on approach. There's the big baobab about fifty metres or so from the store. When we get there, we'll snivel across the road down to the canal and head for the pump-house. Because the canal is down the bank, we'll be able to get there quite easily without being spotted. Manie, I want you to take Tim and Paul to the southern side of the pump-house and spread out on the verge of the canal. I'll take Ant and Jan with me to the northern side. Wait for me to open fire. If they retaliate too heavily, we can always take cover down the bank. Okay? Understood?"

The men nodded anxiously as I lead them through the gates.

"We are going to trot until we get to the baobab. I don't want any kit rattling. Okay?"

The men nodded again in the moonlight, the whites of their eyes staring out ahead. They shuffled their weapons, hitching up their webbing, getting comfortable.

"Okay, let's go," I whispered loudly. "Keep your distances."

The men were veterans and needed no telling, but it was a ritual, a comforting ritual. I led off at a brisk trot, keeping to the grassy verge where possible, but now and again the route faded into gravel and I could hear the soft crunch of boots behind me. It was unavoidable. Just so long as there were no metallic *clinks* of rifles or magazines. Tinny *clinks* that appeared insignificant, but could reverberate through the night and alert the enemy.

We'd run several hundred metres, my breathing hurried, pounding in my ears, when I saw the looming shape of the baobab tree up ahead. I slowed to a fast walk, hearing the men panting behind. The security lights of the store shone beyond, vulgar and synthetic in the moonlight.

I brought the men to a stop, crouching, rifle at the ready. A quick check for anything untoward before the next stage of crossing the road. We'd be exposed, but a quick dash, stooped low, might do it—coupled hopefully with guerrilla complacency. I strained my eyes along the road towards the store. All was still. Not a sound, not a movement. Perhaps Gordy had been mistaken.

Glancing behind to make sure the men were still in a state of readiness, that no idiot had taken off his webbing and was settling down for a smoke break, I raised my arm in an arcing movement. Still stooped low, with my rifle at the trail a bare few inches above the tar, I made a dash across the road and came to rest in the grassy verge on the other side. I tumbled down the slope, out of view, as the next man followed on behind.

There was no time to lose. Already I was on the narrow footpath by the edge of the canal. Without looking, I sensed all the men were now safely across. I broke into a trot. Although seemingly safe and out of sight from the road, this was a dangerous time. It would only take one guerrilla to appear at the top of the embankment and he'd have us at his mercy. The only way out would be up—towards the fire. I could see the shape of the brick pump-house a hundred metres or so up ahead.

Keep going, Chris, I urged myself. Got to get to that pump-house. At least there's cover there. I thought I could sense the men behind me feeling the same. And then we were there. I collapsed in the lee of the brick wall, waiting for the others. Anthony, and then Jan, tumbled heavily at my side, puffing and heaving. Manie was already round the other side with Paul and Tim, in position at the top of the embankment.

"So far so good," I whispered to Anthony at my side. "You ready?"

Anthony hitched the Bren gun on to his hip, facing up the grassy slope. "Sure thing, man," he grinned softly. "Up an' at 'em!"

Still, there was no noise from the store—only the glare of the security lights creeping down towards the canal, casting eerie, distorted shadows. I leopard-crawled to the top of the bank, Anthony and Jan on either side of me.

With my rifle barrel pointing ahead, I cautiously poked my head over the lip of the bank and peered across the road through the mist of the overhead flourescent lights. The double doors of the store were open, that much was clear. But inside was darkness and I couldn't tell if there was movement or not. Wait it out. Patience Chris. If they're inside, they've got to come out sometime.

My nerves had settled and although I could feel my heart pounding, clawing up my throat, I felt confident. We were in position. We had the advantage. We were in control. Wait it out. Wait ... wait ... wait.

And then gradually, low rumblings, murmurings and shufflings and movements from within. They were there!

I strained my ears, trying to pop them by forcing a series of yawns. I could make out faint noises. Boxes being moved, crates of bottles being lifted—and all the while the low hum of muffled voices.

And then in to the glare of the lights, a lone guerrilla stepped out from the double doors, arrogantly, confidently. He had an AK-47 slung casually across his chest. He was wearing blue jeans and on his head an Australian-style bush hat, slouched down on both sides. He stood there for several moments, warily checking to his left and right, perfectly silhouetted under the faded Five Roses Tea and Coca-Cola advertising signs above the door.

So this was our enemy? This was the enemy of that night at the Section 4 compound? This was the enemy that had pounded us with RPGs and mortars from that ridge in the hills? Now I see you, my enemy. Now I have you.

For a long second he seemed to look across the road, directly at our position, not forty metres from him—almost as if he were staring at us, sensing my innermost thoughts, able to comprehend that his foe was in position, ready to kill him. I shrank inwardly, holding my breath. It was too soon. We must wait for the others. Pray God he doesn't see us. Let Manie and Tim and Paul also be dead still. I remember feeling Anthony at my side—my big, bulky, reliable Bren gunner, so calm and so in control. It gave me courage. And Argyle, the new man—also dead still, dead calm. I was blessed.

Seemingly satisfied that there was no danger, the guerrilla turned, presumably giving the all-clear to the people inside. I followed him above the sights of the rifle as he sauntered cautiously to the corner of the store. And then, distracted, the shapes of people began coming out from the store, in one massed group. I was startled. They didn't look like guerrillas. They weren't. They were civilians! Impressed porters, jostling and struggling under the weight of boxes and store goods, some on their heads, some in their arms. Even from my position I could sense their fear.

And then another guerrilla, and then another—stepping out on either side of the mass of civilians, silently shepherding them out the door with the barrels of their weapons.

I could sense Anthony braced over his gun, his whole body quivering, taut with expectation. But what to do? They were civilians. My mind raced. Open fire and hope for the best? Hope like hell we got the gooks and not the civvies? Some hope. I remembered a similar situation in my army days a year or so before—press-ganged porters, the dilemma of killing civilians. Was that my precedent?

In a few brief seconds I turned the problem over in my mind a dozen times. The mass was regrouping and was starting to shuffle away from the store up the road. I couldn't wait any longer. A few more paces and they'd be out of the killing zone. I could almost hear Manie's screaming in my brain to open fire.

I leaned over my rifle, pulling the stock into my shoulder, seeking out the guerrilla farthest to the right—the one most likely to escape first. The glare from the lights was shining through my sights, blurring the target out of focus. No matter. Shoot. The Bren would do the rest.

I squeezed the trigger and the single shot rang out in an almost obscene manner. In that split second my shot changed everything. Seconds before, men would live, now they were to die. For a brief moment time stood still. A brief moment of silence and then the Bren gun opened up at my side, the methodical detonations pounding in my ears. Peering over my barrel, I was unable to tell whether my shot had told, such was the unfolding mayhem before my eyes. Manie and his men had opened up on the other side of the pump-house, as the length of that verge became one super-effective killing machine.

The din was furious, the shooting drowning out the panic and the screams of the people, that pitiful mass of humanity, as they clawed and scrambled for what little cover there was.

A guerrilla, obviously wounded, was crawling desperately towards the sanctuary of the darkness, away from the security lights that a few seconds before had been his ally. But the bullets found him a few paces before he could reach the shadows and he lay still, face down in the dirt, his arms still outstretched towards the salvation that had failed him.

Then a voice was calling out from the stricken mass, imploring, begging. "*Bwana, bwana.* Stop the shooting. For Jesus, please *bwana*, don't shoot."

Anthony was changing magazines and glanced at me, the whites of his eyes ablaze. "Huh? What'n the hell is that?" he shouted to me.

And then from nowhere, I sensed someone was shooting at us. Bullets were cracking above our heads and instinctively I ducked. Someone was shooting at us, only too well, but from where?

I heard a grunt to my side. It was Jan.

Anthony had re-cocked the Bren and was returning fire, sweeping the barrel from side to side, seeking out the enemy, traversing the mass.

"*Bwana*!" the voice came back, shrieking hysterically. "Please, *bwana*. Stop the shooting. It is me. Wellington. Wellington the barman!"

This was madness. I sub-consciously registered that our friend Wellington, the club barman, was there to our front. In the killing field. Wellington, who had served us so many hundreds of brandies and ginger ales, 'Soapies' and canes and Cokes. Madness. It was impossible. And Anthony, unhearing, was furiously firing, his head jarring ever so slightly with the rhythm of the gun.

And then, as suddenly as it had started, it stopped. The enemy gunmen had stopped firing. There was no movement to our front, merely a low moaning coming through the cold and the dust.

"CEASE FIRE!" I shouted, unnecessarily, for the men had already stopped. "Reload and stand by!"

The metallic clink of magazines could be heard along the verge.

"Manie! You okay that side?" I called.

A muffled reply. "Ja, Chris. All in order."

"Thanks, Manie. Can you get one man facing the rear, please … across the canal. They might come back and have a go at us."

"Roger. Copied that."

I looked to the two men with me. One of the flourescent security light tubes was buzzing and flickering across at the store, above the shapeless forms outside the double doors. Anthony, still tense and hunched over his Bren, was waiting for something to move, just waiting.

Jan was moaning softly, his rifle lying at his side.

I started. "Jan, what is it?"

"Agh, it's nothing. I think one of those focken' kaffirs just shot me." He had his left arm outstretched, curiously inspecting it, gently pumping his fist.

I scurried to his side, pulling out my penlight torch. He smiled at me, the wry Charles Bronson smile, and proffered the afflicted arm to the torchlight.

"Shit, Jan! Gave me a fuckin' fright! Are you okay?" I asked, grabbing the arm. There was a lot of blood over the forearm and even in the half-light I could see Jan's face, pallid and drawn, more from shock than anything else.

I tugged at the handkerchief in my pocket and gently wiped the blood from his arm. It smelt sweet and I could almost taste the faint scent of iron.

I laughed, my head bent low, looking for the wound. "It's a flesh wound, Jan. Thank Christ! There's no entry. It's only gashed you. You're fuckin' lucky, you old bastard." I shone the torch on the wound. It was about two inches long and looked like an accidental cut from a blunt machete.

I felt the relief course through his body. I was as equally relieved. I felt responsible. I pulled out the single first-field dressing I had in my webbing and strapped up the wound. There was always a lot of blood with flesh wounds. Then, taking out my hip flask, I took a quick slug before passing it to Jan.

"Drink, Jan. You'll feel better."

He put the flask to his lips and drank long and hard. I almost snatched it from him, Steady on, man. Steady. But I desisted. He grunted with satisfaction, wiping his mouth at the same time, and gave me back the flask.

"*Ja, dankie. Baie lekker.*" Jan was okay. He was out of shock.

And now?

Now the shapes and bundles in the killing ground. There was work to do. Clean-up work.

I instructed Anthony and Jan to maintain their position, covering us from the verge. Jan was to face behind, across the canal; and Anthony with the Bren was to keep the gun trained on the right-hand corner of the store where I believed the enemy had fled.

"Manie!" I shouted over the pump-house. "Ant and Jan are going to cover us. Get into extended line and let's sweep up to the store. Keep your dressing on me."

"Yo! No sweat," Manie called back. He sounded bored. The action was done. Well, not quite—the killing was not quite done.

Low moaning sounds came from the lumpy mass in front of the store. I stood up, but couldn't make out any definition. The overhead lights were still humming irritably, as clouds of insects buzzed around the tubes, hissing and combusting in little puffs as they touched, before plummeting into the mass of lumps.

"Okay, let's go," I signalled to Manie and the others. "Keep your eyes peeled. I dunno if the gooks we got are dead." I wasn't sure if we'd actually got any gooks, apart from the one we'd seen plainly tumble before the line of shadows. He was still there, unmoving, curled up in a foetal position with his back to me. I could not see his weapon. Possible danger. Approaching the body with caution, my *veldskoene* padding silently in the dust, I brought my weapon in to my shoulder, my forefinger resting lightly on the trigger.

Still no movement. No sign. I was at the body now, at his back. I saw the AK sprawled in the dirt a few paces away. It was safe. Only a grenade to worry about now. Maybe he had one clenched to his chest. Maybe he didn't. Maybe he was already dead. I crouched low, inches from his back, listening for the faintest sound of breathing, of breath. If he was alive he would not be aware of my presence. Plan. Pull the body over on to its back, crouching away, ready to hit the dirt if he did have a grenade tucked away.

I yanked on the blue denim jacket sleeve and the body rolled over with an involuntary fart, an arm flopping uselessly with a thud on the ground. He was dead, the flesh cool to the touch. Not yet cold, but the warmth fading fast. I looked into his face, or what was left of it. A bullet had smashed the jawbone away, white shattered bone piercing the lips and the nose. There was not much blood. The eyes were rolled back, grotesquely, vacantly trying to see over the back of the cranium.

A voice called out. "Okay, Chris? That one dead?" It was Manie. I saw him picking his way through the shapes and the lumps.

"Ja, as a dodo," I returned.

"Good! Another one here. Fuck, old Munda can sure make a mess with that Bren."

It was time to move on. Quickly rifling through the dead guerrilla's pockets, I plucked out a few grubby two-dollar notes and shoved them in my pocket.

I went over to Manie. He was standing over another body, this one stretched out in an ungainly fashion over the very store goods he had so recently looted. Sewing machines, blankets, transistor radios, groceries, clothes and bottles of cool drink. The body was seeped in blood, so much that it was difficult to tell where the bullets had struck. It was not important. I see you enemy. I see you as a pulped-up mess. You're fucked good and proper now, comrade.

And then two more bodies, civilians. AMAs, as Special Branch called them. African Male Adults. Though one was still quite young and could have in fact been an AMJ—an African Male Juvenile. They were draped over each other, their faces wretched masks of terror and disbelief.

"Someone's gonna be shy two cotton pickers," Manie jibed, poking the one corpse with his boot.

"Poor bastards," Paul Brown added. "They were forced into this."

"Ag, serve the fuckers right," Manie kicked the other corpse. "They knew what they were getting into.

There was a shout from the shadows to the left. It was Tim. "Hey, Chris! There's one still alive here!" There was a note of urgency, anxiety in his voice.

"Gook?" I shouted back.

"Yeah, gook. He's pretty fucked."

"Okay, I'm coming. Have you cleared his weapon?"

"Affirmative. AKM with fancy wire-cutters," Tim replied through the shadows. "And don't get any ideas. They're mine!"

I smiled. He could have them, if Gordy Gandanga didn't get there first. Ag, fuck him! Where was he anyway? Probably at the club getting blasted.

I went over to Tim and the victim at his feet. He was on his back, his breathing fast and shallow. He was conscious, his eyes staring widely, fixedly up at the white men leaning over him. I studied him. He looked to be in his mid-twenties, probably quite senior in the group. Had to be—what with that AKM and the wire-cutters. They didn't give those kinds of weapons to any old palooka. Like the others he was wearing blue denim jeans, pulled low over his hips like a dude. He was wearing a heavy-duty, olive-green combat shirt under the chest webbing. Good and sturdy. The Commies made good stuff. I inspected the shirt for damage, for bullet holes, but saw none. Maybe he was shot in the back. Pity, it looked a nice shirt. Wouldn't mind keeping it.

"Where's he shot, Tim?"

Tim shook his head. "Dunno. I think the back. He's lying in a pool of blood."

I saw the dark stains in the dust around the guerrilla. "Yup. Back shot."

"What are we going to do with him?" Tim asked, his anxiety fading.

The man was dying.

I looked at Tim, saying nothing, my eyebrows raised in a rhetorical question mark.

Tim was shaking his head. "No way! Not me, man. I'm not doing it. That's for sure." He turned his back.

I couldn't expect him to. Not a civvy in uniform.

The guerrilla was watching the spectacle above, impassively. He knew what was happening but could do nothing.

I went up to the man and put the muzzle of my FN against his temple. Still, the guerrilla looked to the black sky, saying nothing, giving nothing away. I pulled the trigger. The body bucked violently, once, and was then still. Bits of blood and brains and bone spattered over my clothes. Ag, filthy fucker!

The insects buzzed irritatingly under the humming flourescent tubes above as a voice came through the darkness, from the canal. It was Anthony. "Hope that wasn't Wellington you just blew away!"

Shit! Wellington! The barman!

"Nah, don't worry, Munda." Manie chuckled. "Wellington's gone like a long dog. Ten-yard strides, arms flapping like a swastika."

Anthony's hyena laughed boomed through the gloom, as the A76 crackled into life. It was Gordy. He was on his way.

"Lord fucking save us!" Manie laughed cynically. "Here comes the cavalry in the nick of time. Betcha he was at the club. Wonder if the super-cop even noticed Welly wasn't there?"

We wandered around searching for more bodies and helping ourselves to sundry bits of booty. Le Jeune wouldn't know. And anyway, what did he care? He'd be putting in some bloated insurance claim to the Terrorist Victims Relief Fund. Manie took some blankets for his dogs. Tim found some very nice pliers and a hammer. I took some scissors and a T-shirt.

There were no more bodies. That was the final tally—three gooks, two civvies. Not bad. In fact, quite okay.

We sat among the boxes and the bundles, drinking le Jeune's warm Cokes. The Land Rover headlights were approaching, dipping and weaving through the flood bunds. Some minutes later Gordy pulled up alongside, his arm resting casually out of the window. I knew it was an act. He was nervous. Who had we murdered now?

"Soooo, Chris. How many?" he asked nonchalantly.

"Three gooks. Two civvies killed in crossfire." I wondered whether they'd get a mention on the TV communiqué tomorrow evening. Probably not. There were simply too many killed-in-crossfire these days.

Gordy nodded, seemingly appreciatively, as he got out of the Land Rover. We finished our Cokes and tossed the bottles to the side with all the other junk and loot. We stood up.

"Where you going?" Gordy's voice barked.

"Huh?"

"I said, where are you going? We can't leave all this stuff here?" He sounded incredulous.

"What do you mean?" I asked, equally incredulous. "You want us to clean this lot up?" I could hear the edge in my voice.

"Damn right. It's not finished yet."

"Hah!" I snorted. "Get real, Gordy." I looked at him in disbelief. It was like asking children to clean up their room after they'd made a mess.

"Go'n wake up that fucken' Frog, le Jeune," Manie snapped. "It's his shit. Tell him to fucken' clean it up!"

I could see the veins in Gordy's neck beginning to throb. He was getting angry.

But so were we. "C'mon okes. Let's get home." I ignored Gordy. "I don't suppose Gordy will give us a lift so we'll have to walk." We started making our way up the road, back towards Tim's house.

Gordy's shouts faded slowly in the background. "You better get back here right now. Now, I tell you! You'll all find yourselves on a charge. Wilfully disobeying a lawful word of command ..."

"Ag, fuck him." Manie muttered.

It was two in the morning before I got back home. We finished off the Napoleon's and the King Edwards at Tim's. I then dropped the rest of the men off at their respective houses—a time-consuming business in the Hyena. I tiptoed into the house. Carol was sleeping soundly, her pregnant bulk unmoving in the double bed. She'd forgotten to switch off the overhead fan. The room was cold.

I could smell the sweaty, sickly sweetness of the dried blood and bones and brains on my clothes, so I took them off on the verandah and went for a shower. A hot shower which expunged the stench of death from my body. Now I felt clean. Still wet, draped in a towel, I went on to the verandah for a final smoke. The dogs were gnawing at the clothes, tugging greedily at the morsels of human flesh.

"Oi!" I snapped. "Ish! Jasper! Get outa there!"

The dogs slunk off, their tails between their legs.

"Fuckin' animals!" I scolded, muttering. "Where're your bloody manners?"

*

As usual, the following evening I went to the club. Wellington was back on duty behind the bar and regarded me nervously as I ordered a brandy and ginger ale. I smiled at him. He was a good *munt*, as they say.

"You okay, Welly?"

He shook his head vigorously. "*Bwana*, Jesus is my witness. I pray for you, *bwana*. I thank Jesus that you did not shoot me. I was shouting, you know, *bwana*. I was shouting for you to shoot another place. And I know, *bwana*, you lissen. Thank you, my *bwana*, thank you. Jesus he's thanking you." He turned to pour the drink, still shaking his head in disbelief, disbelief that he was still on this planet.

So that was the story of Wellington. Le Jeune never did come and thank us for saving his store. Not a crate of beer as a gesture. Not a word. What would a thank-you have cost? An acknowledgement even?

Ag, well.

Of convoys and cookies

**Intensive Coronary Unit, Parirenyatwa Hospital, Harare:
16 March 1995**

Awake again. In a state of nothingness again. I know I am alive, well
at least my body is functioning—I can hear it, I can smell it, I can feel
it. It is numb from the time in bed. How many days now? But it is of
no consequence. If I were to die at this very second it would make not
one iota of difference to the world. Just another corpse.

And the spirit, God knows where that'd go.

I am remembering that last nightmare. Perhaps that was the one that
tipped the scales. When the black hands came through the thatched
roof, clawing at me in my bed, the fingers like writhing, evil snakes
And I woke my wife and tried to show her but she got scared and
hid under the bedclothes. They were all around the rondavel, in the
garden. They were surrounding us. They were coming to kill us. I
could see them darting along the shadows, by the paw paw trees. It
was just a matter of time now.

I took out the Mokarev pistol from the drawer by the bed and went to
the window, crouching low, out of view. I cocked the pistol and waited.
I was in my underpants. I was sweating. I waited, but no more shadows
came. There were no more hands coming through the thatch.

So I went back to bed, cold from the sweat that had drenched my
body.

Middle Sabi: September 1979

The wheat was turning in the lands, drying from green to golden brown—a colour similar to that in the breakfast-cereal adverts. The hot, dry winds swept along the valley, inciting the *duiweltjies,* the nasty little dust devils, miniature tornadoes that spun crazily out of control, causing minor havoc in its path and lodging the wheat so badly that it became so tangled up in itself as to become unreapable.

And when the *duiweltjies* were gone, the quealea came, in their millions, darkening the sun with their numbers. Like airborne ants, these little birds were the feathered locusts of the Lowveld, the ultimate reaping machine, super-effective destroyers of crops in their swathe-like *blitzkreigs.*

Sitting under the thorn tree on the lawn, the sprinkler still *phut-phutting* after all these months, I heard the roar of a million tiny wings, sounding like rolling thunder. I looked up to the sky and saw the flocks, as wave upon wave of birds zeroed in on the sprawling wheat lands. There was nothing that could be done, but in futile desperation I snatched the shotgun from the verandah and loaded it with Number 8s. Pumping round after round up into the humming, beating mass made little difference. A temporary hole of blue sky was visible for a millisecond, before it closed up, healing itself. And the only evidence of any damage was the *plop, plop, plop* of the victims tumbling to earth and the squealing picannins as they dashed frantically hither and thither gathering up the dead birds in their breasts.

Then, at night, the Agricair crop-sprayer would take off in the evening gloom and seek out the nests along the banks of the Sabi. Loaded with tanks of Quealeatox and DDT, the aeroplane searched for the markers, the masked black men with the torches on the edge of the lands, indicating the quelea nests. And the plane would douse the sleeping birds with the poison and the following morning the riverbanks would be littered with hundreds upon thousands of dead birds.

But still they came and, when they were done and had moved off, the locusts came. But this year the locusts were manageable, the swarms small and ineffective. Not like the previous years when thousands of acres had been stripped clean in a matter of hours.

*

There was great excitement. A trip was planned to Salisbury. Carol, eight months pregnant, was due to see her gynaecologist. As the baby was due in mid-September and we had decided that it should be born in Salisbury at the Lady Chancellor Maternity Home, I applied for a few days' compassionate leave. It was granted. The day came to leave. Carol, in a billowy cotton frock, with her suitcase of stuff, waddled heavily across the lawn to the Renault, saying goodbye to Ish and Jasper sulking under the lean-to. Mrs. Mastak and young Susan Gunn were already in the back seat of the car. We were giving them a lift as far as Umtali.

Mrs. Mastak, a heavily built Polish woman, wife of the hero of Monte Cassino, was in her own right a heroine of the Polish Resistance. I understood she had been a captain in the Free Polish Army during World War Two and, like her husband, had been highly decorated for bravery. She was a good, strong, kindly woman and fussed after Carol in a matronly fashion.

Susan Gunn, on her way back to school, was a young girl around nine or ten. Her father was Peter Gunn who had been executed by guerrillas on his Middle Sabi farm a year before. She was a pretty girl, with long, straight, blond hair, curtaining a happy, open face.

We changed convoys twice. First at Tanganda Junction when Zack and Frik, our escorts, had said goodbye and handed us over to the Chipinga–Birchenough Bridge convoy. And then again at Birchenough Bridge—that imposing, massive steel suspension structure that had been built across the Sabi River in the early days; when gallant, dashing young colonists from Britain, wearing baggy khaki trousers and pith helmets, dreamed dreams of spreading the empire eastward into the wild territories of Portuguese East Africa.

Birchenough Bridge was now simply a dry, dusty meeting place for the convoys converging from Fort Victoria, Chipinga and Umtali. Scruffy Internal Affairs vedettes, the custodians of the bridge, with grubby khakis and red-banded caps, slouched lazily on the parapets, eyeing the convoys with disinterest.

The convoy from Fort Vic was late, so we waited an extra half-hour. When they came, the final convoy to Umtali must have numbered over a hundred cars in total. How could three armoured Mazda pick-ups possibly hope to secure such a length?

With sporadic irregularity the convoy stopped. As we'd been instructed we pulled over onto the verge to allow the roving Police Reserve Mazda access to the front. The halts were never explained and, with the head of the convoy several kilometres up ahead, we had no idea what the hold-ups were about. Perhaps one of the cars had had a puncture; perhaps there was a suspicion of landmines. We never knew.

This time the stop felt nervous. Something was wrong. I pulled over on to the shoulder, opened my window and lit up a cigarette … and waited. There was a stillness in air, marred only by the background screech of Christmas beetles in the bush, and the pounding of Deep Purple in the casette player. *My woman from Tokyo.* I took stock of our position. About thirty or forty metres up ahead was a low-level bridge. We were parked in the shelter of a cutting, our left shielded from the bush by a grassy embankment. Safe enough. I switched off the tape.

"What happens?" Mrs. Mastak asked inquisitively in her singsong Polish accent.

"I don't know. Looks like something up ahead, but I can't see." I got out the car, grabbing my FN from the floor alongside the seat. I cocked it and looked up the road across the bridge. Nothing but the line of cars obediently pulled over.

And then, from the bush across the river, from the other side of the bridge, came the unmistakable *cack-cack* of Communist small-arms weaponry. I crouched instinctively, down by the open car door, noticing the anxious look on my wife's face. Susan was beginning to cry in the back seat.

A man in camouflage uniform came running up the road from the rear. "Ambush! Ambush!" he yelled frantically. "Get out your cars! Get in to cover. In the ditch! In the ditch!" He was brandishing a pistol above his head.

"Shit man, what's this crazy dickhead up to?" I muttered under my breath, flicking my cigarette butt across the tarmac.

It was almost as if they'd turned the volume up, as the noise of gunfire increased dramatically, clearly coming our way. I knew we were safe in the lee of the embankment but still, I felt I had to get the two women and the girl out of the car into the ditch.

I scurried round to the other side of the car and flung open the doors, hustling the women out. With almost Madonna-like serenity Mrs. Mastak shuffled her bulk across the seat, holding Susan's hand, gently cajoling her out from the perceived sanctuary of the back seat. The shooting was now certainly in our direction and I could hear the shots snapping overhead. Carol wasn't so easy. She was in extreme discomfort as I jostled and manoeuvred her pregnant frame out the door. She tumbled into the ditch, on to her back like a stricken dung beetle.

They were as safe as I could get them. I saw Susan clinging to Mrs. Mastak, burying her face in the older woman's bosom. I grabbed my FN and worked my way up the embankment. The man with the pistol had reached the bridge and was lying prone, slap bang in the middle of the road, legs apart, returning fire with his pistol. Jesus Christ! What an asshole! Where in the hell did he think he was? On the shooting range? *Pop, pop, pop*, like some kind of Wild Goose or Dirty Harry?

Shaking my head in disbelief, I pondered the wisdom of sticking my head over the embankment and returning fire. It would only take one accurate, or wayward, shot and my head would be split open like a rotten watermelon. Nah! For what? Let the Dirty Harry on the bridge get nailed rather. Not me. The decision was made for me by a salvo of sudden and violent detonations immediately behind me. Jesus! What now? The gooks had done a flanking attack? I shrank to the earth in alarm. Please Lord, please. Not now. Not after so long. Please.

But I wasn't hit. I glanced behind me, my mouth full of dirt. The roving Mazda was parked alongside the Renault, with the Browning machine gun firing noisily over our heads. I saw the elderly reservist manning the gun on the back of the pick-up, single mindedly, fearlessly, standing to his gun, blasting and blasting the enemy across the river. For a moment I was filled with admiration for this old man standing there, so coolly returning fire.

But did he have to do it right next to us? It had put the fear of God into the women, more so than the enemy fire had done. They were sobbing hysterically, howling and moaning above the cacophony of the Browning. I scrambled down into the ditch and hugged Carol to my chest, trying desperately to shield her face from the violence above. Her body was heaving involuntarily, in spasms. I thought for a second the baby was coming.

And then the gun stopped, the only sounds to be heard being the *pop-pop* of Dirty Harry still on the bridge, obviously alive. I looked up at the man behind the Browning. He had lifted his goggles and was peering earnestly into the bush across the embankment. He banged on the roof of the cab. "I think they've gone, Bob."

Bob grunted from inside the cab and the Mazda roared off, up to the front of the convoy to check things out that end. I wondered whether Dirty Harry had managed to get out of the way in time.

The sobbing had subsided. Carol was crying now, softly whimpering. I put my arms under hers and cranked her up on to her feet. Her entire dress was covered in thorns. She'd landed in a nest of paper thorns and *duiwel* thorns, those evil, multi-spiked devil thorns that could puncture a *veldskoen*. Her backside was liberally peppered with hundreds of them. Mrs. Mastak came to help and, one by one, we pulled them out. Susan had collapsed in shock on the back seat, wailing softly.

I could hear the cars starting up. We were moving out. I hustled the women in to the car as tenderly as possible, levering Carol in to her seat. Her hair was wet from sweat and her face streaked with the tears that had mingled with her make-up.

I changed the tape as I turned the ignition. I'd had enough of Deep Purple. I popped in a Melanie tape. Nice feminine music. Maybe that'd calm Susan down. I glanced in the rearview mirror. She was still crying in Mrs. Mastak's arms, the older woman soothing her, stroking her hair, making low clucking sounds.

The convoy continued on its journey to Umtali and Susan cried all the way.

On 30 September 1979, our son was born. He was named Guy Lamond Cocks. Guy, after his dead uncle, Carol's brother, who had been killed in action in February 1977, and Lamond after my paternal grandmother from the Lamond clan in Scotland. It should have been a joyous occasion, but I wasn't there. I was back in Middle Sabi.

We'd arrived in Salisbury without further incident after the convoy ambush. As Carol's parents were farmers and lived out of town in Mzarabani in the Zambezi Valley, we stayed at my parents' house. The atmosphere was tense. Carol still hadn't forgiven them their hostility and they still hadn't come to terms with the fact that I had married this woman. It was a situation that was never to be fully resolved.

My few days' compassionate leave came and went and there was no sign of the baby coming. It was overdue and then it was late. The gynaecologist decided, unilaterally of course (after all, what did a young couple barely out their teens know about these things?) that nature should take its course and that the baby should not be induced.

I found this all very frustrating. Where was the military precision in this? Where was there any kind of planning? I guess Carol was as equally frustrated, compounded by her immobility and discomfort.

I was more fortunate. I was mobile. I could go out and find my lost youth. And go out I did. Salisbury, the town of my birth, my home turf, held still unexplored treasures for me. Most of my friends lived in Salisbury and I visited them all, leaving Carol to sit it out at my parents' house. I visited 'The Cuckoo's Nest', the mess in Cork Road, Avondale where all my old army buddies lived during their R & Rs. I saw Abbott and Norris and Connelly and Coleman, in fact many of my former comrades from 3 Commando RLI. They had outgrown me, or so I felt and, although we sat at the table in the dining room with the bare Oregon pine floorboards and little else, and smoked joint after joint, rolled non-stop from the never-ending supply in the wooden fruit bowl that sat permanently in the middle of the table, it wasn't quite the same. It was a matter that we weren't actually sharing our experiences. I pined for the 'old days'.

Abbott was on some kind of murder rap for running over a black civvy, allegedly deliberately, while driving an army lorry. There was also talk of his having trashed some Catholic mission station near Fort Vic while on exercise and, for good measure, looting the hospital dispensary of all its drugs. I didn't pry. It wasn't my business and what did it matter? He was still my friend and always would be, regardless.

Connelly would come downstairs every morning in his 'greens', his 'number ones', his regimental dress uniform. He'd been shot up in an action over in Mozambique and was recuperating. I heard later that it had been some fellows from 2 Commando who'd shot him, mistaking him for a guerrilla. They'd visit him, wearing 'I shot John Connelly' T-shirts. He limped badly and his left arm was gammy. He was in a bad way. But that didn't stop him from dressing up for the morning spliff every day. And then, his eyes glazed and maniacal after the first joint, he'd goose-step around the house, boots pounding on the wooden floorboards, pissing everyone off; and when he was tired, stand to attention in front of the full-length mirror in the hall for hours on end. That was it. That was his day. And Janis Ian would be blaring out *Fly too high* and Lou Reed muttering *Walk on the wild side*, which incidentally was my record and never returned, therefore, ultimately, classified as stolen. But I had the Cuckoo's Nest's Jo Jo Zep and the Falcons' *Screaming Targets* LP, the one with that massive hit, *Hit and run*, on it. Some asshole had scribbled, in blue ballpoint, a bullet piercing the pilot's visor on the record sleeve. It looked gruesome but neat.

The nights were simply a darkened variation of the day and we'd all head off to the Inner Circle, a very alternative nightclub that the Rhodies tended to regard as an evil den of drugs and darkness and wouldn't be seen dead near. We'd just sit around on bean bags and pop Lemslim and smoke dope, watching some spaced-out blonde chick called Tree dance all night long—on her own, bouncing up and down like a pogo stick, unrelenting, never stopping. I wondered what she was on.

From time to time the police would come and bust the place, looking for drugs, bursting in like the Gestapo, their Alsatians straining at the leash, desperate to tear chunks of flesh out of us. But Tree wouldn't stop bouncing, not even when the Police's *Message in a bottle* had been ripped from its turntable by some overzealous cop looking for the left-wing revolution. And Abbott and Connelly, unmoved from their beanbags, would laugh at the cops as the cops would steer a course around us, away from us, zoning in on the more obvious, longer-haired 'hippie' targets.

And at dawn, sober from the excesses and the insidious self-guilt, I'd crawl home, back to my parents' house, and creep into the single bed with the sagging coir mattress alongside the sleeping form of my pregnant wife, cold and alone.

The time came for me to leave, back to Middle Sabi. There was just no sign of any baby movement. I pecked my wife on the cheek, wished her well and rejoined the convoy at the Nite-Star drive-in just outside town on the Umtali Road.

I got back home and smothered my loneliness with music, played at volume ten on the PA system. I'd worked out how to run the stereo through the amplifier. The dogs were there which was something. The club was still there, and that was also something. But I wanted more. I don't know what.

It was at this time that I experimented with 'cookies'. They all seemed to thrive on them at the Cuckoo's Nest. I'd heard a lot about them but had never tried them. Normal biscuit cookies like the *tannies*, the Afrikaans aunties, made, but liberally laced with marijuana. The difference between a spliff and a cookie is that the dope gets cooked in the cookie which does something to the efficacy and the potency—the difference between getting high and tripping. It was a challenge too strong to resist. Another of life's experiences that I simply could not let pass me by.

The secret appeared to be the strength and quality of the dope, followed by the quantity tossed into the mixing bowl. Always having erred on the dangerous side, the obsessive side, I pulled out Abbott's recipe and folded in a full cob of dope to the mix of flour and eggs. Ladling the baking tray full, I put it in the oven for the required period. It smelt good, with only the faintest hint of the sweet piquancy of dope apparent—almost like the smell of a nice, homely farm kitchen.

Now the test, the danger time. Being careful and wanting to gauge the strength and effect of the cookies, I fed a few to Ish the Alsatian and watched for any reaction as she gobbled them up. Nothing. So I fed her some more. An hour or two later her legs started buckling, her eyes started rolling and she crept to the corner of the living room, under the cool of the overhead fan, where she sank down to the floor and slept like that for two days. For a while I was concerned about her well-being and periodically checked on her breathing and nose-wetness. She was okay—simply in a deep, deep sleep.

So I tried. Apart from the sawdust-type dryness, they tasted good. Like Ish, no initial effect, so I ate some more. And some more. And then I began to sway and the music seemed louder than ever. It was sensual and I wanted a woman, but there was none. And the room was beginning to spin and the music wouldn't stop, now screaming in my brain. What time was it? Was it day or was it night? The colours of psychaedelia tumbled through the room, enveloping my naked, sweating body. I tried to sleep but was unable to find the bedroom and, still above, the overhead fans, cranking rhythmically faster and faster like the blades of an Alouette helicopter gunship starting up. And I was running to the helicopter, vomitting, stumbling, crying out.

Now the dog was panting heavily, her flanks heaving and her tongue, dry and pale, lying uselessly on the parquet tiles. I registered there was something wrong and with a cup of water spoon-fed the dog, pouring the liquid on her nose and drop by drop down her throat. And then I slept, curled up, still naked on the cool parquet floor next to the dog.

I don't know how many hours or days I slept like that but when I awoke the dog was gone. That was a good sign. She was up and about. The record, long spent, was turning impotently on the turntable, making a gentle *ssh-ssh* sound with each revolution. I found a towel, which I wrapped around my waist, and switched off the stereo. It was day and the dogs were frolicking in the sprinkler water, *phut-phutting* on the lawn.

The telephone rang and I jumped. It seemed so loud. I nervously picked up the handset. It was my mother. Carol had just had the baby—a boy, and all was fine.

Not before my next birthday

Intensive Coronary Unit, Parirenyatwa Hospital, Harare: 17 March 1995

The nightmares kept on coming. Nightmares of the nightmares, until it was no longer definable what was real and what wasn't. The nightmares merged into day and then again into night. Always there was the Mokarev pistol. Such a neat little thing. Not as neat as the Walther .32 I once had and foolishly sold for $25.

My, the Russians were clever—and we always used to pooh-pooh their weaponry—cheap plastic shit, but cheap plastic shit that could kill very well.

The metallic comfort of the Mokarev barrel in my mouth. And the woman screaming, imploring me not to do it. And me, screaming, yelling that, goddamn it, I was gonna fuckin' do it. That would teach her. That would teach them all. Then they'd all fuckin' see, hah?

But where was the Mokarev that night when I tried to kill her? She was a shark, or perhaps she was the shark's victim. Victim and shark became one and in the thrashing, bloodied shallows. I attacked with every ounce of strength I could muster and my hands were round the shark's slimy neck, twisting and threshing.

And again the woman was screaming, but this time screams of such primordial terror that I awoke. My hands were around her neck and there in the sodden sheets she was gasping and choking and crying.

"Fuck you, Chris!" she sobbed. "Fuck you!"

Middle Sabi: October 1979

Carol got a lift home and arrived back in Middle Sabi that hot, dusty

October day with baby Guy. I studied the child with mild curiosity, unable to comprehend that this little bundle of pink, crying flesh was actually the fruit of my loins. My own blood. It was meaningless. But it seemed quite cute in an icky sort of way and I determined to make an effort to be a good father.

I remember being so, so tired, night and day, twenty-four hours a day. And during the nights, I was out on PATU duties and I'd stagger in, exhausted, and the baby would be crying and Carol would be propped up in the double bed, asleep, with the baby clinging desperately to a bleeding nipple. And I'd unplug the baby and put him in his pram and shuffle back and forth along the parqueted passage. And he'd finally sleep and I'd finally sleep, only to be woken a few hours later by the obscene burst of the alarm clock.

It was crop-combining season and Anthony's combines would be revving up on the edges of the wheat lands, drivers masked, squinting into the early morning light.

I dragged myself out of bed. Carol was still sleeping, the baby was miraculously sleeping. I slipped on my *veldskoene* and padded through to the kitchen. Already I could hear the muffled roar of the combine harvesters in the near distance. Today, they were again attacking my section. I filled up the thermos with pre-mixed tea and clambered onto the Suzuki and puttered down the road to the section. Anthony was already there, like a panzer general, marshalling his tanks.

"D'you think you'll finish today?" I asked the big man. The roles were reversed. Now Anthony was the boss. No longer stick leader and Bren gunner, but section manager and Land Prep manager.

He could see that I was anxious to find out how the yields were panning out. He looked at me paternally, like he was saying, "Well, you've tried hard, Chris, but you just ain't gonna cut it this season." But he didn't.

Instead, "Well, it's not going that brilliantly, but it's not that bad either. We finished off Section 8 yesterday and the yields were shocking. Fourteen bags an acre! C'mon! I ask you."

I shook my head sagely. Goodness, that was bad.

"What went wrong?" I asked.

Anthony was slowly shaking his head. "It's the system, y'know. There's no accountability and no incentive. So, what happens? The section managers just don't give a damn. Never check their irrigation, flog the fertilizers to the settler farmers. All that type of shit." He gave me a searching look. "Know what I mean?"

I shrugged. What could I say? He was right.

He went on. "You can tell an estate land a mile off. Burst irrigation pipes all over the place, dead patches in the land. Fuck man, it's an embarrassment."

That it was.

I poured myself a plastic cup of tea and balanced it on the seat of the Suzuki. "So ... what kind of yields can you estimate for me?"

"Hmm ... dunno. Hard to say. Eighteen ... maybe twenty bags."

"That all?" Like it was some kind of auction.

"Ja. But all things considered, that's not too bad, considering you've got the biggest section. Twelve hundred acres plus."

"It's still crap, isn't it?" I stated, dejectedly.

The big man slapped me on the back. "Ja, but by SLA standards it's great." He strode off to shout instructions to one of the drivers who was making last-minute adjustments to his combine head. Getting the cut right, I supposed.

I turned away and wandered off to the section office. Samuel was making a start on the wages. That would need checking. I glanced over my shoulder. In massive clouds of dust and diesel fumes, the great machines were lumbering slowly into the sea of wheat. And behind them the rows of tractors and trailers were standing by, firing up their engines, ready to follow behind and take delivery of the wheat that would shortly be disgorged from the funnels.

There was an apparent lull in guerrilla activity. There was also a strangeness in the air, which I couldn't quite put my finger on. I'd long since given up listening to the mindless drivel of the Rhodesian

Broadcasting Corporation and the Himmlerian Harvey Ward. Well I listened, simply because the spoken English was better than the mindless drivel spewed out by the enemy's radio station, Radio Zimbabwe, broadcast from Maputo in Mozambique. Good Rhodesians weren't even supposed to know about Radio Zimbabwe. Communist propaganda, that's what it was. The same way we weren't supposed to know that the ZANLA guerrillas fighting us on the eastern border were led by Messrs. Robert Mugabe and Josiah Tongogara. Simply mentioning their names was tantamount to treason.

I vaguely knew that the idea of a ceasefire and peace talks was being mooted. We talked about these sorts of things at the club. As ever, Don Hounslow was convinced that the war must go on at all costs—until standards were maintained. This made no sense to us younger men. We could see that we were fighting for nothing.

And our leaders simply made it worse. There was a split in the Rhodesian Front. One or two of the Afrikaner RF MPs were leaving the country. Ian Smith was being politically outmanoeuvred at every turn, but instead of pragmatism, instead of realism, he dug his heels in further and complained how the rest of the world was doing the dirty.

We were ridiculing him in the bar and Don Hounslow was getting angry, his face flushed and florid from a combination of alcohol and rage.

"Ja, how do you like Smith's 'Never in a thousand years' speech?" Nat Pirsons asked rhetorically. He was referring to Smith's jingoistic speech about the continuance of white rule for another millennium ... or so. "I mean, really! What does he think we are? The Third Reich?"

"Well that lasted a good decade or so," Jacklass added. "But we're on the right track. We've got fifteen years behind us already."

Paterson laughed. "Only nine hundred and eight-five to go."

I looked at Hounslow. He was simmering in his drink, slouched over the bar counter in the corner. His body language looked exceedingly dangerous. I smiled thinly at the inevitability of what would happen in a few minutes. The three younger men, like terriers, wouldn't let up.

"Well, we've had the 'never in a thousand years' bit and now we've got the 'never in my lifetime' bit," Paterson continued.

"Fuck me!" Jacklass feigned surprise. "He's dropped a few centuries all of a sudden. What next? No majority rule before my next birthday?"

I spluttered hysterically into my brandy and ginger ale. The irreverence of it all.

Don didn't see it that way. His face was almost purple with rage. He could take no more. His barstool slid backwards with a loud, jarring scrape and he stood up, albeit somewhat unsteadily. Puffing out his chest, his arm extended and pointing like Napoleon, he bellowed, "Fucking treason! You should all be fucking strung up!" He was apoplectic.

"Ag! Sit down, you fucken' old goat," Jacklass said dismissively. "You're pissed. Why don't you fuck off home and go and try and shape with your wife for a change?"

"You come'n say that here, you little punk."

"Fuck you."

Even Zack and Frik had stopped their darts game and were benignly observing. Zack's green pork pie hat was still squashed down on his head. Wellington took a tray of glasses off the bar counter and disappeared into the back.

And then Don lunged at Jacklass. Rather, he lurched clumsily, his fists raised in a quaint Marquis of Queensbury fashion, like a Dickensian prizefighter. Jacklass took a nimble sidestep. Don roared and lunged again and Jacklass slapped him. Don went down on all fours, his dignity destroyed.

But to give him credit, he dragged himself to his feet and stood erect in front of the younger man, the anger dissipating. "If I was twenty years younger, I would have given you the hiding of your life."

"Yeah, yeah, Don. You and whose army?" said Jacklass. "Let me get you another whisky." He put his arm around Don.

So apart from a couple of smarting cheeks, faces were saved all round and Zack and Frik went back to their game of darts, somewhat disappointed. No blood had been spilt—hardly worth interrupting a good game of 301 for.

The conversation developed along a military theme. Obviously politics were now anathema. How to win the war, if it was at all winnable, became the focus. Ron Reid-Daly, the innovative creator of the Selous Scouts, the brilliant pseudo/counter-insurgency unit, had been saying that there was no way on earth that anyone could possibly hope to win a war in Africa without black African troops heavily involved on your side. After all, weren't the Selous Scouts simply duplicating the role that the SAS should have been fulfilling, but weren't? Why? Because the commanding officer of the SAS would not admit black soldiers into the ranks. Well, goodness me, there were no black soldiers in the Long Range Desert Group, the forerunner to the SAS, during World War Two. There had been no black troops in the SAS in Malaya, so for what sane reason would anyone think it necessary to have black troops in an African SAS?

The consensus was that our high command was a bunch of palookas and that, in general, we as Rhodesians had no idea whatsoever about our enemy, no idea what motivated him—apart from, of course, an evil desire to rape our women and drive our Mercedes (and my Renault 12). Even Don Hounslow nodded his grudging agreement.

The facts were clear. We were going nowhere in this war. And now there were rumblings of peace talks, but we pooh-poohed this. After all, how many times had we heard this nonsense? From the *Tiger* and *Fearless* talks of 1966, the Pearce Commission, David Owen, Andrew Young, Cyrus Vance, Henry Kissinger, and all the other *poephols* who just talked and talked and talked.

The telephone rang behind the bar and Wellington answered it, covering his left ear with the palm of his hand to block out the noise of the bar. I glanced at him. Telephone calls were always bad news. Wellington looked up and nodded at me. It was for me. I took the call. It was Gordy Gandanga, phoning from Chipangayi. Police Chipinga had issued instructions that both Middle Sabi PATU sticks were to conduct a sweep up the main Middle Sabi–Tanganda Junction road tomorrow in an effort to cut enemy spoor. If we so chose we could go mounted.

I broke the news to Nat, Jacklass and Paterson, all still animatedly discussing how to win, or lose, the war. Inevitably my news was met with hoots of derision and anger—another complete waste of time. What did they really hope we'd achieve? Bumbling up a tar road on the million-to-one off-chance that a group of incredibly stupid guerrillas had left obvious footprints in the gravel on the side of the road? Hah! *Poephols!*

Quite unsurprisingly, no careless guerrilla had foolishly left his spoor along the side of the road. It took two days of sweeping and patrolling the road from Middle Sabi to Tanganda Junction to establish that this was in fact so. We were mounted and a more ragged set of mounts and riders I had yet to encounter. Fortunately, Paul Brown was kind enough to lend me Melody again. She still remembered me, so there was no problem with our particular relationship.

With Nat's stick, which took the western side of the road, things didn't run quite so smoothly. Very few of Nat's operatives were trained equestrians, if at all. Jacklass, as resentful and disinterested as ever, sat gloomily like a sack of potatoes on his tatty steed. The horse was a pure plodder and I doubt whether a fusillade of AK fire would have motivated the creature. Paterson seemed to adapt okay and at times threatened to look the part. But it was the stick leader, Nat, who faced the real problem. Quite simply, his horse refused to obey his instructions on the reins. When Nat pulled left the horse resisted and pulled right, angrily tossing its head from side to side. And when he pulled right, again the horse resisted. From across the road, I could occasionally hear the cursing and would glance in Nat's direction and see a flurry of tossing horse head, stamping hooves and a horse progressing in a forward direction, side-on, like a crab.

On the second day, without any change in attitude of the horse or in its rider things came to a head. Calling a halt under a shadeless baobab, Nat dismounted. Even from over the road I could see that Nat was very agitated, his face flushed under the mop of blond hair. Still clutching the reins in his left hand he took one long stride to the front of the horse and punched the animal on the nose. Quite hard too. The horse snorted, did what appeared to be a double-take and then was still.

Paul Brown, a lover of horses, burst out laughing behind me. "That'll teach the sod!"

A loud guffaw from Anthony indicated he had also witnessed the little cameo. "Waal, thet'll stop the ornery critter," he said in a Festus-from-Gunsmoke drawl. This obviously triggered some sort of word association in Anthony's mind for he immediately burst into song, loudly singing in a creaky, cowboy style, "I'm back in the saddle again". Over and over he sang the first verse for the rest of the day.

The sounds of a vehicle could be heard approaching from the south. We dawdled to a halt, this time Nat's horse obeying, clearly okay with the newfound rapprochement with its rider. It was Gordy Gandanga in his police Land Rover. He pulled up to a halt and leaned out the window, his elbow resting casually on the door. Garikayi was in the back, propped up against the back window. He looked bored.

"How's it going, guys?" he asked of no one in particular.

The question was met with a wall of insolent silence.

"Well, fuck me! Sorry for asking. Didn't mean to interrupt your little joyride."

I could see that Nat had no intention of talking to Gordy. The mutual dislike had now developed into open hostility. Gordy was looking at me in an attempt to save face. I couldn't maintain the protest.

"It's going fine, Gordy. No signs of any gooks though."

Anthony had briefly stopped his singing. "Ja. Funny that. Thought we'd find tracks like some sort of cattle stampede."

"I don't think they want to play anymore," I added.

The stick on the western side maintained their frosty silence and, in turn, Gordy ignored them. He looked at his watch. It was about four o'clock. "Chris, give it another hour and then knock off."

I nodded.

Gordy revved the Land Rover and did a U-turn, back towards Middle Sabi. So he'd come all this way to check on us? As he executed the turn, the little dog, Gondy, lost its footing and tumbled out from the back and landed unceremoniously on the tarmac. We watched dispassionately as the Land Rover sped off, Gordy unaware that his pet was no longer on board.

I switched the reins gently against Melody's neck as she clicked into gear and ambled forward. Another hour to go. The dog, its little pink tongue darting in and out like a sprightly clitoris, confidently considered his options and decided to fall in behind Jacklass's horse. It made a strange sight—a slumped rider, almost asleep on a low-slung mare with a small mongrel trotting animatedly at her heels. From time to time, the horse would lash out with a hoof, trying vainly to destroy the unseen pest at her rear.

After fifteen minutes I called a halt. "That's it. Home time." Enough was enough.

Jacklass woke up and pulled his floppy hat up from over his eyes. "Hey, already? My word! How time flies when you're having fun."

We turned the horses round and went home.

In the club that night we calculated that we had wasted nearly two hundred man-hours on the patrol. It was as if Police Chipinga felt they needed to keep us occupied. But then, that seemed to be the way with the Rhodesian military. Like the thousands of futile ambushes that were set up in the most ridiculous places. Find a path and put an ambush in. Why? Because the path's there and surely someone will walk on it—hey! maybe even the enemy! Or find a hill and put some dumb fucks up there on OP for two weeks. And why send a helicopter when they can walk—the dumb fucks? Or better still, when the unit is really down below strength send a few of the most experienced soldiers away back to Salisbury on some drill course and use your elite troops for roadblock duties.

We shrugged. They'd never learn. They were determined to lose this war, or at the very least, 'maintain standards'.

I felt irritated when I went home that night, slightly drunk. Carol also appeared to be irritated and upset. She'd had a bad day. The baby wouldn't sleep, had colic and cried all the time. In an exhausted rage, while trying to rock the child to sleep, she'd literally bounced young Guy clean out the pram, onto the soft lawn under the thorn tree … thankfully. Riddled with her own guilt she wasn't about to listen to my monologue on the futility of the war.

I left her alone and lit up a joint on the verandah. The sun was setting beyond the clouds of dust stirred up by the combine harvesters in the lands.

And so life went on, for some.

Chicks 'n' ducks 'n' geese better scurry

Medical Centre, Leopold Takawira Avenue, Harare:
25 March 1995

I didn't know what the woman was—a psychiatrist or a psychologist. Never did know the difference. I just knew her as a counsellor, someone who was supposed to sort out my head. I did recognize that it needed sorting out but I had my doubts about who was capable of such a thing.

As far as I was concerned the events of the past few weeks were now history. What was the point of analyzing them almost to death? But here she was prattling on about my childhood and asking all these inane questions. Had I ever been abused as a child? Mentally, physically ... sexually? I had sisters, didn't I? Had there ever been any kind of 'funny business' there? And what about my mother? Had there ever been any sort of fantasy in that department?

"Are you talking about some sort of Oedipus complex?" I asked. Real clever dick.

The woman did a brief double-take, coupled with the hint of a frown. I wasn't fucking with her, was I? I shrugged. That always threw them—a bit of auto-psychoanalysis. It put them on their guard and made them realize that they didn't have a total fuckwit on their hands. Insane perhaps, but not stupid.

"No, in answer to the question, I have never been mentally, physically or sexually abused as a child."

"Are you sure?"

"Yes, I am positive. One hundred per cent."

"And what about you—have you ever done anything like that to your own children?"

"No."

"Had you ever had any kind of inclination? After all, we are all human and everyone has some kind of latent desire like that in them."

"No. Also hundred per cent sure."

Absolutely, finally, bloody positive.

But still she looked at me like I was lying.

The session came to an end and I felt no different from when I went in. Ah well, perhaps she was building up the case, getting a clearer, overall picture of the lulu she was dealing with.

I stood outside on the landing and lit up a cigarette before descending the fire-escape stairway that everyone seemed to use because the lifts took forever. Huh? Maybe I was a latent paedophile. Maybe I just hadn't realized it all this time. I made a mental note to study the first small child I came across and see if there were any noticeable reactions from within me.

I looked at my watch—still another couple of hours to kill before that interview with that employment agency.

Find a pub.

"Fuck me!" I muttered to myself as I got into the car. "A fucking pervert!"

Middle Sabi: November 1979

The wheat was off and I'd averaged 17.6 bags an acre. Round it up and it came to eighteen, which didn't look so bad. Mind you, over 1,200 acres that came to 21,120 bags of wheat. That was a lot—and an enormous amount of handling to boot. I'd had to more or less excuse myself from the 'bagging-off', the period when the trailers arrived in the yard and the scores of workers scurried about, hooking up the empty grain bags under the trailer shutters and filling up the sacks to around ninety kilograms apiece. It was quite an art and I marvelled at how often they got it spot on. I suffer from hay fever and 21,120 bags of wheat were just too much for me to take. At one stage I found myself choking for lack of air. Almost asthmatic. I'd taken my own pulse and it was around one sixty. Anymore and it seemed it would burst. I went home and lay down for several hours. Imagine—heart attack at twenty-one? Ag shame! And he would have been twenty-two in a few days.

I'd more or less been expecting the call. It was Pirsons. Could he and Paterson and Jacklass come round and do some shooting on the Section 4 lands? The three of them were like a travelling road show, following the just-completed-wheat-land circuit before the tractors went in again and started the land prep for the forthcoming cotton crop. A newly combined wheat land was a magnet to the thousands of itinerant game fowl that came in to the area at the end of winter. For in the wheat stubble lay the equivalent of hundreds upon hundreds of bags of wheat that had escaped the combine drums. Great flocks of Egyptian and Knob-nosed geese, Whiteface ducks, and Whistlers, in wondrous delta-wing formations, would come into the lands around five in the evening. By then, any mechanized activity would be over, and the black women and children, armed with their worn *badzas*, their hoes, would have finished digging in their interminable search for such delicacies as rats and field mice. (A real menace they were too—the holes they left dislodged many a tractor wheel.)

I agreed that Nat and his men could come, but on one condition—it was my shoot and I would take poll position with Tim. No hassle said Nat. Shooting was a thing with him and I often wondered whether he did it for sport or for food. The fact that he often used his .22 Hornet from several hundred metres and would take out a duck or a goose 'not on the wing', that is, while it was happily pecking at the wheat seed on the ground, convinced me it was for food. Not that he had a rapacious appetite for either. It was simply a sensible alternative to actually spending money buying groceries. He'd once boasted in the bar that over the past year he had spent something less than $10 on groceries. His diet was effectively game bird, poached antelope and police ration packs.

We agreed we'd meet at five at the top of the airstrip. I phoned Tim immediately and told him to bring an extra bunch of cartridges. The first evening in a combined land always promised much activity. But a certain amount of cunning was needed. The ducks and geese spooked easily and at the first sight of a human they'd veer away and find somewhere else, somewhere safer. Many were the times we'd come home empty-handed. The problem was that the lands were so vast, so flat and without any form of cover that it was often totally impossible to get in close enough for a shot.

We'd tried all types of tactics such as putting a gun at each corner of the land, or in 'stop' positions across anticipated escape routes, with Pirsons sniping in a sort of beater role. We'd tried full frontals—driving at top speed in Land Rovers directly at the birds, with all guns blazing. But in the main, the terrain played a major role in success or failure. If cover were available, like a deepish contour ditch or a flood bund, we'd invariably come home with something.

Today, Nat, Jacklass and Paterson would position themselves at the bottom of the lands near the canal. Tim and I would try and get in to the middle of the land and find old, flattened antheaps—though they were never fully flattened and generally rose a few inches from the horizantal. It wasn't much but it was our only chance. With our khaki clothing we hoped we wouldn't be spotted by the birds until the last second. So, as the ducks and the geese would land we'd open up with our shotguns. The birds would then wheel and turn and hopefully flee in the direction of the three musketeers near the canal. That way, we'd have two chances at them.

Of course, there was always the consideration that the flocks wouldn't even visit this particular land today.

The other three roared off in Nat's *bakkie* towards the canal. Tim and I made our way on foot to the centre of the land and picked out for ourselves two partially flattened antheaps about two hundred metres apart and more or less level with each other. That way, we planned to open fire pretty well simultaneously. We agreed that kneeling or sitting was no good. We'd tried this before and had been easily recognized by the quarry. There was only one way to do it and that was lying on your back. Lying prone on your stomach was no good as it was impossible to get the barrel elevated vertically. That was where the best shot was to be had—directly above.

We took our positions and waited. I lay on my back, my feet pointing in the direction of the setting sun and presumably the direction of the incoming birds. I figured I'd hear them before I saw them. I hoped they'd only see me when they were almost directly above my position and it was too late for them to alter course. My shotgun lay cradled in my shoulder, flat across my chest but ready to be raised in an instant. There would only be two or three seconds.

The wheat stubble stabbed in to my back and the sun shone directly in my eyes as I waited. Maybe twenty minutes, maybe thirty. It was very quiet. I was desperate for a smoke but desisted. Even the slightest movement would alarm the birds ... if they were coming.

And then I heard the *voof-voof-voof*, the beating of hundreds of pairs of wings. I craned my neck up a fraction and for a moment the sun was darkened. There, a hundred feet up, was a massive delta-wing formation of Egyptian geese coming directly towards me. A hundred geese, maybe two hundred, maybe three hundred. It was a magnificent sight and for a second I didn't want to shoot. They were about a hundred metres or so from my position, descending gently. I calculated they would be landing some way behind me and would be flying directly over me at low level.

My heart was pounding, the old, familiar adrenaline rush of a contact. Action. I slowly levered the shotgun off my chest and nuzzled it into my shoulder, flicking the safety catch off at the same time. No sharp movements now. Slowly does it, slowly, slowly. The delta formation was now at my forty-five degrees, now sixty, now seventy. For a second, when they were almost to the vertical and not much more than thirty or forty feet above me, I could have sworn that I saw the lead goose tilt his head down. In a split-second of alarm he tried to veer of course. But it was too late. The formation had lost speed and could not react in time. In a flash my gun was at the vertical and I fired, taking a bead on the nearest goose. It tumbled groundward as I fired again and again and again until the magazine was empty. And more birds fell, before the panicked flock wheeled in disarray and sped off in any and all direction, leaderless.

To my right I heard Tim shooting—a quick double-tap. Only two shots with the double-barrel. That was all. No time to reload. I pulled myself on to my knees. The dishevelled formation had regrouped and was flying low-level at great speed towards the canal, with only one thought in mind—to get to the safety of the Sabi. And as they reached the canal the other guns opened up in a furious barrage and fowl after fowl tumbled crazily to the earth.

I lit up a smoke and saw that I was shaking. Man, what a buzz! What a rush! I wanted to whoop with elation. I danced a little jig. Today, our cunning, our strategy had worked. The discipline had paid off. I gathered up the birds I had shot. They looked so gentle, so lonely, their feathers soft and downy as they lay there stricken in the wheat stubble. All were dead. Thankfully I wouldn't have to club heads with the stock of the gun. They were too heavy to carry all at once, so I waited for Nat to come and pick me up in his *bakkie*. Presently, the pick-up came bouncing over the uneven lands, Jacklass and Paterson flopping around in the back, perched on the gunwales. They both had beers in their hands and were grinning broadly as Nat pulled up in a cloud of dust and wheat straw.

Nat, normally taciturn, was laughing. "Fuck me, Chris!" he shouted, observing the pile of birds at my feet. "How many you get? Looks like you slaughtered the bastards."

"Three. And you guys?"

"Six between us and two for Bogbrush," Nat replied, taking a long swig of his beer. "Makes a total of eleven. Gotta be our best shoot to date!"

Paterson thrust a cold beer at me as I loaded my victims onto the back of the *bakkie*. "Good one, Chris. You're the master today, that's for sure. And old Pirsons did okay. Now he doesn't have to steal cops' rat packs for another couple of weeks."

I laughed. I was happy. I tried not to look at the dead bundles. So very happy. We sat around the *bakkie*, telling and re-telling the shoot, drinking and laughing until it was dark.

"Oh, Chris," Nat said. "I forgot to tell you. Gandanga couldn't get hold of you earlier. Your stick has got to come and do stand-by at my house tonight."

"What? Both our sticks? How come?"

"Ag, you know those cop fuckwits? Think there might be some gook stuff happening in our area tonight."

I shrugged. Carol wouldn't be too happy about that, but what the hell. It had been a good day. She mightn't think so, but how could I ever hope to convey to her the excitement of the shoot?

"May as well carry on the piss-up at my place," Pirsons laughed. He started the pick-up. "We'll see you okes in an hour or so," he shouted to Tim and me. "Oh … and Chris … bring some of those cookies."

It was about midnight when my A76 radio crackled into life. Luckily, or unluckily as it transpired, I was sitting close by; otherwise I wouldn't have heard it above the music blaring out from Nat's stereo. (The stereo was one of the few pieces of furniture in the house.) It was Gordy Gandanga, no doubt checking that we were all where we should be.

"Go, Gordy," I shouted in to the mouthpiece.

"Roger, Chris," the hoarse voice came back. "I want you and Nat's stick to do a three-sixty around Jacklass's lands. We've had reports of activity down by the river. Copied?"

"Copied that."

"Give me a sitrep when you get back, copied."

"Will you still be awake?"

A humourless double click from his pressle switch indicated that he would. I broke the news to the party of PATU police reservists, most of whom were standing around the dying embers of the braai near the pool, picking at the last bits of a barbecued goose. They were loud and boisterous. Even Manie was in good spirits. Normally he was serious and sullen, not unhappy with the war, but with the way it was being executed.

Jacklass was laughing so much I thought he'd burst. "Fuck me, Chris! What did you put in those cookies? Old Lank's totally fucked. The Dutch Reformed Church is never gonna fucken' take him on as a *dominee* now. That's for sure! Hah! Wanting to be a preacher man!"

I glanced at Pim Erlank. He was lying spaced out on one of the deck chairs by the pool, moaning softly to himself.

"Ag, maybe it got him closer to God," Nat added cynically. "And what did Fuck-knuckle want on the radio?"

"We've gotta do a three-sixty of Jacklass's lands. Says there's activity in the area."

"Fuck him!" Nat spat. "Did you tell him there's also a lot of 'activity' here?"

The crowd burst out laughing, that silly drunken laughter that we were all so good at.

"Nat," I said softly. "He's testing us. We have to go."

"Ag, fuck him!" he repeated. "Tell him to come here and 'test us', the fucken' *poes*!"

Manie interrupted, "Chris is right. Those wankers at Chipinga are looking to nail us. Any excuse and they'll get us up there doing frigging road-block duties."

Jacklass kicked Lank in the deck chair. "Hey, wake up, you fucken' Dutchman. We're going walkabout.'

*

Fifteen minutes later, we were out in the night. Grudgingly making no attempt to maintain any form of silence, we somehow managed to get ourselves in to a file formation. Nat's stick took the inside position right on the edge of the freshly planted cotton lands. My stick took the outside position, on the edge of the bush, where it was slightly harder going.

The nights were still quite cool and for a second I regretted not bringing my combat jacket. But we'd be round the lands in an hour or so, and then back to the party. We'd been walking west towards the river for about thirty minutes or so, and could now make out the looming shapes of the trees lining the Sabi. The moon was almost three-quarters full and I could clearly make out the irrigation sprinklers in the lands. The mutterings at the back had died down and we proceeded in sullen silence.

Nat, abreast of me to my left, raised his hand. "Sshh!" he whispered, crouching low.

Instinctively I crouched too, rifle at the ready. We waited, ears straining. I felt very sober now. After a few moments, I went over to the other stick leader. "What's it, Nat? You hear something?"

He didn't answer. All I could hear was the rhythmic *chuck-chuck* of the irrigation sprinklers in the young cotton lands. There was a soft flurry of movement as Jacklass appeared at our side.

"You hear something, Nat?" he whispered.

Nat nodded. "I heard voices just now. Over there. Just over the flood bund." He was pointing at the bund to our right, offset in the bush, about twenty metres from the edge of the field.

"Hey!" Jacklass snapped, uncharacteristically. "Just watch out. It might be my irrigation gang."

"Well, let's you and me go'n take a recce," Nat whispered to Jacklass. "Okay, Chris?"

I nodded. In situations like this, where there were two stick leaders,

Nat and I worked things out democratically. We thought alike so there was never any conflict over ideas or decisions. Things just worked out. The two men scurried off, half-crouching, towards the flood bund embankment. I lost them in the darkness.

A few minutes later, they were back, panting excitedly, whispering loudly.

"Chris," Nat said, "curfew breakers. Are we gonna do them?"

"For fuck's sake!" Jacklass spat. "They're my fucking irrigation boys!" He was very agitated.

"You can't be sure," Nat hissed. "We didn't get a close look."

"How many?" I asked.

"Six or seven."

"Let's get Manie up here," I suggested. Manie, the voice of maturity, of sanity.

"No fucken' ways!" said Jacklass angrily. "Jesus, Nat ... Chris. You fucking can't! It's fucken' murder!"

I'd never seen him so animated before, so emotional.

"Jacklass!" Nat barked. "Get back to your position now!"

Jacklass stood up, glaring at Nat, his face black with rage and frustration. He turned and stomped back to the rear of the stick, muttering loudly to himself, shaking his head from side to side in despair. "Jesus fucking H Christ. They're gonna murder my goddamn night irrigation gang. I don't fucking believe it!"

Manie was now with us, earnestly crouching in our huddle.

"Chris?" Nat asked again, the urgency in his voice plain. "Your call."

From over the embankment, muffled laughter floated through the darkness. My mind had gone empty. I knew we would do it. I tried desperately to rationalize it all but my mind was blank. It was as if a steel curtain had come down on my heart and I had again reverted to that cold, unfeeling killing machine. I wanted to snap out of it but found I couldn't.

"Yes, we must do it," I heard myself say evenly. "They're breaking the law. Night irrigation boys are only permitted five metres from the edge of the lands. These guys are twenty ... maybe thirty metres off."

Manie was nodding. I knew his feelings. "Ja," he agreed. "They know the law and they're deliberately flaunting it. Like they rule the place. We have to teach them a lesson."

Nat was nodding grimly. "Very well, let's get on with it."

"What's the plan?" Manie asked.

"Simple. We sneak up to the top of the flood bund. My stick on the right. Yours, Nat, on the left—all in a straight line. They're in a hollow, maybe ten or fifteen metres the other side, all sitting in a huddle over a small fire. I'll give the order and we open up. Dead fuckin' easy. Okay?"

Nat and Manie nodded before scampering back to pass on the instructions. Within minutes we were lying hidden in the long grass at the top of the embankment, weapons pointing at the group of black men in the darkness below us. There was a movement behind me. It was Jacklass at the bottom of the bund. He was sitting on his haunches, facing away from us, refusing to participate. Well, so be it.

I turned and glanced at Nat at my side. His eyes were steeled to the task at hand. The men in the hollow were laughing softly around the little fire, a single log flickering limply in the night.

"FIRE!" I shouted.

The embankment erupted in a storm of gunfire. Eight FNs, one long-barrelled FN and a Bren gun—all simultaneously. It was deafening, superceded only by the screams from the hollow. The log fire seemed to erupt as the tracers tore into it, into human flesh, into bones. One heaving, writhing mass of bodies. They didn't even have time to stand up and run and, in seconds, all was still.

Clinical.

"CEASE FIRE!" I shouted.

We stopped shooting, the acrid smell of gunpowder heavy in the night air. In the tangled heap of corpses a body moaned softly below, a horrible, low, rasping, inhuman moan.

A shot rang out to my right. The distinctive sound of a bullet thudding into flesh and the moaning stopped. Already I could smell that old, familiar, sweet smell of human blood. I could almost taste it.

We lay there for some minutes, seemingly astonished at what we had just done. The heap was now still. The smell of shit mingled with the smell of the blood and cordite—shit from the bodies that had involuntarily loosened their bowels.

A voice came from behind us. It was Jacklass. "Well, I hope you okes are fucking happy now!" He turned away from us, his rifle over his shoulder and walked off into the gloom. For a second, I thought he was crying.

We went home and left the bodies where they lay. What else could we do with them? Let the compound come and take them away. I radioed Gordy when we got back to Nat's house. The communication was terse.

"Roger, Gordy," I spoke. "Three-sixty now complete. Curfew breakers taken out."

There was a pause on the other end. "Copied that," a voice said softly. "How many?"

"Six, copied?"

There was no response. He'd switched the radio off.

The Land Rover pulled up to a violent halt on the wet lawn under the thorn tree. Eight o'clock in the morning and already the heat was insufferable. Garikayi was sitting in the passenger seat, gently holding on to the little dog, Gondy, who was panting to leap out and have a go at Ish and Jasper sniffing excitedly at the tyres.

Gordy got out and slammed the door behind him. I knew what was coming. His face was black with anger. I stood at the top of the verandah steps, challenging him to come to me. He did—to the bottom of the steps.

He was shaking with rage. "You've gone too far this time, Chris Cocks." His voice was low and menacing. I could see him shaking, holding back the tears. "Fucking murder, Chris Cocks. Nothing less. Fucking murder, y'hear!"

"Curfew breakers, Gordy," I said, glibly. But inside, I was shaking.

He was pointing his finger at me now. "You ... and that murdering bastard Pirsons. Both of you!" He was choking with emotion, losing the words. "You didn't have to clean up the fuckin' mess, now did you? No! Me and Garikayi had to do that! Before the fucking compound could see what you murdering fucking bastards did to their fathers, to their brothers, to their FUCKING SONS!" There were tears in his eyes.

I said nothing, looking directly in to his eyes. But it wasn't me standing there on the top step of the verandah. It was someone else. Another person. Me? Nah, I didn't do that sort of stuff. Not me. I was a good person. I came from a good background. I had a child of my own. I was a gentle human being. Hah!

I was silent.

"You ... you and Pirsons. I'm gonna see you both fucking *hang* for this. You're both gonna be on a fucking murder charge, d'you hear?" He was choking back the tears.

"Gordy," I said calmly. "They were curfew breakers. You know that and I know that. There's nothing you can do. We're inside the law. Simple. You're a cop, you know the law. We were just obeying the law." I couldn't believe I was saying these things. So cool, so calm, so ... so unemotional.

He turned and, shoulders slumped, went back to the Land Rover. I watched him climb in, the tears streaming down his cheeks. Garikayi was looking at me, coldly, colder than the depths of hell.

I turned and went inside, the gauze door of the verandah banging closed behind me.

Carol was there in the lounge in her candlewick dressing gown. She was holding the baby on her shoulder, trying to wind him. He was gurgling happily, his little pink legs kicking playfully against her breasts. There was look of concern on her face.

"What was that all about?" she asked, her voice edged with fear.

"Ag! Nothing. Just Gordy Gandanga getting his knickers in a knot. You know Gordy. Mr. Do-things-by-the book."

She followed me in to the kitchen. "Tell me, Chris. What's happened?"

"NOTHING!" I snapped. "Just a few lousy curfew breakers, that's all."

She looked at me for a second with a look of such profound questioning, a look that dared me to tell her not to loathe me, that I had to turn away.

I switched the kettle on as I heard the bedroom door slam.

I had a cup of tea and then phoned Nat. "Nat, the shit's hit the fan. Gordy Gandanga's just been here and is threatening to have us both up on a murder charge."

The voice on the other end of the line laughed derisively. "Hah! Let the wanker try. Just let him fucking try. We all know we were just following the rules—the letter of the law. Tell him to go'n tell that to that dipstick Ian Smith. He made the fucking rules!"

"That's what I told him … more or less. But for what it's worth, I'll take the rap here if it comes to that. I made the final call."

"We'll catch up at the club tonight."

"Ja, cheers."

I had another cup of tea and I felt better, for now.

The day had begun. There was cotton planting on the go and I had some geese to hang.

Iain, Lord Carrington and Bill Bailey

**Medical Centre, Leopold Takawira Avenue, Harare:
26 March 1995**

Two days before he smeared his body and his motorbike across the asphalt on that bend on Second Street Extension, just before the Lomagundi Road intersection, Connelly confided in me. For one so seemingly hard-assed, so cynical, so ... wordly, it was indeed a revelation to me. And what's more, he had tears in his eyes when he told me about the nightmares he'd lived with for fifteen long years.

I was stunned, I was grateful, I was astonished, I felt privileged—all at the same time, for here was someone pouring out his soul—to me. I felt very humbled and I also felt less alone. I wasn't the only one. I wasn't cracked. Not like the clinical psychiatrist (or psychologist) who'd recently said at a medical conference that there were no incidences or cases of Post-Traumatic Stress Disorder resulting from the Rhodesian bush war. It was too low-key, of too low an intensity level to warrant it. Well, as an ex-serving member of the army he would have known, wouldn't he?

I related this fact to the woman counsellor, challenging her to agree with the findings of such a renowned specialist. She was shaking her head, tut-tutting. I assumed she didn't agree. Not that I was claiming to be suffering from PTSD. On the contrary, I had it all under control. The drinking, the drugs, the suicide attempts, were merely manifestations of my life's frustrations—broken marriage, fatherless children, zero career—effectively unfulfilled ambitions. And guilt. Always the fucking guilt.

Ah, but Connelly, he was different. Definitely a case of PTSD there. For a while, the counsellor and I discussed the terminology of mind-fucked. From shellshock to combat fatigue (and PMF—poor moral fibre) to the ultimate euphemism—Post-Traumatic Stress Disorder, and tack a 'Syndrome' on the end for good measure. All fancy ways of saying the same thing—fucked in the head.

The stories Connelly had told were simply a variation of the theme. How he'd blown a female guerrilla away at point-blank range, in the face with his machine gun. So what? Well she was surrendering at the time, had her arms raised and was begging to surrender. Ja, so?

Well top this! How 'bout the time he'd fired belt after belt from his gun into a closed door, a door leading down a passage? And not gooks hiding behind the door but women and children … scores of them. And how they'd tumbled out of the passage, the living and the dying and the dead, and how some of the women had crawled to him, clawing at his legs, pleading with him, screaming at him, to stop the senseless killing. But how he'd carried on, like an automaton, until they were all dead—even the ones still clinging limply at his legs.

I was crying … for Connelly … and myself. The counsellor came to me and put her arms around me and was crying too.

Middle Sabi: December 1979

Carol received a call. It was from the Umtali General Hospital. I knew something was wrong as she nodded dumbly into the handset, biting her bottom lip. I could see her body go limp. I could see her face draining of colour. I went to her and held her. Something was wrong. She put down the receiver and I guided her to the couch and sat her down. She was shaking.

"Iain … my brother. He's been in a landmine …" she whispered.

I held her, suddenly feeling a draught. "Is it bad?"

She nodded. "He's in Intensive Care."

"Did they … did they say he'd make it?"

"I don't know," she wailed in anguish. Her body started to buck, racked by violent sobs. "How much can one family take? Please, God. First Guy. Now Iain." She pounded a fist ineffectively on the arm of the settee. "He's only eighteen."

"We must go there now," I tried to sound calm, rational, in control. But she was right. How much could one family take? Christ, were they jinxed or what? "I'll go'n pack now. If we hurry, we can still catch the convoy."

She nodded dumbly, her face streaked with tears. She was looking at me, imploringly, as if I could make it right. For a second, irrationally, I wanted to say that there was only one thing certain in this world and that was death. I wanted to say that Iain was more than likely a mangled, fucked-up piece of meat and he'd end up a useless cripple. I wanted to say that if he was lucky he'd die.

"I'm sure he'll be fine," I said. "These things always seem worse than they really are at first."

She nodded, hungrily accepting whatever useless scrap of bullshit I could feed her.

We arrived at the Umtali General Hospital around midday and went straight to Intensive Care. They wouldn't let us in. They were operating on Iain, evidently trying to save a leg. No, he wouldn't die, but he was 'critical'. That word. Yes, lots of other injuries, but the leg was the worry. No, no internal organs. Oh, almost forgot—lost most of his teeth. Seems he had his rifle between his knees and it got rammed up into his mouth with the force of the blast.

We didn't get to see him that day and spent the night in a seedy motel. The following day, National Serviceman Iain, aged eighteen, was released from Intensive Care and admitted to a general ward, alongside various other casualties, some bad, some worse and some hopeless.

He smiled a drugged, toothless grin as he recognized us. His leg was in traction and he had a bandage round his head, slightly bloodied. We held his hand, weak and cloying. He would live.

Three weeks later, after he'd been released from hospital, he came to stay with us in Middle Sabi to recuperate.

His war was over.

Mine wasn't.

A week later, on 21 December 1979, Lord Carrington announced to the world that a conclusive agreement had been reached at the Lancaster House Peace Talks. Where'd I heard this before? Though this time it wasn't Smith or Vorster or Kaunda speaking.

Under the terms of the agreement a general ceasefire was to come into effect from midnight on such and such a date. (Why did these things always happen at midnight? Like anyone was really awake to notice?) The guerrillas were to be given a number of days to get themselves into designated Assembly Points (APs), which would be monitored by a British peacekeeping, or monitoring, force. Failure to appear at these assembly points within the stipulated time period would render the guerrillas in breach of the agreement and therefore fair game—to be 'legally' shot by the Rhodesian security forces. General elections were to take place within x amount of weeks (there went Smith's millennium promise) and a general amnesty would be implemented in respect of all war crimes, both real and supposed. I was very quick to point this out to Gordy Gandanga, the irrigation-gang slaughter still raw in our minds, but he said it had happened before the agreement and therefore we could still be charged. He just didn't want to give it up.

In spite of all the hype of the agreement, it didn't seem to have much impact on Police Chipinga. Like their junior member in Middle Sabi, they too didn't appear to want to let go and carried on as if nothing had changed. Standing to one's post, no doubt. Got to maintain standards, maintain Christian, western civilization. In fact, if anything, they increased our commitments and started getting bloody-minded about it all.

We were called up to do roadblock duties in Chipinga, a week at a time, a depressing, mindless job, searching buses and vans in the mountain drizzle. How I wanted to scratch the member-in-charge's eyes out and ram a white phos grenade up his ass. I really hated him, that grey, bureaucratic, Smith-junkie dinosaur. I also suspected that Gordy Gandanga might have had something to do with it, a little power play perhaps. If he couldn't get us on a murder rap, he'd fuck us about endlessly with irritating, time-wasting duties, away from our homes.

Didn't these people see it? Didn't they see that the writing was on the wall? That it was all grinding to a halt? Clearly not—just press on as if the war were an institution and we didn't know how to get out of it … or didn't want to.

The fool me for hanging in there.

And then, with the roadblock duties finished, we were summoned again, this time for PATU retraining on Bill Bailey's farm in Melsetter, a small farming district in the border mountains, some kilometres north of Chipinga. Unbelievable! We were to be retrained in counter-insurgency warfare! And peace was coming! Well … nothing surprised me any more.

Bill Bailey, well into his sixties, short in stature, tanned and gnarled, was something of a legend. A founding member, during World War Two, of the Long Range Desert Group in North Africa, and subsequently the SAS, he was the instigator and founder of PATU. I'd never heard the expression, but apparently PATU was nicknamed 'Bailey's Babes', which I thought quite quaint in a Baden-Powellish sort of way.

Bill and I immediately sized each other up. A near-seventy-year-old veteran and a just-turned-twenty-two-year-old veteran. He looked me up and down as if saying, "Well, look at you, you young whippersnapper. Think you know it all, huh? Just because you were in the RLI? Well, we'll see soon enough ..."

And I looked at him and said to myself, "Huh! What d'you think you can teach us, you old fart? This isn't fucking Alamein, grandad!"

For a week he put us through our paces. It was like rookies' course all over again. Waking at dawn, a swim in the ice-cold pond, a run up and down the Gordonstoun-type hills and then a 'hearty' Swallows-and-Amazons-type breakfast.

After which, the earnest stuff began. Jungle lane, range practice, tracking skills, bushcraft, skirmishing, flanking attacks, OP techniques—all the stuff that had become second nature to me over the past four years.

I must say I actually began to enjoy it all. Bill knew his stuff and it became a challenge to do well, to show him that here was a younger generation that was made of the right stuff; and that we weren't all totally useless dope-smoking hippies and that although our values might have changed they were still good, sound values.

Bill studiously made notes during the course, like marking a test, which of course it was. At the end of the week, he sat us down in the bush at the finish of a gruelling jungle-lane exercise. Our faces streaked with running camouflage cream, sweating and panting, we gratefully accepted the cold bottles of beer he'd miraculously produced from a hidden cooler box. The beers proved we had done well. I was proud of my stick—the old, the asthmatic, the untrained. Good men all.

He started going through his notes, making comments on our performance. I listened attentively. He hadn't missed anything and although his points were very minor, they nevertheless showed he knew what he was talking about. And then the coup de grâce.

"Cocks, I can't fault you on your leadership abilities. Your stick has performed excellently and out of all the courses I've run here over the years, your stick's performance rates as one of the best."

I puffed out my chest.

"But!" His steely eyes bored in to me. "I have to fail you!"

My heart dropped. Was this a bluff?

"Yes," he continued seriously. "I would fail you because you are wearing enemy uniform. Fucksakes, man! Look at you! Gook hat, gook shirt, gook webbing. What d'you think you are? The Selous Scouts?"

I made to defend myself.

"Let me finish." He took another swig of his beer, his eyes twinkling. "I know you were RLI and I know the RLI is a bunch of dagga-smoking skates. But we do things differently in the police. A little more conservative." He took another glug of beer. "That's it! Well done, all of you." He slapped his thigh. "Right. Back to the ranch. The missus has a braai on the go."

I smiled, still not knowing whether we'd passed or failed but what did it matter? I liked this man very much. A good, honest, straight-down-the-line, no-bullshit man. I'd wanted to say something caustic about the LRDG dressing up like Arabs, or perhaps having a penchant for cross-dressing, but held my tongue. Point taken, and anyway, what did it matter anymore? Certainly Lord Carrington didn't give a toss.

I heard that my old unit, 3 Commando, was running the Fireforce out of Chipinga. So in the barely mobile Hyena, on our way back from Melsetter, we took a detour via the base. It was good to see my old friends, but they looked haggard and weary, mentally, physically and spiritually exhausted from the ceaseless call-outs.

Abbott was there, as were Norris and Galloway. They looked at me and my men with barely concealed pity. They almost laughed out loud at the sight of Anthony's Bren gun. Our uniforms and matériel did seem hopelessly inadequate when compared to theirs. The major was out on call-out so Abbott raided the armoury for me, loading us up with boxes and boxes of extra rounds, hand grenades and rifle grenades (something we rarely saw in PATU), Icarus rockets, Cordtex, safety fuses, detonators, ration packs, medical supplies and more. The Hyena creaked under the added weight. Thankfully, home was downhill all the way. My men looked at me in wonder—like I was some kind of magician for being able to procure such 'luxuries'. Like it was Christmas—which of course it was.

The Christmas of 1979 came and went without fanfare. All the talk was of the peace process. Would ZANLA stick to the agreement? Of course not—they were Communists, Maoists, without that Anglo-Saxon sense of Christian decency and fair play. And the whites continued to flee the country in their droves, the steady stream becoming a deluge. I don't know why but it never crossed my mind to leave. I wasn't taken in by the RF politicking (a euphemism for lies) that we should stick around and help build the new country—or by Mugabe's posturing that the whites would be welcome to stay because, after all, we were 'Africans' as well.

It was forty-five degrees Centigrade on Christmas Day. Carol had Boney M's Christmassy LP on the turntable. Instead of a turkey we had a roast Egyptian goose in the oven. Iain carved. He looked a sight, hobbling around on his crutches, his hair now long and scraggly, as was his beard. I studied him in the kitchen as he cursed in the heat. He didn't look eighteen now. He looked like one of those Vietnam vets in the movies, a kind of Robert de Niro clone.

"Hurry up and carve, you fuckin' cripple," I joked.

He looked at me and grinned a wide, toothless grin. "What's the rush? The war's over."

Well not quite—there was still a bit of killing to do.

The *pungwe*

I told the counsellor that I took exception to her paedophilic innuendos. In fact, I was a little more direct than that, having been well fortified from a lunchtime session at Sandro's. I felt relaxed and on top, so counsellor, you're talking a crock of shit. Her eyes flared in anger for a moment, which I thought was quite sexy. And while we're at it, counsellor, I'm not sitting in this armchair any longer. It's too low to the ground and you're above me, which gives you the psychological advantage. This is unfair. I don't know whether they teach you this sort of tactic at counselling school, but it's wrong and I'll stand for it no longer.

She shrugged and indicated the upright schoolroom-type chair. I sat and we talked about music. I knew I was drunk, but did she? Well, so what if she did? It was her job to fix my mind—sober, drunk, stoned, whatever. So, fix it counsellor!

She was babbling on about music and its connotations and place associations. I could relate and began to listen. The Tremeloes' number one hit, *Silence is golden*, took me back to the Marandellas road in 1968, on my way to play rugby at Springvale. I was with my parents and we'd stopped off at a dam by the side of the road near Bromley for a picnic. The Supremes' *The happening* took me back to a winter's evening in 1967, around 6.30 in the evening, in my bedroom doing my homework, but listening to the hit parade on the beige Bakelite wireless my father had passed down. Mungo Jerry's *In the summertime*, that smash hit—of lazy Sundays around the pool, with my sisters, gangly teenagers, chilling out in trendy hipster bikinis and me with severe 'lover's balls' from perving over their schoolmates.

Of course, there was a strong time and place association with music. And what about the music of the seventies, she was asking. I squinted at her. Where was this leading? Her skirt had inadvertantly ridden up her thigh and I was lasciviously eyeing her dimpled legs. The seventies? Man, there was some good music then, particularly the late seventies, when disco was waning and punk was waxing. Joe Jackson, Ian Drury and the Blockheads, Elvis Costello and the Attractions, Kate Bush (Ah, sigh!), Donna Summer (Ah, forbidden sigh!), Led Zep, Emmerson, Lake and Palmer (Welcome back my friends!), Uriah Heep (*Look at Yourself*), Genesis, Linda Ronstadt, The Eagles, Yes (*Close to the Edge*—more like over the bloody edge, my friend's mother had caustically remarked), Maxine Nightingale, Tina, 5,000 Volts … and other more commercial stuff.

What did it do for me? Well … it was a time of war. The place was war, so … all that music reminds me of war. The perennial Abba and their *Dancing Queen* and *Thank you for the music* and *Fernando*; Blondie's *Heart of glass* and *Denis*; The Bellamy Brothers' *Let your love flow* and *If I said you had a beautiful body*—they all reminded me of one thing—good ole down-to-earth killing. Sick huh? I challenged her. Who would have thought? Abba? Staunchly pro-liberationist, avid supporters of the suppressed black masses of Africa? And yet their songs inspired a generation of white killers. Weird huh?

She could see that I had become fixated by the expanse of thigh and she hurriedly smoothed down her skirt.

This was going nowhere.

"Same time tomorrow?" She glared at me as she wrote out the receipt. "And try'n not to drink, okay?"

"Sure thing. But what about Bob Marley? Now there's a paradox for you!"

Middle Sabi: January 1980

We'd got to be quite friendly with Rob Hobson and his wife, Lettie. Rob was the fellow who'd dramatically shown us Peter Kenchington's ambushed pick-up truck that first day we'd arrived in Middle Sabi. In spite of his theatricals we liked him. He was a good 'community man' and earnestly carried out his ceaseless community duties with the permanently creased forehead of interminable worry. Lettie, on the other hand, was the epitome of the Afrikaner *vrou*—dumpy, cheerful, practical, hardworking, cook, wife and mother. (I'd always felt I'd marry either an Afrikaner woman or a black woman—they knew how to be a wife—and here I was with a sweet Anglo-Saxon girl ... which at least reduced the risk of being ostracized.)

We were stuck in the mud of the Section 4 lands. The Renault's engine raced, going nowhere and spewing out great gushers of mud all over the young cotton. It was no good. We weren't going anywhere. The baby was starting to cry. We were going to be late for dinner at the Hobsons. And we'd miss Lettie's *bobotie*, her legendary Malay minced-curry dish.

Carol pulled out a breast and plugged the baby on.

"Stay here!" I'd decided on a plan of action. "I'll go back to the house and get the Matchy." Carol looked at me without enthusiasm. Getting dark, an unhappy baby and a dumb-ass husband who thought he'd extricate the family on a Matchless motorbike.

I trotted back to house and fired up the motorbike as the sun was setting. Slipping and sliding through the mud, the bike bullied its way to the stranded Renault. Carol was standing at the bonnet, gently rocking the baby in her arms. There was a sort of acceptance to it all. Without daring to switch off I climbed off and cranked the bike on to its stand. I retrieved the papoose-type sling thing from the car, hooked it onto Carol's back and plonked the baby inside it. He was fast asleep now. Hitching up her floral frock, Carol somehow managed to straddle the great beast, cussing irritably as she burnt a calf on the exhaust pipe.

I grinned at her and climbed on. "Hang on, baby!" I turned the throttle handle, keeping the revs up, not too much, but steady. I could feel Carol's fingernails clawing at my midriff.

It was a ride that Paul Revere would have been proud of—certainly Rob Hobson was. He couldn't believe his eyes when he saw the apparition of man, woman and child arriving through his security gates on an antiquated Matchless 500cc.

He slapped me on the back, hugging Carol at the same time. "Well I'll be damned!" he gushed earnestly. "Well done, bugger! This has got to be the meaning of true friendship! I mean … to make such an effort! Lettie! Come and take a look at this!"

Lettie came out and eyed me sardonically. She wasn't impressed. "Blerry fool! What if he came off in the mud? Then what? *Bliksem!*"

Undaunted by Lettie's lack of enthusiasm, Rob led us inside. The *bobotie* smelt good.

Two hours later, I was at Pirsons's house, Lettie's *bobotie* repeating on me. The phone call had come through from Gordy Gandanga sometime during pudding. Somehow he'd tracked me down.

Gooks in Pirsons's compound. Confirmed. They were having a *pungwe* … right now! Right now as we speak, right now as you shovel that spoonful of lemon meringue pie into your mouth.

I stalled for time. "What about the ceasefire?"

But that had been covered. All cleared with Police Chipinga. The ceasefire no longer applied to guerrillas who'd not checked into the APs. These guys were clearly, illegally, in violation.

I stalled again, pointedly. "What about civvies?"

Gordy made some caustic comment about curfew breakers and how civilians in their own compound were hardly breaking any curfew.

But 'killed in crossfire' was a different matter, no?

Finally, grudgingly, I told Gordy I'd get the rest of the stick together and RV at Pirsons's house. I informed Rob who took me aside, earnestly. His brow was now very creased, with anxiety, as if he were playing out a scene from *Hamlet*.

"*Pungwe*, huh!" he stage-whispered knowingly. "Means the gooks are mobilizing for the elections."

"What the fuck's a *pungwe*?" I stage-whispered a reply.

His look was patronizing. "*Pungwe*! Don't you know? It's a political meeting, a rally, to indoctrinate the *povo*."

"Oh right! Like Harvey Ward does on RBC?"

But it was lost on him and, as an aside, he added, "You know 'the *povo*' don't you? The masses?"

Rob Hobson was motivated. He couldn't get me off to war quick enough. Carol and the baby would stay at their house. You just never knew. The shit could really hit the fan! He phoned Paul and Manie and Tim and Anthony and Jan Pieter Casper, then bustled me out the door. No time to get the Hyena. He took us to Pirsons's house in his white Peugeot 404 pick-up truck himself. He had done his duty.

Pirsons, Jacklass and Paterson were braaing a White-faced duck, wholly unconcerned by my driver's theatricals. ("Lissen, buggers! If you need any help, just shout! I'm a radio-call away.") The duck looked lean, immature and worm-ridden. Jeff, the Doberman, slavered hungrily under the blackened carcass, receiving an occasional slap on the nose from Pirsons for his attentions.

Paterson ripped off a wing and gnawed hungrily at it, grease oozing down his stubble. The dog salivated obscenely, its eyes red and pig-like. Paterson finished the bone and tossed it on the lawn by the pool. The dog pounced and swallowed it whole in a painful gulp.

"Must taste better than that *munt* he ate today!" someone quippped.

"Ja, and the fucken' *munt* had the cheek to come and ask Nat for some bandages!"

"Well, whaddya expect? If the *munt* bathed more often, then he wouldn't smell so much like a fucken' baboon and then Jeff wouldn't bite him!"

"Fucken' amazing! More cheek than a white man!"

The duck was finished and the men gathered up their webbing. The night was dark and overcast, with the threat of rain. We would walk to the compound, about a five-kay walk across the lands.

Nat closed the security-fence gate behind him, catching Jeff's nose in it with a yelp. "Home, Jeff!" Nat hissed. "You can't come. Go'n. Fuck off!" The dog cocked its head and sulkily trotted back to the remnants of the duck.

We marched off down the dirt road in file, past the paw paw plantation, then through the cotton lands. We passed some nightshift 'boys' changing irrigation pipes in the lands. Although only a few metres from us as we passed they did not acknowledge us, nor us them. It would not be good for them to know that their boss, *Baas* Nat, was also a *musoja*, a soldier. Not good for them, not good for Nat.

We came to the compound, a neat array of brick structures with tin roofs, with a few traditional pole and *dagga* huts interspersed. As was African custom the pathways and areas around the huts were swept clean. Tall, overhead flourescent lights hummed in the darkness like stadia lights. Clouds of midgies drifted carelessly in their glow. But something wasn't right.

I crouched down beside Nat, kneeling next to the wall of one of the houses on the perimeter. "Nat," I whispered. "None of these houses have their lights switched on. What time do your *munts* go to bed?"

I glanced back at the men. They'd automatically gone into all-round-defence positions—one at the lone thorn tree on the edge of the compound and a couple in the cotton lands, crouched low. The rest were against the walls of the buildings, some facing in, some out—all with weapons at the ready, ready at any given moment.

He was nodding. "It's far too early for them. Normally, there's activity here till after midnight."

"And dogs?"

"Nah, no dogs. Shot the lot a couple of weeks ago."

I peered round the corner of the building into the innards of the compound. Row upon row of unlit houses. No sign of any activity whatsoever. "Maybe they've all been abducted," I stated. It was not beyond the realms of possibility.

"Maybe," Nat replied. "But maybe for once, Gordy Gandanga's right. Maybe they *are* holding a meeting. My bet is that, if they are, they'll be at the beerhall in the centre of the compound."

We quickly agreed on the plan of action. We'd leap-frog, buddy-buddy system, from hut to hut towards the beerhall, with Nat's men on the eastern perimeter, nearest the bush, to cut off any escape routes, and my stick down the middle, to flush them out.

Simple. Now the hard part—stepping out into the open. Nat gave me a thumbs-up and scurried off with his stick into the darkness. I summoned my men and briefly explained the plan. Anthony, with the Bren, was to stick to me and cover the rest of the stick as they moved forward, hut to hut, one by one.

"Don't split up too much and don't lose contact with each other. And at all times have me visual."

The men nodded.

As normal, Manie took the lead. He was my scout, my pathfinder. He stepped a step into the open ground between the lines of huts, waiting a fraction. Nothing. He stepped another step and waited again. Nothing. He turned and pointed at his target hut, his immediate destination. I gave a thumbs-up and he trotted, half-crouched, across the open ground. Anthony tensed at my side, the Bren snuggled into his shoulder, his head over the sights.

Manie disappeared into the shadows of the hut.

I turned to the next man. "Okay, Tim. You next. When you get to the hut where Manie is, you take up the position on the far side."

Tim nodded, licking his lips before padding off, the only sound the faint rustling of camouflage denim cloth.

"Paul. You and Jan next, then me an' Anthony right behind."

A few blobs of rain splatted onto the dry, smooth ground. I glanced up at the sky. It was low and menacing, the heavy, black clouds pressing earthwards, set to dump their loads. Ah well! Good for the cotton, I thought irrationally. The irrigation just hadn't been keeping up with the evaporation figures—sometimes twelve or thirteen mills a day. That was the equivalent of half an inch of rain. Half an inch of water being sucked out of the ground every day—no wonder the cotton was wilting.

I nudged Anthony and we clambered to our feet and moved to the hut where the other men were waiting. A few more drops of rain. I tried to think logically. Was the rain good for us or not? Now I mean. Would it compromise us ... or the enemy? One sure thing was that the people at the *pungwe*, if in fact that's what it was, would run for the nearest cover—their huts.

There was an urgency now. The rain was our enemy. It was coming too soon. No bad thing if it were to hold off until we were in position and set to open fire. Then it would simply add to the confusion—to our advantage. But for now it was not good.

I tapped Manie on the shoulder and pointed to the next hut. He could sense my urgency and went scurrying off. Then Tim, then Paul, then Jan Pieter Casper, then Anthony, then me.

It was indeed a *pungwe*. A crack of lightning lit up the entire area, and there, fifty-odd metres to our front, for a brief moment, I saw the crowd of people, sitting obediently on the ground in the open outside the beerhall, illuminated in the surreal, white light. And when the thunder rolled away I could hear the rumblings of the people as they responded, like zombies, to the guerrilla chants. It was eerie. For a minute, I crouched, mesmerized by the scene in front of me.

A few globs of rain thudded on the corrugated-iron roof of the hut next to me. Another crack of lightning and this time, more clearly, I saw several guerrillas standing tall among the *povo*.

What to do? It was clear we had to engage the enemy very quickly, before they sought shelter from the rain.

But again, that age-old dilemma. Between the enemy and us sat the people, the compliant *povo*. 'Killed in crossfire'. But 'killed in crossfire' during a ceasefire? What if Gordy Gandanga had simply been bullshitting? What if there had been no such clearance from Police Chipinga? How would the newly installed, venerable British governor, Lord Soames, handle that one? Easy—throw us to the wolves.

I could sense Manie at my elbow, rifle in his shoulder, taking aim. For a moment, it appeared he was going to open fire … with or without my orders. He was right. There was no time to lose. There was no dilemma. It was like old times. Shoot first. I felt the adrenaline pumping, that feeling so difficult to describe. I checked for the men. Anthony was lying prone on his stomach at my side, his Bren in the shoulder. He was ready. Paul and Tim were at a neighbouring hut. They were ready. So too were Paul and Jan Pieter Casper.

"Stand by for my order to fire," I hissed. There was no requirement for me to warn the men to aim off of the civilians. But I prayed that none would aim at them deliberately. That way, in spite of any civilian deaths that might occur, my conscience would be clear. It had worked for me before. Not always, but mostly.

I was whispering into the handset of my radio. "Nat, we have the Charlie Tangos visual." Although speed was the priority I needed to make sure that Nat's stick was ready as well. "Are you in position, copied?"

A double click from Nat's pressle switch indicated that he was.

I prodded Manie on the shoulder and bent down close to him, my lips brushing his ear.

The crowd mumbled another response, a low, menacing rumble.

"Manie, open fire when I tap you. I want you to try and take out that tall oke standing up over there. Probably the political commissar. As soon as you open up I'm going to send up an Icarus."

He nodded quickly, as if saying, "C'mon, man. What are you waiting for?"

I fumbled in the kidney pouch on my web belt and pulled out the Icarus flare. Unscrewing the base cap, I unfolded the firing chord and grasped the tubular rocket firmly in my left hand.

I tapped Manie on the shoulder and he opened fired, the closeness of the detonations ringing loudly in my ears. Gunfire erupted from Anthony's Bren as tracers arced beautifully towards the *pungwe*. Tim and Paul were firing, and in the corner of my eye I could make out Jan Pieter Casper's shoulder bucking and bucking with each shot. I extended my left arm, aiming the Icarus skywards at a ten-degree angle. I tugged on the firing string and in a violent *whoosh* the rocket sped from its tube, clawing at the blackness of the sky.

Another flash of lightning and I could vaguely make out the seething mass of people, of movement, absorbing the tracers, fleeing this way and that, towards us, away from us, towards Nat and his men waiting hungrily in the wings.

The Icarus was faulty, or I'd fired it incorrectly, and in mid-flight suddenly spun angrily out of control, looping the loop several times. For a horrible moment it appeared it was turning on itself and was heading straight back towards our position. It fizzled and crackled like a firework before embedding itself in the thatched roof of a hut to the left of the *pungwe*.

Our gunfire continued furiously, but I could not see anything for the smoke and the dust. The dry grass on the thatched roof sparked and in an instant was burning. And then, the unmistakable sound of AKs. Fuck me! The bastards were returning fire!

I still hadn't fired a shot. I needed to be in control, aware of what was happening. This wasn't the bush. The gooks could swamp us in minutes if they had the mind to, with a flanking attack around the back of our position, using the huts as cover. Several huts were now burning, fully on fire, the rafters and the thatch crumbling inwards, cracking and spitting.

In the dancing shadows of the flames, fleeting figures of guerrillas ran towards the apparent safety of the bush on the eastern side of the compound—towards Pirsons and his men.

The *povo* had miraculously disappeared and, within a few minutes, a few seconds, there was no sign of movement in the killing zone. But the gooks were still there. Some had run but some were still there. I could sense it. I knew it.

"Cease fire!" I shouted.

The men stopped shooting and peered nervously over their hot barrels.

To the east gunfire erupted, muffled by the roaring fire of the huts to our front.

"Tim, Paul. Watch our back!" I shouted.

"Chris," Manie said softly, without looking at me, his eyes trained to the front. "I might be wrong, but I'm bloody sure I saw a couple of them dive into one of those huts to the right of the beerhall."

"Civvies?"

"Uh-uh. Gooks. The tall one. I'm pretty sure I hit him with my first shot, but he didn't go down. I reckon he gapped it to the nearest cover … that hut," he pointed.

I considered a moment. "We'll give it a couple of minutes and see if anything breaks. He might try and make a run for it. If not, we'll sweep in and clear the huts."

Hut-clearing—our dread.

Manie nodded. "Ja, okay. Sounds like Nat and his merry men are having a fine old time!" The firing to the east continued unabated.

I got on the radio, "Nat, Nat. You okay there?"

"Affirmative," came the animated reply. "Like a fucken' turkey shoot over here."

"Need any back-up?"

"Negative. Winding up now."

"Copied that."

Almost as a signal, the firing stopped and the compound was enveloped in a shroud of silence, save for the soft whimpering of a wounded person somewhere in the distance. Now was the time. I whistled to the rest of the men and indicated extended-line formation. We were going to sweep in towards the burning huts and the beerhall.

The men rose to their feet and we spread out, ten paces or so apart. I led off, taking the centre axis, the direct route. We got to the *pungwe* position. I scanned the debris of overturned benches and abandoned clothing and shoes. Anthony was gingerly stepping over the shapeless form of a corpse. Gook or civvy? I couldn't tell. Must be civilian, for Anthony hadn't stooped to pick up a weapon.

Then the oddest thing happened. I heard shouting from the hut where Manie had said the two gooks had taken cover. We crouched instinctively, weapons trained. There were two voices, shouting in Shona, shouting defiantly, incoherently. I picked up the occasional phrase among the babble.

"*Pamberi ne hondo!*" (Forward with the war!)

"*Viva* Robert Gabriel Mugabe!"

"*Viva* ZANLA!"

Manie was at my side, gabbling excitedly, "I knew it! They're in there! Looks like they want to go down guns blazing!"

I nodded in agreement. "I reckon they know they're trapped. They've seen us coming." The thought briefly crossed my mind that I should, perhaps, try and get them to surrender. But I dismissed the idea. For what?

"You wanna do it, Manie?" I asked. "A grenade probably."

He nodded, his Adam's apple bobbing hard as he swallowed. "Frag or white phos?"

I dug out my M962 fragmentation grenade and handed it to him. "Whatever. Take this as well. You might need a few. We'll cover you."

Manie sank to his belly and, like a snake, leopard-crawled towards the door of the hut. There was only one voice shouting now, almost drunkenly.

"FUCK YOU IAN SMITH! FUCK YOU BISHOP MUZOREWA!"

"*PASI NE* SELLOUTS!" (Down with sellouts!)

And then a cackle of defiance, followed by the loud ranting of a seeming madman.

Manie was now at the door. He nudged it open with the muzzle of his FN. The mutterings inside continued, oblivious. He gently lobbed in a grenade, and then another, rolling away to the side as two muffled explosions tore out the guts of the hut. In a flash he was on his feet, kicking in the door and firing shot after shot after shot into the hut.

"Asshole!" I muttered. "He didn't have to do that. Could have got himself killed."

He emerged from the hut, grinning. "All clear, Skip! Looks like we got ourselves a political commissar and maybe a detachment commander!" He was brandishing what looked like an AKM above his head. "And the bayonet's mine, *comprende?*"

No wonder they hadn't given up easily. Hard core.

And then the heavens opened. A few drops at first, but within seconds a deluge of such frightening proportions that we dashed to the nearest hut and took refuge from the fury of the storm—the hut with the two dead guerrillas—the floor awash with the blood that oozed from the mutilated corpses. The eyes stared vacantly at us, dull and wide.

Anthony was singing loudly above the din, a Kinks' song, "What a day for a daydream, what a day for a daydreaming boy. I'm just lost in a daydream, dreaming 'bout my bundle of joy ..."

The last waltz

Medical Centre, Leopold Takawira Avenue, Harare:
28 March 1995

She was making good money out of me. A daily session for an indefinite period until I was sorted out. She thought Prozac was a good thing. Anything to help. I'd been on it for about a year now, but I hadn't noticed any discernible difference in my life, apart from some sort of levelling out of my moods. Well, at least the sessions were claimable from medical aid, as was the Prozac.

The day before I'd registered with another employment agency. Me, the mighty—having to stoop to such a level. The pages and pages of forms that needed to be completed, the inane questions, like 'salary required'; and in the end it made no difference anyway because the woman (who called herself a human resources consultant) disliked me immediately and was downright rude, saying who in the hell did I think I was applying for such an exalted position. The bloody nerve of it. I had no qualifications and the advert specifically stated MBA, nuclear physicist, blah blah blah.

I'd apologized for wasting her time and slunk out of her office, my dignity shattered. Sandro's was two blocks away, so I went there and got pissed. Slouched over a triple vodka and Coke, I swore to myself that I was going to go back to that shitty, little employment agency in that seedy, crappy shit-hole of an office and tell that fucking bitch just quite what to do with her crappy corporate world and to stick it. But I didn't. Instead, I had another triple vodka and Coke.

I was relating this to the counsellor, the shit knocked out of me, my self-esteem at an all-time low. I'd gone through this before, so why should I be worried? But I was.

The counsellor could see that the cynicism, my standard defence, was absent. She didn't quite know how to take it. She tried to make light of it, but I wanted her to feel my hurt.

"What is it, man? It must be me. I've been down this road so damned often. I know every goddamn employment agency in town. And when I do get short-listed for some job or other, I'm pipped at the post … every time a fucking coconut!" I knew I was whining.

She was making notes. "So, to solve it, you go and get drunk?"

I shrugged petulantly. "Yes. What else!"

"Were you drunk when you went in for the interview?"

"No."

"Promise? You hadn't had one drink? Not one?"

"Well … one or two. But I definitely wasn't drunk. I know myself. I know when to stop. I can handle it, man."

She didn't believe me, but had the grace to pretend otherwise. "Only you can control the drinking. My suggestion is that you stop altogether."

I stood up. "Stop?" The idea was simply preposterous. "Stop? What'n the hell would there be to look forward to in life. C'mon! Get real!"

She continued with her notes. "As I say, it's purely my suggestion. But it's your choice."

I wanted to get angry. Why wasn't she fighting me? Why wasn't she shouting and pointing her finger at me, accusing me, being her normal, judgmental self? Was it because she'd given up with me? That she no longer cared? I felt a momentary sense of panic. Not her too? The steelhead human resources manager—yes! But not the counsellor!

Middle Sabi: 16 April 1980

On 16 April 1980, we had our last contact of the war. Robert Gabriel Mugabe and his victorious Zanu (PF) party had swept the board in the elections a few weeks before. I hadn't been in the least bit surprised, though the majority of whites were suitably mortified. After all, they'd been fed for months by the politicians, the generals and the police hierarchy that the 'voice of reason' (Muzorewa's UANC) would sweep all before them. The independence celebrations were due on 18 April, the day when 'Bob, as he'd come to be known by the whites, would be sworn in as the new prime minister of Zimbabwe. The presidential position would go to the part-time priest, part-time chicken farmer, part-time football referee and full-time closet sodomite, Reverend Canaan Banana.

There was every likelihood that the contact on 16 April was the last contact of the war. There was also every likelihood that no one really noticed. The only certainty was that the couple of dead gooks we left to rot in the sun on that little kopje near Tanganda Junction wouldn't be attending the independence celebrations at Salisbury's Rufaro Stadium two days later. Bob's victorious army minus two. Certainly the screaming, singing, chanting, ululating, jubilant crowds with fists raised wouldn't notice. Nor would Bob Marley or any of his Wailers, performing at Rufaro, notice.

Pirsons wasn't involved in that last contact. He'd effectively boycotted the war soon after the last action in his compound, and had gone fishing on the Zambezi. No amounts of pleas or threats from Gordy Gandanga could persuade him otherwise. The answer was always a straightforward "Fuck off. I'm not doing anymore." So that was that.

But for Manie Dreyer and J.J. Fourie it was different. For weeks they'd been talking about setting up a two-man OP on Mutema Mountain, the formidable peak that sits between Tanganda Junction and the Sabi River. From there they'd see all. No one had ever done an OP from there, and certainly not an ultra-clandestine two-man operation. They were under no orders whatsoever, not from Ground Coverage, Chipangayi, nor from Police Chipinga. It was a wholly voluntary operation which the rest of us failed to comprehend and refused to support.

"What on earth for, Manie?" I asked him at the bar.

Tim concurred, shaking his head at such madness. "Yeah, Manie.

Shades of things to come. A squatter's humble abode in the Rhodesian bush. *Photo by Tony Young*

Sunset over the Zambezi. *Photo by Tom Argyle*

Top: The mighty Zambezi River. *Photo by Tom Argyle*

Above: With the Chilojo Cliffs as a backdrop, Gemma, the author's daughter, strikes a pose by the Runde River (formerly the Lundi) in the Gona re Zhou game reserve, Lowveld, 1985. *Photo from the author's collection*

Top: Carol ponders the practicality, or wisdom, of Geoff Higgs' crocodile trap on the Runde River, Chiredzi 1985. *Photo from the author's collection*

Above: Trapped! A young crocodile gets snappy. *Photo from the author's collection*

The drought-stricken Sengwe Communal Lands, adjacent to the Gona re Zhou national park in the Lowveld, 1985. *Photo from the author's collection*

Centre: The 1987 *Gracelands* concert in Harare. Here Paul Simon harmonizes with Miriam Makeba. *Photo from the author's collection*

Left: Ladymith Black Mambazo performing at the *Gracelands* concert. *Photo from the author's collection*

Top: The back view of the house the author built in Glen Lorne, Harare. The cliff face is on the other side of the house. *Photo from the author's collection*

Above: By the late eighties, the Zimbabwean honeymoon was fast coming to an end. Here, unemployed wait hopefully, but in vain, for jobs in Harare's industrial sites. *Photo from the author's collection*

Top: Harare's bustling 'informal sector'. Mugabe was to destroy this utterly in 2003/04. *Photo from the author's collection*

Above: A blind busker plies his trade on a Harare street, 1990. *Photo from the author's collection*

A Harare busker playing what appear to be homemade pan pipes. *Photo from the author's collection*

A common sight in Africa—a pavement tailor—Harare, 1990. *Photo from the author's collection*

Top: The Pungwe River, the border with Mozambique, north of Mutare (formerly Umtali). *Photo by Tony Young*

Left: The Moulin Rouge nightclub in Beira's docklands. Inside was no less salacious. *Photo from the author's collection*

Opposite page:

Top: A food-aid truck bringing a load of maize into Beira, early 1990s. *Photo from the author's collection*

Middle: A timber-processing factory in Beira, early 1990s. Massive hardwood concessions were granted as Mozambique's economy opened up in the nineties. *Photo from the author's collection*

Bottom: The Mozambican port town of Vilanculos, more or less closed for business while awaiting President Chissano's visit. *Photo from the author's collection*

Top: A tug outside the port of Beira at sunset, early 1990s. *Photo from the author's collection*
Above: Chicamba Real Dam at dawn. *Photo from the author's collection*

Above: The author with Afonso Dhlakama (centre) in the early 1990s, outside Renamo's Beira headquarters. The man on the left, Dhlakama's closest lieutenant, went by the name of Generale João.
Photo from the author's collection

Left: A local Mozambican fisherman in his dugout, Chicamba Real Dam.
Photo from the author's collection

Top: The quayside at Vilanculos. *Photo from the author's collection*

Above: 1993 bass-fishing competition at Chicamba Real Dam in the Manica Province, Mozambique. *Photo from the author's collection*

The author's sideline businesses tended to stretch him financially. Here women workers process loofahs on a smallholding south of Harare, 1994. *Photo from the author's collection*

Frank Neave and his lovely wife Angie, circa 1980. Frank electrocuted himself on a swimming pool pump shortly after this photograph was taken. Angie then remarried, but her second husband died under cruel circumstances in the mid-eighties—murdered execution-style by ZIPRA dissidents near Gweru—with Angie forced to watch. Just another African story. *Photo by Tom Argyle*

John Coleman, US Special Forces, Vietnam and RLI veteran. He died of cancer in 2002 in California. *Photo by Tom Argyle*

Right: Carl Oosterhuizen committed suicide in Cape Town in 1981. *Photo by Tom Argyle*

Below: Bob Smith died in a most bizarre accident. While mowing his lawn in Georgia, USA, an 18-wheeler came round the corner, lost control and careened across the lawn, killing Bob instantly. *Photo by Tom Argyle*

Malcolm Nicholson committed suicide in
South Africa, early 1980s. *Photo by Tom Argyle*

The war's finished. So what if you see something? What are you going to do about it?"

Manie laughed. "Uh-uh, Tim. You've got it wrong. What will *you* do about it?"

"How d'you mean, Manie?" I asked. I felt aggrieved that this operation was going to be conducted without my say-so. I hadn't been consulted for obvious reasons as I'd have opposed it.

"J.J. and I have cleared it with GC and Police Chipinga. PATU Middle Sabi will still be expected to react. Any gooks still not in the Assembly Points can be taken out."

I held my tongue. What could I say? That I felt piqued because I hadn't been consulted? And worse—we were expected to be at the beck and call of these two aging warriors that quite stupidly didn't know when to call it a day? Or perhaps Manie had for all these months been niggled by the fact that I had led the stick? And that this was his way of usurping my authority and saying he could do it better?

Ag! Let the fools go.

So they went, stealthily one night. Gordy Gandanga informed me the next morning that Manie and J.J. had successfully reached the summit of Mount Mutema without compromise and were now in position … observing. Well, bully for them, I told him and promptly forgot about them for a week.

Several days later the call-out came, at two o'clock on the afternoon of 16 April. Gordy Gandanga phoned me and gave me the map co-ordinates of the OP sighting. Manie and J.J. had spotted a bunch of gooks holed up on a small hill just off the main road, a couple of kays south of Tanganda Junction. He'd already advised Paterson, the PATU south stick's temporary stick leader, to RV in twenty minutes with my stick at the Chipangayi turn-off on the main road. Both sticks were to react.

In spite of my apathy, I felt the adrenaline rush. I knew that this was a definite sighting. Manie and J.J. were too professional and too dedicated for it to be otherwise.

We met Paterson and his men on the road. They were yawning, having been interrupted from their afternoon nap. Gordy Gandanga hadn't bothered to turn up.

"So, Chris. What's the plan?" Paterson asked.

I shrugged. I was damned if we were going on some long, convoluted march-in. It was too hot. "Easy, Nev. We all pile in to the Hyena, drive up the road and when we get level with the kopje, we all pile out and sneak up on the bastards."

"Won't they get suspicious if they hear a vehicle stopping?"

"Good point. We need someone who can drive us there and slow down as we get to the kopje ... as if he's changing gear. We then de-bus on the move."

"Better be in first gear," Jacklass quipped. "I'm not getting out of anything at more than five miles an hour."

"The fucking Hyena can't go more than that anyway," Anthony guffawed.

But who would drive? Errol! As a good citizen who understood these things, he'd oblige. I radioed the workshops and finally got hold of Errol. He was delighted. Into action again—it was an honour!

We waited a few minutes, smoking languidly on the side of the road. Presently Errol, still wearing his grease-stained white coat, arrived in his Renault 4. With some difficulty, he hoisted his gammy leg onto the Hyena and manoeuvred his body into the cramped space behind the steering wheel.

"Fuck me! D'you mean to tell me you okes have been going to war in this fucking thing for all this time?" he laughed.

"Don't be rude. Just drive, Police Reservist!"

Errol knew the hill. After all, he'd passed it every day for the past two years on convoy duty. Lank at the back swung open the metal door as Errol dropped a gear in a very smooth double-declutch, keeping the revs up and the speed down. We tumbled out easily enough, without fuss, and soon found ourselves taking cover in a storm drain on the side of the road.

The Hyena spluttered on towards Tanganda Junction and disappeared from view. The bush was silent, save only a few Christmas beetles screeching lazily in the heat. Paterson came across to me, his freshly applied camouflage cream already running, mingling with his sweat. He was wearing a floppy hat, turned up at the brim. With his droopy moustache he looked like a very dirty Pancho Villa.

He was pointing towards the kopje, double-checking his map which he had out in front of him, folded neatly, the pertinent segment upward. He was taking his leadership duties seriously. "That's the one, Chris," he whispered. He was licking his lips. It was a nervous time for us all.

Two days to go to the official end of the war, the day we could all hand in our FNs and tell Police Chipinga to ram it. Undoubtedly though, they'd try and keep us on under some guise or other. (Probably something to do with maintaining standards.) Still two days to get blown away. Maybe even now one of us was going to die on that little hillock in the African sun.

I nodded. I had a good feeling working with Paterson. He knew what he was doing. I scanned the kopje. It looked innocuous enough—about a hundred feet high (sometimes I work imperial, sometimes metric—that 'crossover' generation of slide-rule-to-pocket-calculator converts), tall, brown grass waving softly in the breeze, and liberally scattered with outcrops of granite boulders. It was reasonably well treed, right up to the top. Lots of good cover for the enemy—but it would also work for us when making the approach.

Paterson was looking to me, unsure of himself. I don't know why. He was a good soldier.

"Let's see what Manie and J.J. have to say about it all," I suggested. "They're high enough on that mountain. Should get good comms from here." I cradled the radio handset in my shoulder, ensuring the volume wasn't up too high.

"Manie, Manie, do you read?"

There was a pause, before the radio burst into life with a static-filled splurt. It always filled me with gratitude and wonder when the radio worked. "Roger, Chris. I read you strength threes."

Threes, huh! Not bad for such a range—in fact a miracle for the A76. "Manie, we're at the base of the target area. Do you still have Charlie Tangos visual?"

"Roger, affirmative. We have you visual as well. CTs are still in position. Suggest one stick sweep up from the west and the other from the east, copied?"

"Copied that. Stand by. Will commence sweep in figures five."

"Copied. Will maintain comms. And ... good luck."

I double-clicked the pressle switch. "D'you get all that, Nev?" I asked.

He nodded, his lips dryer than before.

"Okay, Nev. Can you take your stick round to the eastern side? When you get into position at the base of the hill, give me a shout on the radio. I'll be in position at the foot of the hill on this side. We then sweep up simultaneously. Okay?"

He nodded again and turned to his men still huddled in the ditch. In a minute they were gone, wraith-like through the bush. Lank's one water bottle was clanging a bit. Maybe a metallic buckle on his webbing somewhere. I made a mental note to remind him of it.

I signalled to my men, indicating extended line in the direction of the kopje. They spread out as we clambered over the lip of the storm drain onto the more open savannah towards the hill. The going was relatively easy and within a few minutes we came to the base of the hill. I signalled to the men to stop. We crouched low in cover, eyes straining upwards to the target, waiting for the radio call from Paterson.

It came some minutes later, Paterson breathing heavily into his mouthpiece.

"Okay, Nev," I said softly, trying to sound in control. "Let's move out, but take it slowly, huh! There's no rush."

"Copied," he breathed. "See you at the top."

I signalled to the men and we warily stood up. Still there was no sign of enemy activity. The going became more difficult as the incline and the foliage increased. We weaved our way around the rocks and the jesse bush, losing our dressing on several occasions. This was a sensitive time. Out of line, out of breath, looking down at your footing. It would only take the metallic clank of a rifle barrel against a rock to alarm the enemy. Just one little thing like that could change the entire complexion of the action—the difference between victory and defeat—the difference between life and death.

We were about half way up the slope when we heard voices. For a second, I thought it was one of Paterson's men, who couldn't be too far away now, stupidly compromising the operation. The voices continued, blabbing away unconcernedly. But they couldn't be *that* foolish, surely?

No, it was the gooks. They were there, not twenty or thirty metres from us, among the granite boulders, like *dassies*, rock rabbits, sociably sunning themselves. I stopped to get my bearings and to confirm that there were no pickets out. And then, for a second, silhouetted against the summit, the figure of a man with his back to us. He had an assault rifle slung over his shoulder.

I signalled to Anthony that I had the enemy visual. He peered through the bush but was unsighted. I slowly raised my rifle and took aim. It was a difficult shot as the man was bending down doing something, and I now only had his head and shoulders visual. To fire or not? To miss would possibly give them an opportunity to escape and undo any advantageous position that Paterson might have got himself in to. Yes, it was premature. As I made the decision, the man ducked out of sight anyway.

I again signalled the advance and we cautiously crept forward, step by step, watching out for twigs and loose stones—weapon in the shoulder, forefinger extended, caressing the trigger guard. Step by step, yard by yard.

The chattering on the summit was getting louder. Then a shout. A shout of alarm and the hillside erupted in gunfire. Paterson's stick had opened up. I could hear Lank's heavy-barrelled FN barking distinctively above the barrage of rifles. I could see nothing but could clearly hear the shrieks of panic and the clattering of bodies and matériel as the guerrillas attempted to take cover, or flee, or whatever they were doing.

The shape of the man appeared again and even from that distance I could sense the agitation. In a flash, my rifle was up and I fired off a quick double-tap. But the man was gone before I'd squeezed the trigger.

Paterson's fire was continuing unabated, getting closer as his men neared the summit. And then the same man appeared again, his back still away from me, behind the same rock. It was bizzare. I lifted my rifle again, but the man was slowly collapsing, holding his head in his hands. He crumpled behind the rock, out of sight.

And then on my left flank, I could hear Tim and Paul shooting, and shouting at each other, "Get him! He's getting away!" Anthony was desperately looking around, trying to get the enemy visual, any enemy, but he was still totally unsighted. I could see him leaning into the Bren, swivelling it on the bipods mounted on a rock, traversing the top of the kopje. It looked like he was going to rake the top of the hill—more out of frustration than anything else.

"Hold you fire, Anthony!" I snapped. "Paterson's on the top there!"

And said not a moment too soon, for at that moment, Lank's great bulk came in to view—on the boulder where the guerrilla had been shot. He was making no attempt to seek cover and was standing victoriously on the rock, clasping the heavy-barrel in his right hand like a toy. He spotted me down the slope.

"Howzit, Chris?" he asked conversationally, grinning happily. "Got one fucker here." He pointed somewhere behind the rock with his rifle barrel.

The firing on top of the hill had died down. A sporadic shot or two on my left flank indicated that Paul and Tim were still busy but, by the sounds of it, they were letting off an occasional shot more out of hope than anything else. The gooks would be long gone.

Paterson appeared on the rock next to Lank, looking as equally relaxed. "Well, we got one at least," he said. "We should have got more, but this one spotted Lank and we had to open fire. It was too soon. I would have liked to have got a bit closer."

"Have they bomb-shelled?"

"Fuckin' right. They'll be half way to the border by now."

A series of whoops to my left indicated that Paul and Tim had got lucky.

Paterson was laughing. "Well, seems like we might have got two! Anyone'd think they've just caught a trophy tiger fish!"

I laughed at the analogy. It was exactly the same kind of whoop that fishermen make when the hook 'the big one'. I scrambled up the final few metres to the top of the hill and took a seat next to Paterson on the rock. I pulled out my cigarettes, the pack damp from the sweat of my chest, and lit up a crumpled cigarette. It tasted good. Two dead. It was good.

Lank's guerrilla lay at our feet at the base of the rock, his head skewed uncomfortably against the granite at an obscene angle. He'd taken a head shot. The bullet had entered above the top lip, travelled up through the brain and exited at the back of the skull, taking most of the back of the cranium away with it and smearing a trail of goo on the rock. I studied the face for a while, methodically inhaling and exhaling the smoke. The gook's top lip was partially torn away in a grotesque sneer, exposing his gums and part of the skull. With most of the back of his head having been blown away, the profile of his skull was only a few inches thick, like it only had a face, or was wearing some kind of mask.

I finished my smoke and took aim, attempting to lob the stompie into the gook's mouth. It missed and landed in an eye socket.

"Lank, have you checked him out yet?" I asked.

"No ways, man. I don't touch the bastards."

I shrugged and hopped off the rock. As routine, I felt in the trouser side-pockets for money. Nothing. I half-rolled the corpse on its side and patted the back pockets. Nothing. The shirt pockets. Nothing … just a half-finished ten-pack of Kingsgate cigarettes.

"Fuckin' cheapskate!" I spat, tossing the cigarettes away.

But he had a very nice canvas bag, maybe a medic's pack or something. I unclipped a swivel hook and slid it from the body. It was indeed a nice bag, robust and well made—not like our crappy Rhodesian kit which fell apart in no time at all. Probably East German. They made good stuff. I undid the buckle and scratched around inside. A couple of grubby field dressings with Chinese lettering on the torn plastic wrappings, more half-finished packs of Kingsgate, a couple of tins of sardines with 'Product of Norway' written on them, some Cafenol headache pills and that was about it.

"Nice bag," Paterson quipped.

I tossed it at him. "Have it. Your stick got him."

The cigarette was still smouldering in the guerrilla's eye socket, emitting a wisp of blue smoke that smelt disgusting. It looked totally weird, like some sort of sick special effects.

Clattering and panting on the one flank announced the arrival of Tim and Paul, grinning eagerly, out of breath.

"Yeah, got one of the bastards. Trying to gap it our way. Fucking great shot man! Got the dude as he was sprinting down a gully. Fell like a sack of mielies!"

They were very excited and I congratulated them.

Well, they can't say we didn't go out in style … of sorts.

Tim had an SKS slung over his shoulder. "Wouldn't mind keeping this—make a great hunting rifle."

"Wouldn't bother," I replied. "Gordy Gandanga'll have you for it. You know those okes!"

The sun was sinking over the Sabi. I got on the radio, looking for Errol and the Hyena. He'd be waiting at Tanganda Junction for my call. It was time to go home. The women had organized a Bingo and supper evening at the club.

It'd be more than our life's worth to be late.

*

Independence came and went, with no ostensible change in Middle Sabi. The cotton still grew, the bolls still ripened and opened, the aphids and the loopers still came and Wellington still ran the bar at the club.

We heard stories of the latest white exodus, of panicked congestion at the Beitbridge border post, of moonlight flits. There were nasty rumours going around that Ian Smith was relocating his cattle to South Africa on the quiet. This was strongly refuted and the nasty rumour evolved that it was his wife Janet's herd, not his. Of course.

There were rumours that RF cabinet ministers were smuggling out Reserve Bank bullion under police escort.

Nothing surprised me very much.

We heard stories about the British Monitoring Force and the Bobbies who'd come to police the polling stations—Mr. Plod bringing his western civilization to this grubby little corner of Africa. We heard how the other white farming districts had taken the Brits to their hearts. Good guys, they'd said. Just like us, really. It's just the politicians who stink—Wilson and Carrington and Thatcher and Soames. But it all goes back to that bloody Harold Wilson and those other bloody Commies—David Owen and that Yank *munt*, Andrew Young. Rabid, man! That's where the rot set in. And to think that at one stage we very nearly went to war with the Brits! I ask you! Our own kith and kin! Good guys like the Monitoring Force. Oh, it's all just such a waste. Well at least this Mugabe fellow doesn't seem too bad. He isn't hanging every white man from the lamp posts by Cecil Square. That's something.

Hell, who knows, maybe it'll all work out?

Prince Charles was 'out in Africa' as the British chap who'd do the actual handover of power and lower the Union Jack, which had only recently been run up the pole after a fifteen-year absence. We read about him in the press having a gay old time on safari, and how dangerous the buffaloes could be. ("What about my four years of warfare?" I wanted to interject ... petulantly.)

I was feeling unsettled, uneasy, but I couldn't put my finger on it. No one had come and told me to hand in my rifle or my PATU kit. What was happening? The war was over?

A few in the valley were making plans to leave. Zack Prinsloo had a job lined up in the Eastern Transvaal. Nat Pirsons was making plans to immigrate to Australia and was spending his every waking minute trying to fish out the Zambezi. J.J. Fourie vanished overnight, taking his entire fleet of tractors and combine harvesters to South Africa, across a drift on the Limpopo.

But, in the main, most of us hung around, not quite sure what to do, where to go, what to think.

So I woke one morning and decided I needed to do something about it. I felt an urge to take control, somehow. I went to the SLA offices, got Max's sultry secretary to type out a letter of resignation, signed it with a flourish and submitted it to Max. We sold up all our furniture, everything—even the new, imitation-kilt, four-piece lounge suite we'd recently bought from Mashonaland Furnishers in Umtali. With the money I bought three return air tickets to Mauritius, drew our miserable holiday allowance from the bank and went on holiday to La Morne Brabant for a fortnight.

part 2

Peace 1980–1995

Transition

Salisbury: 1980

1980 was the year that the war stopped and the peace began. Though, for many of us, I've often wondered if the war ever really stopped. I looked about me, at everyone else who seemed to be knuckling down and getting on with his or her life—living, loving and making money. I was in my own personal whirlwind, frenetically standing still.

I can't remember if it was during the seventies or the eighties when they changed the name of Peking to Beijing. And Mao Tse Tung to Mao Zedung, or something like that. I remember at the time feeling indignant that I hadn't been told about it. Was this some sort of new ZANU (PF) political correctness, or was it a universal thing and there'd been some sort of resolution passed in the United Nations? It took me fifteen years to realize that I'd simply missed it. The world had passed me by and was moving on. Maybe it had occurred when I was bogged down trying to recall all my battles, the guerrillas, and civilians, I had killed—trying to etch the faces of my dead victims into my mind. I'd lie awake for hours at night trying to remember. That's when I started writing them down. So I wouldn't forget.

We came back from Mauritius, suntanned and with no future. I was broke and I had no job. For a while we squatted with Carol's parents on the Tilcor Estate at Mzarabani. There, at least, I could live my memories in the vastness of the Zambezi Valley. There I could drink my brandies, orange and water (cheaper than brandies and ginger ale) in the thatched pub by the pool. I could talk to others who appeared to think like me—the farmers who came down from Umvukwes

196

and Centenary every weekend to go fishing in the Msengezi River, teeming with eight-pound Mozambica bream.

The river, untouched during all those years of war, was yielding a rich harvest and the people knew it. The white anglers, the sportsmen, were climbing in, hauling them out, and breaking the national angling record every other week. And the black fishermen, the hungry, would form human nets and wade upstream the waist-high river, legs touching, driving the bream into a corner and then saturating the water with their spears. And the whites would mumble about the bloody *munts* and how they were screwing the place up already and that there'd be nothing left in the not-too-distant future. For Christ's sake, the cops stopped a bus the other day going into Salisbury and confiscated two tons of dried fish! Two tons from one bus! And dried at that! What'n the hell d'you suppose its wet weight was? Six, seven tons? More! Eight! That's a shit-load of fish from one river. This place is fucked.

For a time, Carol's father, Colin—a big, flaming-red-bearded giant of a man—gave me a part-time job supervising the laying of a massive underground pipeline for a new irrigation scheme that would water thousands of acres of crops being opened up from virgin bush. But the workers knew what they were about and carried on regardless of what the young white man on the motorbike said.

I was vaguely hoping for some sort of permanent job offer but it never materialized, so I took my wife and child back to Salisbury, where I began the rounds of the employment agencies. Forms and forms and forms and forms. But no job. No one wanted to know.

"I have to tell you Mr. Cocks," the elderly, bespectacled Scottish lady said, "that the business climate in Zimbabwe is very depressed. No one's taking on new staff and, when they do, they take on ... well, you know ... our darker-complexioned friends. They're scared ... affirmative action an' all that mumbo jumbo."

The battle-axe at another agency was more direct. "Mr. Cocks. Quite frankly, you're the wrong colour and what's more you have no qualifications. To be fair, there are literally thousands of blacks the same age as you who have got better qualifications than you."

It was getting very difficult to support my family, my Lemslim and my drinking habits. Each empty bottle was carefully hoarded and stashed until a large enough deposit to buy a half-jack, or quarter-jack, was warranted. I did a few music gigs with my friend Fraser at the Clovagalix restaurant. We'd learned to play guitars together in our youth. We were paid $25 apiece for a night's work, with as much food and drink as we could consume. This kept the family going until I was offered a job by RAL Merchant Bank as a clerk, on the starting salary of $400 a month. We rented a house in Greendale for $250, so after tax and other deductions (pension contributions at twenty-two!), I was left with a little under $100 to see us through the month. I'd take the bus to work to save money and I'd eat at the Anglo American canteen across the road at Charter House in Jameson Avenue (RAL was part of Anglo American).

The country was being racked by a new kind of capitalism. White carpetbagger 'businessmen' were getting rich, supplying the Assembly Points with milllions of dollars worth of rations. Black businessmen, fronting for black politicians and white businessmen in need of an affirmative front, having been ignored during the years of white power, were getting themselves 'empowered' with all sorts of lucrative government contracts and tenders falling into their laps. A post-war situation is always ripe for sickening opportunism and Zimbabwe was no exception.

My old 'Communist' tendencies re-surfaced during my short time at the bank. Here I was, a clerk, handling these massively valued cheques and treasury bills—literally millions—from the grey, faceless corporations that had got fat on the war, fat on my sweat and the blood of my comrades. I began dreaming of ways of ripping the bank off. After my lunchtime visit to the Dae-Night Pharmacy on the street below to stock up on Lemslim, I'd sit twiddling my pencil over the bulky ledgers, concocting ways of opening up bogus accounts and siphoning a few of the millions into them. And then the grey, faceless, middle-management bankers with their grey suits and geeky spectacles would interrupt my reverie and ask me if I'd balanced. Like something out of Dickens. It was bizarre—Pickwickian characters in Africa, looking out from the chrome and glass modernity of their corporate idolatry onto Jameson Avenue (shortly to become Samora Machel Avenue).

All the names in the country were changing—the victors' purge of things colonial. Salisbury was to become Harare ("But what're they gonna call the *munt* township? Harare too?" "Nah, Mbare."); Railway Avenue was to become Kenneth Kaunda Avenue (KK had supported ZAPU so didn't get a prime street); Manica Road was to become Robert Mugabe Way (in a fit of prime-ministerial modesty); and Moffat Street was to become Leopold Takawira Avenue (most whites had never heard of him). The whites got to fume about these changes—major inconvenience with letterheads and company stationery.

But I simply dreamed and at five o'clock would board the Salisbury United Omnibus Company (shortly to become HUOC) bus on the corner of Second Street and Samora Machel Avenue and head back to Greendale, walking the last half-mile or so home from my drop-off.

Home? Hardly. We still couldn't afford any furniture. Apart from a cot, a double bed (and bedclothes), an old fridge (borrowed) and a two-plate electrical cooker (also borrowed), we had nothing. It struck me one day that we didn't even have a chair, so I dug out a few termite-eaten gum poles from the shed round the back of the house and fashioned together an armchair of sorts. For weeks, apart from the upturned beer crates, it was the single piece of 'furniture' in the living room.

At night, I would escape to town again, leaving Carol to look after the baby. There I'd meet up with my friends at somewhere like Club Tomorrow and pretend we were back in 1975. We'd smoke dope, get stoned, get blasted and then in the early hours I'd scrounge a lift back to the house and invariably pass out on the porch, too afraid to wake my wife, fast asleep with the baby.

After three months at RAL, Colin came to town with grand visions of me farming. Having been at Mzarabani for several years, he'd got to know most of the Centenary farmers quite well. (It always surprised me that they never changed the name Centenary, after all it was named in honour of the centenary of Rhodes' birth.) One of the farms, Charmwood, on the edge of the escarpment, was up for grabs. It had originally been owned by one Tommy Koen, but he'd been executed by gooks in his farm shed during the war. Since then the farm had been leased and now the leasee was moving off. Tommy's sister, who farmed in Hartley (shortly to become Chegutu) and who oversaw the farm, was looking for a manager to run the place, with an option to buy 'sometime'. This was a golden opportunity, Carol's father enthused, but clueless on where we'd ever get the money to buy the place.

I thought about it. I looked at the gum-tree chair and the bare lounge. I imagined the depressing bus trip down the Arcturus Road the next day. I thought of all those grey, faceless bankers. Yes, farm life—that was it! That was what I needed. Good, healthy outdoor stuff, away from the Lemslim, away from the booze. Farm life—it couldn't be worse than what I was doing now.

So I agreed and the next morning handed in my resignation to an unhappy Mr. Merry, the bank's secretary. I cleared my desk, folded shut the vast ledgers and walked out.

We packed our stuff into the Renault 12 the following day, piled in Guy, Ish and Jasper and drove north out of Harare, in the direction of Centenary—to a new adventure ... away from the world

Bad *mtagati*

Charmwood Farm, Centenary: 1981

Charmwood Farm was beautiful. Nestled in a picturesque valley, it was the northernmost 'white' farm in the Centenary Block. It was the last farm on the Alpha Trail, the twisting, turning tar road that wound down through the Mvuradona escarpment to the Zambezi Valley below. Several hundred feet lower in altitude than most of the farms in the area, it was an ideal Burley-tobacco-growing farm. Or so I was told. Tommy Koen had won the Burley Grower of the Year Award when he was still alive, before he'd been butchered in his farm workshop.

We turned off the main road near Altena Farm—where it had all started back in 1972 when ZANLA guerrillas had attacked the farmstead, immediately followed by the Rhodesian high command declaring Operation *Hurricane* to be open ... work in progress.

So, here I was ... now farming, now a civilian, but still unable to get away from the roots of the war. Perversely, I felt part of history, like a trail-blazing pioneer.

The farm labourers looked at the new arrivals—a young white couple, a baby and two dogs—with grave suspicion and scepticism. I looked at them with a measure of aggression and distrust. They were lurking around the sheds, eyeing us as we unpacked the car. They were dressed in long, tatty bell-bottoms, T-shirts with grubby pictures of Mugabe and the ZANU (PF) *jongwe*, the cockerel, screen-printed on the front (no doubt by a firm of Caucasian screen-printers back in Harare). All in their late teens and, without exception, they all wore their hair in the same fashion as the guerrillas had during the war—unkempt, Rasta-style. Undoubtedly they'd all been *mujibas*, or aspiring *mujibas*, during 'the struggle'. *Mujibas*—the civilian eyes and ears of the *vakomwana*, 'the comrades', 'the boys in the bush'. And undoubtedly, some of them had had a hand in Koen's murder.

"I see you, you bastards," I muttered under my breath.

"We see you, white man. Do not ever forget Koen," they seemed to mutter in return, sullenly resentful that their circumstances still hadn't changed, that they were still labourers, in spite of the heroic execution of the white Boer settler, *Baas* Tommy.

The farmhouse was pleasant enough in an unstartling way—the windows still encased in metal grenade screens. The one feature was the number of homemade wooden bookcases that had been built in to almost every room in the house. Roughly hewn from the *mukwa* forests of the Mvuradona Mountains, they added a scholarly, yet homely feel to the place. Either Koen was a consummate man of letters, or his carpenter could only make bookshelves. Having stacked my paltry, half-shelf library (Ayn Rand, James Michener, Leon Uris, Ernest Hemingway and John Steinbeck), I filled up the empty spaces with my war memorabilia—my RLI beret and stable belt, my parachute wings, my dog-tags, my farewell silver beer mug from my 3 Commando mates (with 'Cheers and good hunting' engraved on it) and assorted captured guerrilla items such as bayonets and canvas webbing.

We settled into the house in quick time and began the wait for the tractor and plough and other such implements to come from Chegutu. Two months later, still nothing had arrived. I began to fret. The rains were imminent and we had as yet to turn a clod of soil. The cropping programme was modest—a hundred acres of maize and a few acres of tobacco, more as a stop-gap measure to present an illusion of productivity and a white presence. Squatters from the neighbouring TTLs had already moved on to the vacant farm next door.

During this period of inactivity I occupied myself, fixing up the barns and the workshops. I kept the place clean and I ripped all the grenade screens off the walls and made a fine chicken coop out of them. Carol's parents, still farming on the valley floor at Mzarabani, gave us some day-old chicks, which we adequately reared, infusing us with a feeling that we really were farming.

A firm of Harare accountants managed the farm finances. I was paid $150 a month with no benefits, other than a rent-free house and one tank of petrol a month. A four-tree orchard of lemon trees presented an opportunity to earn some pocket money. I picked all the lemons and, with two sacks bulging, went to Harare and sold them for $10 apiece to a market-garden outfit in Greendale, something like 'Mr. Potato' or 'The Cabbage Patch'. With the cash I promptly bought two bottles of Mellowood brandy. Not a bad return.

We became very friendly with our nearest neighbours, Chris and Dawn Pohl. Although in their mid-thirties and therefore a good thirteen or fourteen year older than us, we related well to them. Nothing was too much trouble for them and they made us feel very welcome. Chris was farming on Mvuradona Farm, which was more rock and hill than arable land. He'd also leased Altena Farm, marginally better, but with two dams teeming with bass. We spent many happy hours together thrashing the waters with Rapalas and ticky spinners.

While on PATU duties, Chris had been severely shot up during the war in an action at St. Albert's Mission, a few kays east up the Mount Darwin road. Goodness knows how he survived—his body was racked with scars. Chris, as down to earth and unpretentious as they come, went down in Rhodesian farming history as the man who, as a young farm manager in the early sixties, ripped down the partition in the Umvukwes Club. Umvukwes, eighty-odd kays south of Centenary on the Salisbury road, had a fearful reputation for intense snobbery. So much so that in the country club the bar was subdivided, apartheid-fashion, into three distinct drinking areas—one for the farm owners, one for the farm managers, and one, barely in the pub at all, for the farm assistants, travelling salesmen and other such low-life riff-raff. It went without saying that 'darkies' weren't even allowed near the waiters' (fezzed, of course) serving hatch, let alone on to the property.

I could never understand, or tolerate, the dreadful social strata, an archaic colonial hangover, that had been introduced into the country. I was unfortunate enough to experience first-hand this ugly, Kenyan-type 'Happy Valley' snobbery, which persisted for many years post-independence in certain farming districts. But Centenary and Umvukwes, then and now, took first prize. Many of the original settler farmers were ex-servicemen (of that strange breed—the officer class), demobbed after World War Two, and given an opportunity to purchase 'Crown land' at something like tuppence an acre, or perhaps sixpence. Many were incompetent, Darjeeling-sipping, G & T-swilling twits, with no agricultural, let alone African, experience, who soon went bust, in spite of prefixing their names with 'Captain' or 'Major'. (To be fair, many persisted and turned their wild, virgin farms into viable, economic propositions.)

Messrs. Mugabe and Nkomo did indeed have a justifiable cause—land. No wonder my 'boys', lurking around the sheds, were surly and sullen.

St. Albert's, conversely, had had a fearful reputation as a hotbed of Communist agitation—a virulent Leninist den of white-hating iniquity. Staffed by German and Irish Catholic nuns, it was widely known that the mission overtly offered shelter and succour to the guerrillas during the war (as Chris Pohl discovered at his peril).

So it was with immense trepidation that I found myself in the position where I was obliged to seek the help of the nuns. After all, was I not one of the racist enemy? Baby Guy, now a boisterous two-year-old, had been romping on the bed one morning and cracked open his forehead on the wooden edge of the headboard. Straight off I could see the gash, which was bleeding buckets, urgently needed stitches. The nearest 'proper' hospital that attended to whites was in Centenary, a good fifty kays away. And even that was more of a 'native' clinic than a hospital.

I bundled the screaming child into the car, Carol white with shock, and made all haste to St. Albert's Mission. There, to my surprise, we were met at the doors of the casualty department by an anxious Irish nun, who took one look at the child, gathered him up in her voluminous arms and rushed him through to the theatre. I followed her in, leaving Carol still blanching in the outpatients' waiting room.

I went in nervously and was immediately put at ease. The nun was a qualified doctor. She was friendly and in no time at all had young Guy sedated and sewn up with a dozen stitches, her lilting Irish brogue soft and soothing for both father and son.

"There we go!" she smiled at me. "All done. Just as well yer brought him in as quick as yer did. Much longer an' he would a' scarred sumpin' terrible." She took my hand and squeezed it. "Yer a good dad, me boy."

I felt the tears welling inside me. I wanted to confess that I was one of the hated enemy and why had she shown such compassion. I wanted to take back all those years of death and misery. What could I do to make amends?

As if reading my thoughts, she patted my hand. "Now run along to that pretty Colleen o' yours ... an' take care o' this lad. He's very special."

She smiled a smile of such infinite love and compassion. The lump in my throat bobbed as I took the child and, mumbling my thanks, asked if I could pay. She said no and told me to "Be off with yer now."

It made no sense.

The tractor, a Buffalo (a blue one!), and a few implements arrived in late November, a few days before the anticipated onset of the rainy season and I felt I was now truly a farmer of some worth. I had the tools. In no time at all the lands were ploughed, harrowed and rolled. Fertilizer was applied by hand and the planting stations holed out, ready to drop the maize pips into when the rains finally came.

I also prepared a few acres for Burley tobacco and scrounged some seedlings from a very kind farmer called Fitzgerald who farmed near the village of Centenary. I was happy—king of my little domain.

Waiting for the rains brought on another period of idleness and I took up my old shooting habit, but this time animals not people. Most of the farm was bush and teemed with antelope and bush pig, the latter proving a real scourge on the maize crop in weeks to come. Sable, kudu, bushbuck and the smaller antelope—duiker, klipspringer and grysbok—they were all there. Brother-in-law Iain had come to stay for a while and, being an avid hunter, he and I would head off in to the bush every night, his battered Land Rover bristling with rifles, shotguns and powerful spotlights. We shot dozens of bush pig and a few antelope, but it all came to an end the one night when the spotlight picked up a pair of red eyes gleaming tantalizingly in the blackness. Iain stopped the Land Rover and I quietly climbed out. I had the shotgun as I thought the eyes belonged to a bush pig, but they didn't. Blasting off several shots brought on a loud squealing of such immeasurable anguish and pain. It wouldn't stop. It was a duiker, mortally wounded and crying like a human baby—like it was begging, asking the question, "Why, why, why have you done this thing?" I could face it no longer, so Iain drew his .38 revolver from his holster and put the poor creature out of its agony.

But didn't farmers hunt? Was it not a manly thing to do? Like war, of course there were casualties. Didn't Hemingway hunt?

I never shot another animal again, except my dogs, that is. My faithful dogs, Ish the Alsatian and Jasper the fox terrier. It is still too painful to relate and I want to vomit as I write these words. Ish the Alsatian—she never left little Guy's side, lying for hours on end by the pram, following him and Carol wherever they went, protecting them with her life. And I repaid her by taking hers. And her friend, Jasper's.

We'd come back from a drunken Sunday at the Mzarabani pub, having braaied a vundu, one of those prehistoric catfish, by the pool. A good day of drinking, eating, darts, swimming and more drinking. It was dark when we finally got in the car and wound our way slowly up the escarpment. We turned into the Charmwood road at the Altena store and within minutes the headlights were beaming down the driveway towards the homestead. For a second, the lights swung across the porch of the front door and I vaguely noticed a pile of something, dumped unceremoniously on the steps.

"What's that?" I asked my wife.

"What?"

I stopped the car, reversed a bit and aimed the lights at the porch. Immediately I knew what had happened. The dogs had got into the chicken run and killed all the chickens. Perhaps out of boredom, but perhaps they'd 'turned'—become gratuitous killers. Then, having done with the slaughter, they'd dragged all the dead fowls out from the coop to be displayed on the porch for our return.

There was a stunned silence from my wife as she took in the scene of carnage. And then softly, her voice low and menacing, "My dad says that once dogs start doing this, they'll never change."

The dogs had seen us and came trotting happily up to the car, tails wagging and tongues still dripping with blood. She slammed her door closed to keep them away, to keep the blood away.

"What are you saying?" I looked at her. I knew very well what she was saying.

"Chris, my dad gave us these chickens. He'll have a bloody fit if he knows what's happened. You have to do something!"

That same old brain mechanism kicked in. This time it was dogs, not civilian curfew breakers. I knew what had to be done and I felt something inside me take over. Like a zombie, I felt myself get out the car, ignoring the dogs at my heels, as I strode purposefully to the front door. And then, through the front door. Down the polished cement passageway to the bedroom. To the gun cabinet. I was shaking as I opened it and took out the shotgun. It was an FN automatic and I loaded it up with cartridges. Some force was inside me. I felt the anger rising, possibly psyching myself up for the bloody task at hand.

Out the kitchen door, to the open rubbish pit near the lemon trees. I called the dogs and they came happily, at last some attention. I ordered them to sit by the edge of the pit and they dutifully obeyed, panting with anticipation, like I was about to play a game with them. I stepped back a few paces and raised the shotgun, the dogs looking directly at me. I was shaking. What spread did the gun have? I must make it quick. Get them both with the first shot. But Jasper became restless and sauntered off a few paces, sniffing some interesting smell in the grass.

"Shit!" I cursed and lowered the gun. "Jasper!" I snapped. "Sit!"

The terrier looked at me, ears cocked and dutifully went and sat down next to Ish. I raised the gun and squeezed the trigger. The blast was thunderous in the still night air. But as I'd shot the dogs moved. There was a terrified barrage of squeals, both dogs clearly wounded. I shot again and again … more yelps and screams of agony. The dogs went racing off with Ish dragging her back legs in unimaginable pain. Irrationally, I noticed that Jasper's uncropped tail was firmly, bloodily clamped between his back legs. Somehow or other both dogs scurried in terror to the nearest shelter—the outside scullery, a lean-to affair. They staggered, slipping and sliding into the room, desperately clawing the smooth, polished floor. I chased after them and switched on the light. They were hiding under a low table, peering out fearfully, whimpering, eyes trying to look away from the man and the gun.

I brought the gun into the shoulder again. This time there was no escape for the doomed creatures. I fired five shots at short range and in moments the dogs were still. Dead.

But still reality did not come to me. I remember hearing my wife, pitifully calling out from inside the house. I could hear little Guy crying.

It was done. By God, and how it was done!

The scullery floor was awash with blood. Uncaring, I slopped through the mess of entrails, fur, blood, urine and faeces. Grabbing the dead dogs from under the table, I dragged them by the legs to the rubbish pit. Slinging them in, an awful emptiness of such indescribable proportions came over me. Clean. I had to get the place clean. Like Macbeth. Like an automaton, I dragged the hosepipe around from the front garden and started hosing down the floor, hosing down the walls, the ceiling—everywhere—where there was blood and bits of flesh—real or imagined.

I don't know how many hours I stood like that, hosepipe clamped in my hand, spraying and spraying. I was wet through.

The sun was starting to peep over the eastern horizon when I switched off. Shotgun still slung, I went to the compound and woke up Chataika, the horse boy. I told him to get some labourers together and get the rubbish pit filled in.

Then the memories would be gone, would they not?

Never.

For nearly twenty years I have lived and re-lived this nightmare. I still see their faces as I shoot. I still hear their whimpers. I howl and I hit the wall with my fists. I bite my bottom lip and I attempt to draw blood.

What am I?

The maize and the tobacco were doing well. The rains had been good and there was promise of a fine harvest. But then the bush pigs came and devastated great swathes of the fresh, green plants. Then the aphids came and the tobacco was attacked by a virus and never grew more than two feet high.

We had two horses, which we'd bought from a neighbour, Alf Jackson. Fine, strong Arabs. The mare was in foal when we bought her and the filly had just been broken in. Then one day the filly died. Just lay down and died. The mare had her foal, a beautiful, skittish creature. Barely a week old, she too died inexplicably. Was it Chataika, the horse boy? Did he have some sort of *mtagati*, evil medicine? What nonsense! I took the mare back to Mr. Jackson and asked if his stallion would cover her again. The second foal was born dead.

Chickens, dogs, duiker, horses. All dead. The farm was jinxed. Was it the spirit of Tommy Koen coming back to wreak his revenge? Or was it the spirit of Chris Cocks, alive in flesh, but dead in soul, perpetuating his own living nightmare?

The maize was ready for harvest when a letter arrived from Mr. Vermaak, the accountant in Harare. It was terse and succinct. The farm had been sold to a Mr. Thorn from South West Africa. Mr. Thorn would finish reaping the crops and please would I vacate the farm within fourteen days.

I pleaded with Chris Pohl to take the mare, which he kindly did.

I packed the car. Carol was pregnant again.

I went to the where the rubbish heap had been, now a bare mound of earth, and planted my crudely fashioned cross.

The year of the Mkorekore

Viewfield Farm, Centenary: 1982

Chris Pohl again came to our rescue and at the eleventh hour organized a farm assistant's job for me with a neighbour. Doug Davies, owner of Viewfield Farm, came across as a dour, stolid Geordie, but was in fact a very kind man. I was grateful for the job, and in short time we'd moved in to the small cottage perched literally on the edge of the escarpment. The view across the Zambezi Valley was simply stunning and on a clear day we could make out the shimmering waters of the vast Cahora Bassa Dam, far away in Mozambique. The house, red farm-brick under *marata* (corrugated iron) hadn't been lived in for many years, and had been used for tobacco storage. As a result, it needed much cleaning and, with our new cook/houseboy, Scot, we set to the task with gusto.

We had first met Scot the previous year when he had been the estate tea-boy at Mzarabani. He was an enigma was Scot, or Mr. Scot Chigede, as he preferred to be called. He was a local *sabuku*, a headman, under Chief Kasikete's jurisdiction and like all Mkorekore tribesmen was very dark-skinned, almost pitch-black. (As a white man I found it difficult to reconcile that a man of such stature, a headman, could 'demean' himself by working as a lowly tea-boy.) He didn't know how old he was, but he must have been well into his sixties when he started working for us. As thin as a rake, with droopy, lidded eyes, he looked like a tortoise without a shell. Cottage pie was his speciality.

The Mkorekore peoples, inhabiting the northeast corner of Zimbabwe, straddling the Mozambican border across the Zambezi

Valley, are a sub-group of the Shona race. They are the target of much scorn by their haughtier Mzezuru cousins living on the highveld. It was common practice when picking out a farm worker to say: "What's the matter with you Ephraim? Are you a Mkorekore, or what?" In other words—dim, interbred, poor, black trash.

There was even a fish nicknamed a 'mkorekore'. This was the dreaded 'squeaker' or 'grunter' that was found in the warmer, lowveld waters of the Zambezi and Msengezi rivers. Rarely exceeding seven or eight inches in length, without scales, this slimy, pig-like scavenger was the angler's scourge. No sooner had you cast your delicately prepared bait into the water than you'd feel a sharp, urgent tugging on the line.

The problem came in trying to remove the hook from the fish, which had invariably been swallowed to the depths of its gullet. The fish, angrily wriggling and making those fart-like grunts, would flip and flop all over the place and the poor fisherman could sometimes spend several minutes at the task, forever wary of the steel-strong spike of its dorsal fin. A pair of pliers was always necessary. As a greenhorn angler, I once inadvertently trod on one of these spiked, upright fins, little realizing that they are designed to secrete a poison into the puncture of the victim's foot. Swelling up like a football, my foot was unbelievably painful and I couldn't walk on it for several days. A 'mkorekore' took a long time to die and, without being clubbed on the head with a rock, it could lie in the hot sun for several hours before finally expiring.

Doug, with that avid Anglo-Saxon, Protestant work ethic, was a hard taskmaster. His cropping programme was ambitious—three hundred acres of Virginia tobacco and six hundred acres of maize. But the bonus scheme, on an incremental sliding scale as yields increased, motivated me no end (as it was intended to) and I set to the job with energy. Doug's hours were long and arduous. His day and, it followed, mine as well, started at four o'clock in the morning. Quite what we were supposed to do at that time of the morning, I wasn't exactly sure. I implemented all sorts of records' systems—for the fleet of tractors, the hours worked, the diesel used and so on. Records for the wages, for the amount of fertilizer used, for the amount of seed, chemicals, time spent on tasks—ad nauseam. Doug used this early-morning time to swot up on his Masonic programme.

I was allocated an old, yellow CZ motorbike. CZ is apparently a Czechoslovakian make. Prague is not, and never was, a leader in motorcycle manufacturing. It was a shocker and until the day I left Viewfield, it gave me no end of trouble. I lost track of how many times I stripped that carb. It would rarely start and invariably needed pushing.

The day would wind up at dusk, around six o'clock, but of course there was the de-brief of the day's activities and I'd ususally only get back to the little house on the prairie after seven or eight o'clock. Of course, during tobacco-curing time, I'd be obliged to wake up every four hours or so through the course of the night, 'to check the barns'— an institution with tobacco farmers.

I very soon came to realize that tobacco farming was an arduous, repetitive and uninspiring pastime. I suppose if you are the owner and making a bundle of money, there's some merit in it. But for a young assistant, earning $300 a month, with vague promises of a 'nice' bonus, which could easily be manipulated by an unscrupulous boss at the end of the season, the sixteen-hour days somehow didn't warrant the effort.

It was also a lonely existence. The farm was fifty kays or so from the country club at Centenary and, apart from the fact that we couldn't afford the petrol let alone the club fees, I had little desire to mix with the local farmers. Our friends were the Pohls and another older couple, Pip and Pam Thorneycroft. Pip, a highly successful farmer, was very much a kindred spirit. He played the double bass, of all things, and once a week we'd get together for a jam session with Pip on bass and me on guitar. But Pip and Pam? A more unmatched pair, you'd unlikely see. Pip was quiet and unassuming, while vivacious, redheaded Pam was a fire-eater. After a year or two, the couple sold the farm and immigrated to Canada, where they got divorced. With enough

steelhead salmon fishing for a lifetime behind him, Pip returned to
Zimbabwe before moving to war-torn Mozambique. He married a
black woman and lived happily on the shores of Chicamba Real Dam
in Manica Province, Mozambique, where he ran a very successful
guest house and restaurant. (I was blessed to spend a forthnight with
Pip at Chicamba in 2003, playing music and drinking beer on the dam
with him, little knowing he had cancer. He died a few days after I'd
left.)

I still recall the days and days of excruciating boredom perched
on top of a water cart, overseeing the tobacco planting—all done by
(black) hand. Only achieving five acres a day, it was several weeks
before we finished. During that time, I closely studied the workers,
their habits and their mannerisms, as there was little else to do. I made
an effort to learn Shona and managed to pick up a reasonable amount
from the workers. I studied the women and began vaguely to see that
some were not unattractive in terms of an Anglo-Saxon perception of
beauty, in spite of their dirty, ragged frocks and Mkorekore heritage.
They made little effort to hide their sexuality and were unashamed
of it. I could understand why Pip did what he did (although he was
cruelly shunned by his white 'friends' for doing it).

A distraction came in the form of a Fireforce arriving one day on
the farm. I was sitting on top of the water cart in the middle of the
lands, when I heard the unmistakable throb of Alouette helicopters. I
looked up at the cloudless skies and, sure enough, three choppers were
coming north over the horizon. The helicopters swung low, setting
their course on me, on top of the water cart. I mused. What now?

The helicopters, causing much excitement among the Mkorekore
maidens, buzzed over us, stirring up swirling dust clouds. I looked
up and saw a young white man leaning out the lead chopper—a
blond-haired white man. Norris! It could only be. And it surely was.

The choppers scudded off in the direction of the homestead and I excitedly jumped on the CZ and push-started it, chugging home as fast as it would go. By the time I arrived, the three Alouettes had landed on the lawn and shut down. Air force pilots and gunners, in their grey flying suits, were nonchalantly chatting under the rotors.

"Hey, howzit, my buddy!" Charlie Norris, in an army jumpsuit, came striding across the lawn to greet me. I noticed the three captain's pips on his epaulettes. Captain Norris! Who would have ever believed! Not six years before, when we'd first met in 3 Commando, Norris was a young trooper with a shaven head, having just completed twenty-eight days in DB—Detention Barracks—for sleeping on guard.

We shook hands and, amidst a lot of backslapping, we caught up with each other's news. Charlie was now the adjutant of 1 Commando Battalion, the successor to the RLI. Now fully integrated—that is black, white, former Rhodesian and former guerrilla soldiers—the battalion was on exercise in the Zambezi Valley, sniffing out Renamo insurgents who might be basing up in Zimbabwe. Renamo, the Mozambican National Resistance Movement, had been founded in the mid-seventies by the Rhodesian Central Intelligence Organization, with the express purpose of countering Frelimo and their allies, the ZANLA guerrillas, by fighting terror with terror. Losing their Rhodesian support at the end of the bush war, the South Africans soon filled the void in terms of logistical support. Now Renamo was getting cheeky, and Charlie as adjutant of 1 Commando Battalion had been tasked to seek out and destroy his former allies in the Zambezi Valley.

"Lissen, bud," he asked. "Is it okay if we bivvy up here tonight?"

"Erm, ja, sure." I eyed Carol on the verandah. "What, all of you?" I could sense her suspicion even at that distance.

Charlie laughed, sensing my uncertainty. "Nah. I've already spoken to your boss, Doug, an' he said he'd look after the Blue Jobs. So it's just the two of us ... me an' Fletcher."

"Who?"

"Fletcher. My right-hand man. Converted gook. He's a great guy.

We talk for hours about all the ops we were on. Y'know, he was at Chimoio? Telling me about how they ran like fuck when we came in in the Daks. Fascinating stuff ... like the tactics they used to counter our Fireforce ops."

"Sure, no problem," I said, a little too glibly. "I'll get Carol to make up the beds in the spare room." Rather, I'd get Carol to tell Scot to make up the beds in the spare room. I glanced over to where Fletcher was squatting on his haunches next to a helicopter. He looked presentable enough—certainly more so now that he was in camouflage uniform and had had his hair cut.

But I hadn't bargained on Carol's attitude.

"What! D'you mean to tell me we're gonna have a *munt* sleeping in *my* house and sitting in *my* chairs and sitting on *my* toilet!" She spat the words. "*And* he's a bloody terrorist as well!"

"Aw, c'mon, man. Don't be ridiculous. The war's finished ..." I muttered.

"Maybe for you! But what about my dead brother, huh? Maybe that bloody terr killed him. And what about Iain in the landmine, huh? Huh!"

"It was war. He was a soldier ... same as us."

"I don't care! He's ... he's black! He's a murdering, bloody *munt*!" She burst out crying and, nearly knocking over young Guy happy beetling up and down the verandah on his trike, she stormed off to the bedroom.

I explained the situation to Charlie and casually finished with, "Ag, don't worry about it, Charlie. She'll get over it."

So Charlie and his 'tame' gook, his converted guerrilla, spent not one night, but two, with us. Carol grudgingly emerged from the bedroom a few hours later, glared at Fletcher sitting in the armchair and skulked off to the kitchen. I followed her through, to try and settle things, but she'd have none of it.

"Chris, I don't care what you think about it. I'm not going to change. And that bloody Charlie! How dare he! Who does he think he is?"

"Well, we know Charlie ..."

"Bloody right we do. Manic bloody depressive! What pills is the little bastard on now? I'm going to talk to Tan when I see her next." Tan was Charlie's long-suffering wife, back in Harare.

So that night, Charlie, Fletcher and I all got rat-shit drunk. It was good. Former enemies, former comrades, talking war talk. We laughed a lot and we reminisced about the good times and about the bad times. I liked Fletcher.

We decided to get another dog. It was a difficult decision and re-opened the wounds of the previous year. But, perhaps a dog, a new dog, a different breed, would help heal. We opted for a Labrador. With a new baby on the way we wanted something gentle. Labradors are good with children. So scanning the week-old newspapers, we found some people in Arcturus, near Harare who were advertising 'pedigree' golden Labrador puppies at $25 each.

Carol, who was something of a dog buff, said that at that price they were possibly pure bred, but certainly not pedigreed. Did they have papers she wanted to know. So, on our next trip to Harare, we made a diversion to Arcturus where we bought a golden Labrador puppy. We called him 'Tex'.

After what seemed an age, the tobacco crop came and went. I sent two young workers to the now-stripped lands to gather up the tobacco stalks in piles on the contours and burn them. It was law that tobacco stalks had to be burnt by a certain date, to prevent any carry-over of disease or virus to the next season. The cut-off date loomed. Logistically, destroying six hundred acres of tobacco stalks is a massive exercise. Doug didn't seem that interested in the chore as he was too busy watching the prices on the auction floors in Harare. Prices were disappointing, he said. It was becoming clearer by the day that my anticipated bonus was rapidly diminishing.

I don't know how the two fools did it, but somehow, while burning their piles of dry stalks they allowed the flames to creep back along the contour ridge, sparsely grassed as it was, towards the dry grass of the waterway on the edge of the lands. Within minutes, like a tinderbox, the dry winter grass in the waterway became a raging fire. Then, to make things worse, a strong wind blew up. The fire quickly spread and roared up towards the main tar road, taking out a young gum plantation en route. Surely it would stop at the road? There was no ways it could cross the road. But it did. Two days later, exhausted and dispirited, we gave up the fight. The fire was out of control and had destroyed thousands upon thousand of acres of maize, grazing land and gum plantations.

Like the neighbouring farms, I was devastated. I accepted full responsibility for the damage. Doug didn't say anything but I knew he was seething inside. Already the neighbours' lawsuits were being set in motion against him. There were mumblings of bankruptcy and the suited insurance men came and went, looking grim. They spoke to me, taking endless statements—like talking to a recalcitrant child. My guilt was immeasurable and, to make matters worse, I learned that my friend Chris Pohl had also been burnt out. He was struggling enough as it was. This was the last thing he needed.

I was stunned. Mvuradona Farm was over ten kilometres away from where the fire had started. How'd it been put out? Where had it burnt itself out? The Msengezi River, I was told, some forty kilometres to the west.

I resolved that there was no option but to tender my resignation. It was the honourable thing to do. Besides, I was getting obvious vibes from Doug that my time on the farm was limited. Curious questions like, "So, Chris, what have you got planned for your future? Are you going to stay in farming?" were asked.

So, one evening in June, I went home to the cottage and wrote out my letter of resignation. Carol was now heavily pregnant, with the baby due in six weeks or so. I looked at my family—my wife; happy, innocent, little Guy; and Tex, the fluffy Labrador pup. And soon, another baby. A feeling of hopelessness engulfed me. What now? How could I support them?

I made a decision to leave Centenary. There was nothing for me there and, at any rate, I wasn't really cut out to be a farmer. For God's sake who had I been kidding? I knew nothing about curing tobacco. All those long, cold winter nights, checking barns—I'd just been going through the motions. In reality I had no idea about 'pushing temperatures' or opening and closing vents. I just didn't have it— period.

But Centenary hadn't done with me just yet—no, not by a long shot. In the early hours of the following morning, I was woken by the sounds of vehicles outside on the lawn. The beams of headlights flashed across the verandah, piercing the bedroom curtains and blinding me, as I tried to shield my eyes from the glare. Loud voices were shouting in Shona.

I scrambled out of bed, little Guy soundly sleeping in the cot next to us, and peered cautiously through the curtains. There, on the lawn were several grey police Land Rovers. Figures were running, rifles in hand, around the house. Even through the gloom it was clear they were surrounding the place. I shrugged on my old dressing gown and slip-slops as Carol stirred. She sat bolt upright when she heard the noises outside.

"What's happening?" she asked sleepily.

"Ssh!" I whispered. "It's the cops, I think. They're surrounding the damned house. God knows what for."

She switched on her bedside light and swung out of bed, putting on her slippers as she got up. "Well, I don't know what they want, but I'm going to give them a piece of my mind!" She was making to storm out and confront them.

"Hey!" I hissed. "Slow down. They might get violent. What if they're pissed? I'm going. You look after Guy." I grabbed my torch and stepped out on to the verandah. A tall, black policeman, I think an inspector, came up to me, shining his torch in my face.

"Are you Christopher Cooks?"

"Cocks. Yes, I am. Who are you?" I tried not to sound antagonistic. "It's three o'clock in the morning. What's going on?" I lit a cigarette to calm my nerves. Why was it that black people, like Afrikaners, could never get my name right? Either Cooks or Cock or Kok—never Cocks—as in Cox.

"I am Inspector Mudakiwa. I have instructions to search your property."

"Huh? What for?" I was confused.

He was looking past my shoulder, in to the house. Two of his constables were waiting at the French doors that led into the lounge from the verandah.

"I am not authorized to tell you."

"Well, how about I authorize you to tell me? I mean, it's only my house. And how about I ask you for your search warrant?" I said sarcastically. But it was missed on him.

"We do not require a search warrant under the Emergency Powers Act."

I was stunned. Emergency powers? That was insurgency sort of shit. I tried a different approach. "Well, what if I were to co-operate? It will save you a lot of time." I noticed Carol, silhouetted against the bedroom door, holding the child in her arms.

The inspector noticed the woman. "Good evening ma'am," he nodded politely. "Very sorry for the inconvenience."

Carol, not renowned for her diplomacy was aggressive. "I should bloody well hope so. What in the hell do you think you're doing?"

The inspector gave a deep sigh. "Very well. We have been instructed to search for weapons. Weapons of war." He pronounced it "weeporns".

"What!" Carol and I blurted out at the same time.

He was nodding, almost regretfully. "Yes. The station received a call from the Fifth Brigade at Mkumbura. They were the ones who were supposed to come and search the house. But they got lost and radioed us to do the job ..." he tailed off, almost embarrassed.

"Fifth Brigade! Jesus! It must be serious!" I stammered.

"Yes. It is too serious," the inspector replied softly.

Christ! Fifth Brigade! They were rabid, man. Trained by the North Koreans, they had become Mugabe's roaming hit squads—cruelty personified. Whispers seeping through from Matabeleland indicated they were on the rampage against the Matabele, slaughtering and burning entire villages, wiping out whole regions.

"Mr. Cooks. A report was made to the Fifth Brigade HQ at Mkumbura that you are caching weeporns of war and, through your father at Mzarabani, this MacAllister ..."

"Father-in-law," I corrected.

" ... that you and him are together supplying weeporns to the M. N. Urrer."

I was totally bewildered. The MNR? Renamo? What absolute fabrication was this? What horrible, scurrilous lies were these? It was a set-up. It had to be—or a very, very big mistake.

"We have already searched your father's house in Mzarabani and he has been arrested for possession of weeporns of war." Before I could interrupt again he continued, his hand raised to stop further discussion. "I only ask for your co-operation. Otherwise, we will be forced to turn your house around." He indicated the door to the lounge. "Please can you unlock all doors, all cupboards, so my men may continue with the search."

"Very well. But I'm telling you now I have nothing. I've sold my weapons. A shotgun and a .22 rifle. I was broke and needed the money."

I led the inspector in to the lounge and they began the search. It was very thorough. After two hours they were done, a pile of things lumped on the verandah. My heartburn was hurting, from too many cigarettes and too much coffee. Carol had gone back in to the bedroom and was tidying up the clothes scattered over the floor and the bed.

A constable with a clipboard was making an inventory of the things laid out on the floor. A box of .22 rounds, an AKM bayonet and three metres of yellow Cordtex detonation chord. That was it.

The inspector drew himself up and cleared his throat. "Mr. Cooks, do you admit that these items are in your possession?"

"Erm, yes, I suppose so. But those aren't weapons, for Christ's sake! I use the bayonet as my fishing knife!" I'd forgotten about the .22 rounds when I sold the rifle. And the Cordtex ... I wasn't even aware of it. I think it was being used to tie up an old sack in the garage.

"Christopher Michael Cooks," the inspector continued mechanically. "You are under arrest for possession of weeporns of war. We are under orders to take you to the police station at Centenary for a statement and charging." He nodded to the constable at his side. The constable stepped up to me and took my wrists, snapping on a pair of chromium-plated handcuffs.

Carol was still in the bedroom so was unaware of my arrest. I'd long since changed out of my dressing gown and was now wearing a T-shirt and boxer shorts. I was barefoot.

"What about some clothes? ... and I need to talk to my wife."

The inspector shook his head, looking away from me. "Take him!" he nodded curtly at two constables.

The two policemen, one on either side of me, grabbed my elbows and, at a fast walk, bundled me into the back of the nearest Land Rover. I tumbled painfully onto the ice-cold, metallic floorboards, as the drivers fired up their engines and switched on their lights. As they reversed up the lawn I caught a glimpse of Carol running from the verandah. She was shouting something and, even amidst the roar and smoke of the diesel engines, I could make out the unmistakable fear and panic in her voice.

The Land Rovers bustled up the driveway as I peered anxiously out the back at the fast-disappearing figure of my wife. She was standing stock still on the lawn, her hands up to her cheeks, a forlorn, desolate figure.

The vehicles bumped and ground their way over the dirt road on to the main tar road and I was hard-pressed to keep my balance.

There was a subdued grunt behind me. "Hello, Chris," a voice called out.

I spun round. Up against the back window of the cab was the bulky figure of Colin, my father-in-law. He was sitting on the floor, his handcuffed wrists between his knees. Like me, he was barefoot, dressed only in shorts and a thin cotton shirt. The temperature was surely sub-zero by now?

"Colin! What the fuck ... you too!"

He grunted. "Ja. Searched me first. We didn't know how to warn you."

"But ... but is this for real?" I asked, ignoring the lone constable sitting on the metallic bench beside me. I thought briefly of giving him a good elbow in the face and baling out.

"It's for real all right. The bastards! They've confiscated all my rifles and shotguns. Twelve of them."

"But they're legal aren't they? I mean, you've got firearm licences for them all, haven't you?"

The big man appeared very uncomfortable, almost embarrassed at being subjected to such demeaning treatment. After all, he was the big white *bwana* of the Zambezi Valley, a man who commanded much respect.

"Ja, they're all legal, but I haven't got the licences on me. We had to send them all in to Central Firearms Registry in Harare for verification and renewal."

The Land Rovers were picking up speed as the bitterly cold night air rushed against my skin. I was shivering involuntarily. My teeth were chattering. The constable next to me was unfazed and peered silently ahead up the road, ignoring our talk.

"But didn't you tell them? I would have thought a phone call to Harare would have cleared it up?" The handcuffs were beginning to bite into my wrists. They'd been done too tightly.

"Of course I told them. But they weren't interested. I think they're so shit scared of Fifth Brigade that they came to arrest us, regardless."

"But on what grounds?" I persisted. I could see he didn't want to talk, but I had to know.

He sighed wearily. "Oh, I don't know. I reckon it was one of the *munts* who worked in the garden. I fired one for stealing a couple of weeks ago. I'm guessing he got all bitter and twisted. Maybe he'd seen all the weapons in the cupboard, maybe when he was weeding outside the bedroom window. Dunno what else it could be."

"So you reckon he ran off to Fifth Brigade and made up this little story?"

Colin didn't answer, but nodded briefly. I think he was trying to hold back the tears. I left him to his silence and clumsily tried to extricate my cigarettes from my shorts' pocket. Finally, I managed. Now to light it—in an open-backed Land Rover travelling at eighty or ninety kays an hour. I ducked behind the driver's cab, as the constable reached for his SLR rifle in momentary alarm. I manipulated a match into my right hand, the matchbox clenched in the left. After several attempts the cigarette took, glowing comforting in the blackness. I offered Colin a drag and held it up to his lips for him. He leaned forward and inhaled deeply, nodding his thanks.

We sat in silence for the rest of the journey. An hour later, with the sun peeping over the gentle, undulating hills to the east, we arrived at the police station. The station's perimeter lights were still on, glowing feebly under the encroaching daylight. We clambered off, stiff with cold and were led to the charge office. The escort constable indicated a bench and we sat. He leaned his rifle against the counter and started gabbling loudly to the member on duty.

And so began the three-week nightmare.

We sat on the bench like that for the whole day, with nothing to eat or drink. At least they had the grace to take the handcuffs off. Policemen came and went, as did an array of civilians—women with babies on their backs filing complaints against unfaithful husbands who'd beaten them up; women who'd been beaten up for refusing their husbands sex; drunks being let out of cells, and others being taken in; a farm worker arrested for stealing maize—in fact, a normal day at a districts' police station.

A white farmer came in and I vaguely recognized him. He knew Colin and came and greeted him. "Hi Colin. What are you doing here, old boy?" All jovial.

I could see Colin wanted to crawl under the bench. He muttered some lame excuse and rudely turned his head away in the general direction of the ubiquitous portraits of Mugabe and Banana, hanging cockeyed on the wall. The farmer, discouraged, looked a mite hurt but shrugged and continued his conversation with duty officer—something about an overloaded maize truck that had been impounded. But surely, the farmer would have noticed that we were barefoot? It was usual for barefooted white farmers to loiter carelessly on a charge office bench? I wanted to blurt out that we weren't okay and that there was a gross miscarriage of justice in the offing and that we were under arrest for caching weapons of war for Renamo. And please, could he do something about it for us, for Christ's sake!

But I held my tongue, for Colin's sake. The humiliation would have been too much for him to suffer.

The day wore on and nothing happened. It was forbidding … the fear of the unknown. Occasionally we'd visit the toilets, unescorted, slipping and sliding in the piss that covered the floor. The one window was barred so escape was out of the question. And anyway, where'd we run to? We drank cold water from the tap that didn't turn off. My cigarettes ran out mid afternoon.

Dusk was approaching when I heard a Land Rover draw up outside.

The inspector was back. He sauntered in to the charge office, barely glancing at us. The constables braced up.

He rattled something off in Shona and the constables nodded deferentially, reaching for their caps and greatcoats and rifles.

A sergeant came to us and told us to stand up. We did. He clamped the handcuffs back on. "Come, we go!" he snapped.

Colin looked about him. I could sense his panic. That grubby little charge office had perversely become our comfort zone. "Where ... where are we going?" he tried to sound authoritative but instead came across as petulant. "I say, this is really not on. I *demand* to know what's going on. We have rights. I demand to see the member-in-charge!"

"Shut up, please!" the sergeant snapped again. "And get on the vehicle." He pointed at the inspector's Land Rover. He pronounced it 'vay-hee-cule', which I thought quite funny in a childish way. In fact, I was feeling infantile, like a naughty schoolboy who'd been caught trying to piss out of the lavatory window as I had in kindergarten. That was when I learned about humiliation and the erosion of self-esteem and self-respect. I'd had to clean it all up during break.

There was a different constable in the back with us this time and he was friendly. I cultivated his largesse and scrounged a Kingsgate cigarette from him, which he lit and passed to me. Colin had gone into his shell again and silently refused the gesture from the black man. I knew his biggest worry at that stage was being recognized by any farmers who might happen to pass us on the road. But thankfully for him, darkness was closing in.

We were on the main road to Umvukwes, or Mvurwi as it was now called. I asked the constable where we were going.

"Bindura. Mashonaland North HQ," he said lightly, dragging noisily on his cigarette, now down to the butt. I could smell the filter burning.

"What are they going to do with us?"

He shrugged nonchalantly. "Aiee, I don't know. I am not too very much familiar with the case."

"But surely they have to charge us?"

"Not really," he rolled the 'r'. "Only after twenty days. There is still the Emergency Powers in position."

Bindura was Colin's original home turf, a mining town in the middle of the fertile Mazoe Valley with some of the most productive farms in the country. It was cotton country. Before moving to Mzarabani he'd farmed in the area, towards the neighbouring town of Shamva.

Near the Glendale turn-off, the constable pulled out his last cigarette, and apologized to me that he only had one left, but if I didn't mind we could share it. I didn't mind. It might be the last cigarette for a while.

The Land Rover was winding its way along the dimly lit, deserted streets of Bindura, lined with Asian bazaars and Greek cafés. The last time I'd been here had been in the army, during the war, when the town was a vibrant, bustling mass of soldiers and army lorries. Now I was back … as a prisoner.

We drove through the gates of the police station. I'd been here before during the war and recognized the low, red-roofed, colonial structure, with the grey-enamel-painted walls, just like any other government institution in the country.

The vehicle pulled up outside the charge office and we alighted. Inside, a yawning sergeant signed us in and took our watches, Colin's belt and pen and a few loose coins—for safe keeping. Prisoners weren't allowed these sorts of things. If we'd been wearing shoes they would have taken those too—in case we hung ourselves with the laces.

The friendly constable unlocked the handcuffs and put them in his pocket, property of Zimbabwe Republic Police, Centenary. He smiled at me and said, "Ciao, my friend."

I smiled weakly at him and said 'ciao' back. Then he and the inspector were gone, their charges safely off their hands.

The duty sergeant hollered out the back and a sleepy constable shuffled into the room. He had an old, single-shot Greener shotgun slung over his tatty greatcoat. The sergeant said something in Shona. I recognized the word 'cell', said in English.

The constable nodded to us. "You come with me."

We followed him outside, along a gravel path, lined with whitewashed bricks, angularly embedded in an attempted chevron pattern. Arriving at a fenced-off area, with the cell block like a row of stables visible in the background, he extracted a large bunch of keys and unlocked the padlock. The diamond-mesh fence was interlaced with barbed wire, woven in among the mesh, with three strands strung on top, facing outwards at forty-five degrees. Apart from the tower lights glaring at each corner of the compound, the cell block was in darkness. The gravel was painful underfoot as he led us to a cell door. Using a torch, he pulled out another large set of keys and dragged open the steel door. It was about a foot thick, with a small, unglazed, barred hatch about six inches by six.

There was a tree in the compound yard. One lone gum tree. The gravel was littered with leaves. The constable stood at the door and ushered us in. With a cursory flash of his torch across the interior of the cell, he grunted and slammed the door shut, his job done.

"Hey!" I shouted. "What about some lights?"

There was a grunt. "No lights."

There was a rattle of keys outside, then quiet. There was an overpowering stench of faeces and urine. I could hear Colin's breathing, echoing in the confined space—short, agitated breaths. We stood like that, stock still, for several moments, unable to comprehend. I closed my eyes tightly. It was an old trick I'd taught myself in the army—to get accustomed to the darkness—for when you opened your eyes it would seem you'd been in the darkness for a lot longer than you actually had. It worked.

I opened my eyes and could vaguely make out the boxed perspective of the cell. It appeared to be about twenty feet by ten, and about twelve feet high. The cement walls and concrete ceiling were unpainted. I reached out a hand and brushed against Colin's shirt.

"Sorry. Is that you, Colin?"

"Who'n the hell d'you think it is?" he said sourly. He hadn't spoken in over an hour.

I laughed feebly, trying to make light of it all. "Well, at least we've got some privacy. Thank God there's no one else in here."

I shuffled around the cell, afraid I might bump into something. My foot scuffed against something on the floor. I bent down. It was a threadbare, government-issue blanket. I picked it up and gagged. It stank and clearly hadn't been washed in years, or ever. I tossed it on the floor, out the way, and shuffled to the far end of the cell. The cement floors were cold and smoothly polished. There was another small window at ceiling height. A faint shaft of light shone in and that's when I noticed the toilet. It was a galvanized-lined hole in the floor. It was almost full to the brim with human waste—encrusted shit. I retched violently and stumbled back.

"Jesus Christ!" Colin whispered. "They're fucking animals. I've fucking had it!"

"Doesn't look like it's been flushed for weeks," I stated, the bile rising in my throat. I fumbled against the walls, trying to find a chain or something that would flush the filth away. There was nothing. "They must flush it from outside."

"GUARD!" Colin's angry bellow boomed through the darkness. I got a fright. "GUARD! Please can you come and flush this bloody toilet!"

Nothing—just the cold wind whistling eerily through the gum tree in the yard. I sat down against the wall, hugging my knees to my chest. I was shivering. A headache was throbbing in my brain. My resolve was waning and I felt an uncontrollable impulse to cry. But I couldn't—not in front of Colin. I had to be strong. Well, what could they do to me, huh? Kill me, huh? I'd been in worse situations, deathly situations. At least here, I was alive. That was something, no?

Colin was still shouting. He would shout and shout until someone came. For now, it was his life's only purpose. It became mechanical.

"GUARD!"

"GUARD!"

"GUARD!"

Standing ramrod-straight at the little window of the cell door, he'd got the timing down pat—six seconds between each shout, each yell identical in intonation, timbre and volume.

Some while later, an hour, perhaps two or three, we heard the crunch of boots on the gravel. A man came up to the little window.

"*Iwe!* Hey! Why this bruddy-fuckeenie noise?" a voice barked.

Colin adopted a tone of sarcastic politeness, asking that someone please flush the toilet outside.

The voice outside *tsked* and clicked, annoyed. The voice ignored the request and faded with a diminishing cruch of boots on gravel. "Too much bruddy-fuckeenie noise. You shut up! *Wazinzwa?* Understand?"

"GUARD!" Colin shouted after the man. "GUARD!"

I closed my eyes and tried to sleep. Colin was still shouting. It was bitterly cold. I couldn't sleep, but my body ached with exhaustion. My mind was numb with emptiness—so lonely, so hopeless … so desolate. And still Colin was shouting.

"GUARD!"

I woke at dawn, having barely slept. I took in my surroundings in the grey cold of a winter's morning. It was real. I hadn't been dreaming. Colin was lying, stretched out on his back against the wall, snoring loudly. Glancing over at the corner, I saw the toilet, the black crud of half-dry shit spattered and smeared up the walls and across the floor. Using the wall as a crutch, I levered myself upright. The cold was in my bones, my flesh like ice.

I made my way over to the toilet and took a piss, the hot, yellow urine sizzling and steaming as it splashed against the shit. Colin stirred, moaning softly. He sat up. His hair was awry, his eye sockets black and hollow. He looked at me without greeting, without expression. He stood up and urinated noisily into the galvanized hole. We wandered silently around the cell, looking at the illegible graffiti gouged in the cement. Then, for a very long time, Colin stood at the cell door, staring vacantly out the hatch.

In time, we heard the crunch of boots on gravel, the rattle of keys in the door and it swung open.

A constable placed a tray outside the door on the gravel. "Breakfast," he said. "You come out. In thirty minutes, I close." He turned and, unlocking the compound gate, let himself out. He re-locked the gate and sat on a rock, his shotgun across his knees, rubbing and cupping his hands, breathing hot breath on them. He took no further interest in us.

I regarded the tray. Two battered tin dishes of watery mielie meal porridge, two battered aluminium spoons and two battered enamel mugs of weak, warm, insipid tea. I squatted on my haunches and gulped at the porridge. It was tasteless, but it was something. I gulped at the tea. It was sweet, which was okay. I was craving for a cigarette.

Colin was wandering about the yard, occasionally stooping and picking up leaves from the ground.

"What are you doing?" I called. "Aren't you going to eat?"

He grunted. "Eucalyptus leaves. Rub them in your clothes and in your skin. Might stop the stench."

"Good idea."

So, this became our routine for the next two weeks. Thirty minutes outside in the morning, thirty minutes at midday and thirty minutes in the evening. Lunch was a bowl of watery soup, butterless bread and tea. Supper was a bowl of *sadza* (maize meal) and gravy, with a rare lump of meat ... and tea.

I started counting the days, scratching notches on the wall with a sharp piece of gravel. Really corny—like the Count of Monte Cristo, or Spook in *The Wizard of Id*. But I did. And every day, three times a day, Colin went on his eucalyptus-leaf safari, bundling handfuls in to the cell, scattering them all over the floor, around the toilet. One day, a guard confided that the toilet flush was broken. The member-in-charge had put in a requisition to the Department of Works several months before for it to be repaired, but they were still waiting.

I asked the same guard whether we could make a phone call. Wasn't that a prisoner's right? Like they did in *Starsky and Hutch* and *Hill Street Blues*? He said he'd see what he could do, but he never came back to us. Perhaps he was posted off elsewhere. The new guard didn't talk to us.

A white lawyer from Harare came to see us one morning. He was wearing a navy blue pin-stripe suit and looked extremely uncomfortable and out of place as the guard let him in the cell. I knew him vaguely. He didn't shake hands with us, his distaste clear. He said my parents, who in turn had been contacted by my wife and mother-in-law, had contacted him.

"Have a seat," I said, jokingly.

The attempted humour was disregarded and the lawyer stood, ill at ease. He really didn't want to be there. I sat, unmoving, on the floor in my corner. Colin was standing, also distinctly ill at ease. This was the hardest part for him—the humiliation, the loss of dignity, particularly in front of another white man, another middle-aged, middle-class, upstanding citizen.

The lawyer had no good news for us. He understood that Police Bindura were waiting for a directive from Police General Headquarters in Harare. Apparently PGHQ were in a dither whether to charge us under the Firearms Act or the Law and Order (Maintenance) Act. The latter carried a mandatory five-year sentence. Apparently no one at PGHQ was prepared to make what was clearly a political decision.

"Well, not a lot's changed since the old Rhodesian days, has it?" My sarcasm was also disregarded. I could see the lawyer just wanted to be out of there as soon as he could.

"So, how long can they hold us?" Colin asked. "Surely they have to remand us?"

Not necessarily, was the lawyer's reply, but take it from him he was going "to move heaven and earth" to sort this little lot out. I didn't take it from him, which was just as well, for we never saw him or heard from him again.

A white Special Branch policeman came to see us. Although based at Bindura he had been on leave at the time. I liked him. He was a north-country Englishman, no bullshit. He wore only safari suits, with his immaculately combed, shiny hair curled over the collar. He'd adopted the Rhodie trait of carrying a comb slipped squarely into the top of a long sock. His name was something like Eddie or Norm.

He was almost apologetic and assured us that, had he been around at the time of our arrest, we would have been out long ago and this nonsense would have been squashed. Unfortunately, the local magistrate, who also happened to be white, was on leave in South Africa and was only due back in a week or so. The priority was to get a remand, hopefully out of custody. It seemed that had this magistrate been around then this too would have been a formality.

"Look, what I can do is get you across to Umvukwes. Court's in session tomorrow. It's a black magistrate, but he's okay, good guy," he said earnestly. "If you're prepared to take the chance, I think I can swing it to get a remand hearing for you."

Colin was sceptical. "Well, what if we get remanded *in* custody?"

"That's the chance we have to take. If, and I stress *if* that happens—very unlikely, mind you—then they'll send you back here to await trial."

"And how long will that take?"

Eddie (or Norm) smiled without humour. "Anything from a week to a year. But I know the Bindura beak and I'll get him to fit you in pronto. So, worst case, they'll send you back here, remanded in custody. Best case, you'll be remanded out of custody, until they formally charge you."

"Does 'remanded out of custody' mean we can go home?"

"Yes."

I looked at Colin and he looked at me. I nodded to him.

"Okay, Eddie, we'll take our chances," Colin said. "One thing … would you do us a favour? Could you give my son Iain a ring and ask him to get round to Central Firearms Registry in Harare and try'n get back my gun licences? And then tell him to get to the Umvukwes courtroom ASAP tomorrow."

Eddie (or Norm) nodded. "Sure. I'll try my best. Give me his number."

The Special Branch man stood up off his haunches and patted Colin on the back. "Don't worry. We'll get this bullshit sorted out."

"Thanks, Eddie. We owe you," Colin half-smiled.

The following morning, bright and early, the duty sergeant came to the cell and, having handcuffed and put us in leg-irons, escorted us to a waiting Land Rover. We shuffled uncomfortably up the gravel path. I was uncaring. Perhaps freedom was a couple of hours away. Unlike Colin, I didn't suffer from any worries of humiliation or loss of dignity. I'd been through similar before in the army when we'd been reduced to nothing. I'd also suffered the indignity of driving through Bulawayo in handcuffs and leg-irons in a Military Police Land Rover, under armed guard, on my way to Detention Barracks, for the heinous crime of an accidental discharge (of a weeporn). From kindergarten to adulthood, Southern Rhodesia to Rhodesia to Zimbabwe–Rhodesia and finally to Zimbabwe—they were all the same when it came to humiliation—countries of fear and oppression, perpetuated with Stalinist laws such as the Emergency Powers Act and the Law and Order (Maintenance) Act. I'd fought for two of those countries. Now here I was a victim of those very same laws, conveniently manipulated by the last.

We arrived at Umvukwes after a short forty-five-minute journey. It was good to get out into the open, into the fresh air of a sunny winter's day. It was another world—passing farmers and their wives on the road, the rich, green crops of wheat in the lands and the lumbering trucks with their loads of cotton bales off to the gin. The Land Rover pulled up under some *msasa* trees, their leaves ochre and yellow and brown, rich autumnal colours. Court was in session and we were told to wait in the Land Rover.

Colin anxiously scanned the scattered cars in the dusty car park for Iain's beaten-up Land Rover. No sign.

"Shit! I wonder if he got the message from Eddie. Those licences might save our hides."

Our turn came and still no sign of Iain. Colin looked as if he'd aged ten years. His lips were dry and bloodless. We were led to the dock in the bright, airy courtroom—more like a classroom. The black magistrate peered over his spectacles as we came in, an eyebrow faintly raised at the sight of the handcuffs and leg-irons. He was wearing a black cloak and looked harassed. The previous case had obviously got up his nose. Some desultory black people sat silently in the gallery, possibly waiting for another case—what could their interest have been in ours?

"Right, get on with it!" the magistrate muttered in a distinctly English manner.

The public prosecutor, a ZRP section officer from Umvukwes, stood up. He'd clearly only been handed the docket a few minutes before. His brow knitted as he read out the charges, struggling with the handwriting.

"Get on with it, man!" the magistrate snapped. "We haven't got all day."

After the longest five minutes of my life, the public prosecutor finished his summation with a strong recommendation that we be remanded in custody until trial. After all, we had been found in possession of weapons of war … we were clearly traitors of the state.

The door of courtroom opened a fraction and I noticed Iain's bearded, toothless face peeping round, wondering whether he was in the right place. In his hand he was clutching a bunch of papers. Colin signalled to his son, urging him to bring the papers to us.

The magistrate banged his gavel on his desk. "Remanded in custody until trial," he stated matter of factly. "What's next, Public Prosecutor?" he queried, at the same time languidly scribbling some notes on a piece of paper.

I was stunned. I could sense Colin's shoulders slumped next to me, beaten. Had Eddie conned us? Was this all pre-arranged?

Iain, half-crouched in a deferential manner, came scurrying through the gallery of wooden benches, unnoticed or ignored by both magistrate and public prosecutor, and breathlessly thrust the papers at Colin. "I got 'em, dad. All the licences."

Colin snatched the licences from his son. "Thanks my boy. Chris," he whispered. "What do we do? Should I say something?"

"Ja! Damned right! Quick, before they take us away."

Colin cleared his throat loudly, as if embarrassed. "Erm ... excuse me, m'lud. Am I allowed to say something ... please? In our defence?"

The magistrate, taken aback, glanced up from his scribblings. "Yes, you may speak. But make it quick."

Colin brandished the bunch of firearm licences in the air. "M'lud, we have been charged with illegally being in possession of weapons of war. But, m'lud, I have here all the firearm licences for these weapons."

The magistrate frowned, confused. "What? Let me see those."

Colin shuffled forward in his chains and handed the papers to the magistrate. The public prosecutor was flicking through his notes. Something was wrong. For a very long time the magistrate studied the documents in front of him.

"Public Prosecutor! Come here!" he snapped. "Do these licences match the weapons on the docket?"

The prosecutor studied the licences, cross-referencing them against the docket. After a few minutes he mumbled, "Yes, m'lud. They are the same ... I don't understand ..."

The magistrate's face was dark with rage, his voice low and menacing as he glared at the section officer. "D'you mean to tell me that the charges on this sheet are incorrect?"

"I ... I ... don't know, m'lud."

"Well, it certainly appears that way. This makes me very, very angry. Do you realize that two innocent men might have gone to prison because of your incompetence? This whole case has been handled with gross ineptitude and I shall not become party to a clear miscarriage of justice." He banged his gavel again. "My previous judgement is reversed. I refuse to remand these men. Now go and prepare your case properly. Next case, please!"

"What does that mean, Colin?" I asked, as our escort led us out. My euphoria had been short-lived. Something was wrong.

"I'm not sure," Colin replied. "From what I can make out we haven't been remanded in *or* out of custody. Back to square one."

And so it was. Back to the cell in Bindura. Nothing had changed. We were being tossed around in the middle of legal no man's land. Eddie (or Norm) was furious and said that on that basis the magistrate should have thrown the case out of court. "But, look. All is not lost. The Bindura magistrate is back in three days from his leave. He's a mate of mine and I'll see if we can't swing it … that he gets to hear your case. We'll have to get you formally charged though. Can't have a trial without charges. And unless PGHQ pull finger, I'm going to try and twist the beak's arm to see if we can't do a Firearms Act number. Okay?"

Colin and I nodded dejectedly. It would never end. I felt sick to my stomach.

Eddie (or Norm) was a good man and the next day came back with some hamburgers and cigarettes. It was like Christmas. I felt light-headed from the cigarettes.

The following day we had more visitors—two black men in civilian clothes, from CIO—the Central Intelligence Organization. I knew the second they were let in to the cell what it was about—the eighteen-inch-long section of rubber hose made that quite clear. They were both slightly overweight. The one with the boyish features wore a perpetual smile. The other, slightly balding, held a revolver loosely in the one hand.

Colin gasped in fear, his breathing fast and shallow. He shrank to the floor and for a second I thought he'd had a heart attack. I was shaking, but hoped it didn't show. Fuck them! I kept telling myself. The two black men were talking to each other in Shona. I could understand some of what they were saying, the gist that this *murungu*, this white man in Special Branch was being too soft, looking after his own … a sellout! And how these stupid uniformed branch *mapolisa* had blown everything by fucking up the docket. Well, perhaps one last crack?

The beatings that followed were done more out of malice than anything else, perhaps a release of frustration. I accepted the blows from the rubber hose with as philosophical an acceptance as I could muster. I tried not to cry out but I suspect I did, all the while attempting to look the baby-faced goon in the eye. I remember the spittle at the corner of his mouth. I remember his spit in my face, warm and smelling of beer. He did not beat me about the face or head but across my body, across my buttocks and the top of my legs, where it wouldn't overtly show.

Colin, still crouched in the corner, shielding his head with his arms, took a barrage of blows and kicks, crying out, screaming in anger and pain.

We were perhaps fortunate. There was no interrogation and it was over in minutes, but as a parting gesture, the two apes dragged Colin by his beard and thrust his face in to shit-filled latrine.

"Now you eat shit, comrade," the one laughed, as he rammed the head down.

And then they were gone, laughing as the door swung shut behind them. I don't know how many hours we lay, motionless on that cold cement floor. My body was stinging with excruciating pain, the bloodless weals now purple and angry. Colin hadn't moved and was lying face down by the toilet, sobbing great, heaving sobs. I dragged myself to my feet and, with the putrid blanket, turned him on to his side and tried to wipe the filth from his face. It was matted in his hair, in his beard, in his eyebrows. It was in his mouth.

Three days later, Eddie announced he had spoken with the magistrate, now back from leave. If we both agreed to plead guilty to contravening the Firearms Act, we'd each be fined "a nominal amount" and it would be finished. Eddie knew something had happened, but Colin, who hadn't spoken a word since the ordeal, kept silent. I too. There was nothing Eddie could do as CIO was the ultimate security organ and to speak out might have put him in a compromising position.

And anyway, what could be done? What was there to do?

I agreed with Eddie. The deadness in Colin's eyes agreed. We would take our chances.

And so, we went before the Bindura magistrate. We both pleaded guilty to contravening the Firearms Act. For a moment, the magistrate nearly blew the gaff by asking whether a bayonet was 'a weapon of war' or simply a knife. The black prosecutor assured him it was an illegal weapon. Colin was fined $400 or six months in prison. I was fined $300 or four months in prison. One of Colin's old Shamva friends, at Eddie's request, was on stand-by with the cash to pay the fine.

At the charge office we paid the money over to the duty sergeant and, with our receipts, watches and other bits and pieces that were returned to us, we walked barefoot to Iain's battered Land Rover waiting in the car park—free men.

Until his death six years later, Colin never once talked about our ordeal. Nor I … until 1999.

A month later, our second child, a girl, was born.

Going nowhere slowly

Lomagundi and Chiredzi: 1982–1988

The mid-eighties and I'd lost track of what was happening in the music world. I knew then I was losing track of my life—if it'd had ever been on track since the war. A new crop of groups and new styles of music were emerging. Good stuff, but I wasn't in at the birth; it was other people's music—Tears for Fears, Wham, Duran Duran, Spandau Ballet, The Cars and The Pointer Sisters. Blondie had gone and a part of me died, pining eternally for Debbie Harry. Genesis still lumbered on but were never quite the same once Peter Gabriel had left. Dire Straights were getting bigger and bigger. But I related to some—Talking Heads and their *Burning down the house* left me breathless. Radical stuff.

I was still waiting for this thing to happen; this thing called a career. After Centenary, I got a job with a canning factory in Rusape. Gibcan was owned by the Gibbs family (of Sir Humphrey fame) though I understood they'd recently sold out to a large corporation. I didn't understand these corporate mergers and buyouts.

Gibcan lasted three months for me. I found Rusape an incredibly depressing little town. There was a large Asian community of traders in town and most of the farmers were Afrikaners. The big dam outside town was fast drying up and with it the renowned bass fishing. An advert appeared in the newspaper. Shell Chemicals were looking for a sales rep (or more accurately, an agronomist). I took a flyer and applied. A Mr. Colin Shade, the agricultural manager at Shell, also took a flyer and hired me in the face of some stiff opposition from everyone else in any hierarchical position, including the managing director.

I was delighted with the job. For the first time in many years, here was someone, Colin Shade, who'd shown a bit of faith in me and what's more he'd put his neck on the block for me. My salary started at $900 a month (double what I was getting at Gibcan), plus company car, plus all the other fringe benefits that go with a multiational company. I was posted to the farming town of Banket to look after the commercial farming area of Lomagundi—from Banket to Karoi, from Chinhoyi to Raffingora, from Trelawney to Mhangura—an area of roughly forty thousand kilometres in extent.

We rented a cottage from some kind farmers in Banket and I started my job with relish. The job was reasonably straightforward—selling agricultural chemicals to mainly white farmers. I soon built up a large client base and found I could get on with people. My farming background, as limited as it was, ensured I had a vague idea what I was talking about. My agricultural knowledge increased in leaps and bounds with Shell's ongoing training courses. The company had some of the finest technical people around in the form of plant pathologists, weed experts and entomologists—all strange terms to me—except 'weed expert'.

Suddenly, there was an element of security in my life—a reasonable salary and bonus (not subject to the vagaries of the weather, shifting tobacco prices and shifty bosses), a car, medical aid, pension and so on. Of course, the economy was anything but secure. Within a few weeks of starting my new job, the country was hit by a chronic fuel shortage—finger trouble in some ministry or other. Queues of cars, miles long, built up at filling stations. I couldn't do my job and found myself drawn to the Banket Country Club. It became a habit, a bad habit. I'd find, in time, when the fuel was back on tap, that I'd be totally on top of my job and by midday I'd have finished my rounds. I'd end up at the club. My friends became the other 'travellers'—the National Foods rep, the insurance salesman, the used-clothes hawker, the Marathon Retreads man—all a lot older than me. The barmen, Enoch and Silas, knew me intimately and would field phone calls for me. They knew my drinking pattern and they knew exactly what food I would order and at what time.

I became proficient at dice, darts, snooker and cards. I was now an alcoholic. I was well aware that I had a drinking problem and had had for many years, but I found alcohol 'loosened' me up. I could communicate with people. I was witty, I was fun. So much so that I hooked up with the Banket Players, the local amateur dramatics group. I thrived and started off as Rolf, the nasty little Nazi postman in *The Sound of Music*. My singing came to the fore and in the next production, an old-time-musical-hall variety concert, I played several larger parts. Then came my 'big break' as tight-jeaned Curly in *Oklahoma*. I convinced myself I was an actor.

At the same time, the creaky PA system I'd bought while at Middle Sàbi was dragged out of storage and I set myself up as a one-man band, doing gigs in Harare at various hotels and bars (some seedier than others), three or four nights a week. The 250-kilometre round trip was a grind, but the music put me on a high that I hadn't experienced for a long time, not since the Clovagalix days with Fraser. The money was good and the 'fans' appreciated me and, in some extreme cases, liked me. I felt good, I felt wanted. Naturally, I couldn't strum a chord or sing a note without at least a couple of joints and half a dozen brandies inside me.

But still, happiness eluded me. My life was empty and it shouldn't have been. I had two beautiful children, growing up fit and strong. I had a wife who loved me (for the moment) and I had a good job. Was it the country? Zimbabwe? A country that was standing still, still not of the real world as I perceived. Was it me—unfulfilled ambition? Must be.

But I found in time that the more I drank, the more morbid I became and very soon the nightmares of the past began. The war was somehow still there. I could never quite get away from it. Not as Rolf, not as Curly, nor as the bar-singer from the Wine Barrel and The Usual Place. Carl Oosterhuizen, my good friend from 3 Commando, committed suicide. Frank Neave, another close friend, died soon after I joined Shell—electrocuted himself on his swimming pool pump. Deliberately? Probably not, but it mattered not. He was dead.

I could never reconcile the fact that there was a whole white population out there who managed to go about their lives and their business like nothing had ever happened. Yes, they moaned and bitched about the government and the farmers moaned and bitched about the poor producer prices. But the war? That was never talked about. It had been compartmentalized and forgotten by the white tribe of Zimbabwe. Whether it was a normal human reaction, obliterating it from the universal consciousness, or whether it was fear—paranoia of the Mugabe government and the evil security police—I don't know. All I know is that I could not come to terms with it.

And then the death and the violence crept back in to my life … insidiously. I wasn't conscious of it at the time, but a series of events in the mid-eighties led me to believe that I'd perversely become some sort of death magnet. Perhaps this was my penance for being alive, for not taking an intermediate 7.62 round in my face, like maybe I should have. At times, I envied Carl and Frank. At times, I considered joining them.

The first incident happened late one afternoon as I was travelling to Karoi. I had a farmers' field day to attend the next day and was going to stay overnight with my friend, Monty, our Shell agent. I enjoyed my trips to Karoi—with Monty the ever-effervescent host—and there was always the mouth-watering possibility of bumping into Monty's vivacious assistant who controlled the Shell stock. (Stock-take was something to look forward to with the ethyl di-bromides, methyl bromides and cypermethrins overshadowed with a shroud of frustrated testosterone.)

The road between Chinhoyi and Karoi is undulating and at times winding. Getting stuck behind a truck on its way to Zambia might add an extra thirty minutes or so to the one-hundred-kilometre journey. I don't know what made me glance to my left when I did but I did a double-take. There, forty or fifty metres off the road in the bush was a car, upside down, its wheels still spinning. A young white woman, staggering desperately with a bloodied child in her arms, was making her way towards the main road.

I screeched to a halt and reversed onto the verge. As I opened the door I saw she'd somehow got tangled up in the barbed-wire fence, the barbs tearing at the bare flesh of her arms. Like the child, who was perhaps three or four, she too was drenched in blood. Her hair was matted with blood and sweat and she was clearly in a highly agitated state of shock. I rushed to the fence and, taking the limp form of the child from her, somehow extricated her from the barbs.

I guided her to the car and sat her in the passenger seat, giving her back the little boy to hold. He was still alive, his breathing shallow and weak. His leg was broken and hung limply at an ungainly angle. I jumped in and sped off, in the direction of the Karoi hospital, still another thirty or forty kilometres away. The woman was very grateful and, sobbing, thanked me over and over. It transpired the accident had occurred not two minutes before I happened on the scene. Her husband had been driving and, I suspected, they'd been fighting. During the course of the argument, he'd lost control and the car careened off the road and flipped, rolling several times. The husband was apparently okay but she asked if I could go back and pick him up after I'd dropped them at the hospital. I said I would. Well, there went the prospects of getting stuck into Monty's unrivalled Scotch collection that night.

Her dress had hitched up around her waist. She wasn't wearing pants and I could see her lower body was covered in blood. Well, there went the car seat covers. The boy started whimpering softly and, unconsciously, I accelerated. She begged me to slow down but I didn't. We got to Karoi as it was getting dark and I dropped my charges off at Casualty. It so happened that there was a state-of-the-art ambulance on stand-by, ready to rush the victims off to Harare. The ambulance was sponsored and run by one of those charitable-type organizations—either Lions or Round Table (and a fine job they did too, considering the government health services were fast collapsing). The driver, an officious little man, the type that thrives on drama and feels important, had unfortunately and foolishly lost the keys to the padlock that locked the back doors of the ambulance. Rushing around like a headless chicken, trying to take charge, he asked if anyone had some tools so he could break open the lock (his tools were locked inside). Like the good citizen I was, or aspired to be, I lent him my large screwdriver. Snatching it from me, he started to destroy the lock. I tried to mention that the husband was still at the scene, and perhaps the ambulance could pick him up on the way to Harare. I don't think he realized that I'd been the rescue driver and in no uncertain terms told me to keep out of it.

As it turned out the husband appeared a few minutes later, having hitched a lift shortly after I'd picked up the wife and child. The family was re-united and together climbed in the now opened back of the ambulance. It was satisfying—all's well that ends well. Now I could go and drink Monty's Scotch. I went to the little man sitting behind the wheel of the ambulance, no doubt filing his flight plan to anyone who'd care to listen, and asked for my screwdriver back. His sudden vitriol astounded me.

"Hey!" he snapped. "Just who in the fuck do you think you are? You've been hanging around, pestering us all afternoon. Can't you see we've got an emergency on our hands? And all you can think of is a bloody screwdriver? Unbelievable! Some people! I ask you!"

Totally gobsmacked, I mumbled some sort of grovelling apology and went back to my bloodied car, humiliated. "It's just a screwdriver," I muttered to myself. "Don't make an issue out of it."

I drank my humiliation away at Monty's and related the story. Monty's retort, a big, booming guffaw, was, "Oh, that little prick! Don't worry about him. Here ... have you ever had a Chivas before?"

I heard later that the accident family survived though the little boy never fully recovered. A few months after the accident they got divorced … finally finishing off their argument, I guess.

The following year, Carol's grandparents were murdered. They lived in an old house (that 'Gramps' had himself built several decades before) on the Enterprise Road, just up the hill from Newlands shopping centre. Two black youths had broken in to the house late one night and bludgeoned the old couple insensible, before stealing whatever they could carry away. Gramps, a boxer in his time, had apparently put up a solid fight, but finally succumbed. I understood the grandmother was raped. The couple was left for dead, the beautiful, old Oregon pine floorboards and Persian carpets, soaked through with their blood.

Gramps died the following morning and several months later, after endless surgery, the grandmother, by then crippled and deaf as a result of the brutal attack, also died.

The two youths were caught and hanged.

I was staggered, made worse by the fact that at the very time the grandparents were being assaulted in the early hours of the morning, I had driven past the house, after a drunken evening of music and ribaldry.

In 1986 the company transferred me to Chiredzi. It wasn't a compulsory transfer but I was told that if I accepted the position it would assist with future promotion prospects. I knew that our marriage was faltering, exacerbated by the late nights of music and drinking. Chiredzi might help things, being far away in the Lowveld, over four hundred kilometres south of Harare. The temptations of the city nightlife would simply be out of reach. And promotion? Well, there was a thing. I'd been promoted once in my life—from trooper to lance-corporal. Suppressed ambitions bubbled to the surface. I began to discover what it was like to be ambitious … a feeling I didn't particularly like. Ambition meant trampling over people to get to the top and most (not all) of the people 'on top' at Shell, with the exception of Colin Shade, were ingratiating assholes.

Chiredzi, with a rabid social life which effectively consisted of drinking, wife-swapping and extra-marital affairs, was a 'frontier' community. Set around a vibrant sugarcane industry the town thrived, in spite of the excruciating, debilitating heat. Though, by midday, everyone was indoors and didn't reappear until later in the afternoon when things started to cool down a fraction.

Colin died soon after our arrival in Chiredzi. He had leukemia and was eventually diagnosed by what my grandmother called the 'knife and fork' doctors of the country, when the disease had almost, like Colin, run its course and it was too late. It was dreadful to see him waste away—from the big, jovial, larger-than-life man he'd once been—to the frail, wizened, skeletal form he became.

I found the workload in Chiredzi even simpler than that of Lomagundi. There are very few agrochemicals required for sugarcane, apart from the odd herbicide and they're generally only needed once a year. There was no pressing need to visit the farmers regularly and, at any rate, I saw most of them socially, either in the pub or on the tennis court or cricket field.

So, I began writing down my memories of the war. By suppertime each day I'd bashed out on the little, portable typewriter, pages and pages of horror stories, inspired by a daily bottle of brandy and half a cob of dope. I was a Byron, a Keats, a Shelley, a romantic poet, but instead of opium or laudanum—alcohol and marijuana. Occasionally, clad only in a Mauritian sarong, I'd amble out to the pool and slide in to the tepid waters—the life and world of an 'artist'.

After six months I surprisingly discovered I had a book on my hands and enthusiastically sent a couple of dozen copies of the manuscript to various military publishers around the world. Of course, it was rejected out of hand. Rhodesia was still politically too fresh a pariah to have any meaningful significance in the modern western world. We were unreconstructed racists, bigots and baby-killers.

Eventually, I submitted the manuscript closer to home—to Galago Publishing in South Africa. Surprisingly, a Mr. Peter Stiff was enthusiastic about it and rushed through a contract, which I signed without reading. I was ecstatic. A published author and still only twenty-nine! At last, here was my career beginning to unravel before my eyes. I was needed in Johannesburg, so Mr. Stiff told me, for the launch!

I applied for leave and drove down to Johanesburg, where I was royally entertained by Mr. Stiff. I appeared on the SABC early-morning breakfast programme, *Good Morning South Africa*. I was interviewed 'exclusively' by the *Sunday Times,* who saw me coming a mile off and ate me up and spat me out, the headlines screaming, "Rhodesian killer confesses to atrocities". But it was exciting, invigorating, glamorous stuff and I felt on top of the world.

I came home with an earring in my left ear. Peter Stiff had told me it was "Commie" and Carol told me I looked like a faggot. So I took it out and the whole ear went septic.

At the time, I was unaware that Mr. Stiff was embroiled in an unsavoury legal action in the South African Supreme Court. It appeared that Lieutenant-Colonel Ron Reid-Daly, author of the book, *Selous Scouts: Top Secret War,* was suing Mr. Stiff for plagiarism. The case was to become a landmark case in the legal and publishing world. Reid-Daly won the case and Stiff was forced into liquidation.

I discovered what submitting claims to liquidators was all about. Several months later a cheque arrived in the post from the liquidators for an amount of R157.40. To add insult to injury the cheque was only valid for thirty days and, by the time I received it, it was stale. I should have framed it.

*

Our marriage effectively died in Chiredzi. Fleetwood Mac's *Sweet little lies* was number one on the charts and Carol was pregnant again. A promotion opportunity arose at Shell but I was overlooked. So with a petulant 'fuck-you' attitude I resigned, but with nothing lined up. No point in sticking around in a dead-end job and a dead-end marriage. But I stuck out the marriage for a couple more years after we'd moved to Harare, more or less at the same time as I suffered my first 'nervous breakdown'.

Piano wire

Harare: 1989–1995

A nervous breakdown comes in many guises, but my various bouts affected me uniformly—uncontrolled self-pity brought on by a manic desire for love and acceptance. Invariably it would begin after a long, unbroken period of alcohol and drug excesses, themselves the perceived cure or escape, which merely perpetuated the downward, self-destructive spiral. For many, my friends, they never came out of this spiral and, either by design or accident, are now dead. Perhaps they are the fortunate ones. Some of us never quite have the guts to hit the nadir of the vortex, instead bouncing around near the bottom, wishing and praying that we'd be sucked away into eternal peace. For some, they drag themselves up to the lip of the inverted twister, peep over and then, overwhelmed by the frenetic activity of the real world, allow themselves to slide back down again to repeat the cycle ad infinitum.

But for a few, they stumble clumsily over the precipice and are absorbed in to supposed 'normal' mainstream society. That's what I aspired to, even during my blackest moments. I did not crave wealth, I did not want position—only inner peace, to be able to live with myself.

My breakdowns of 1988/89 were very black. I found myself jumping at a rat's squeak. A dark void—neither the past, the present, nor the future—always accompanied by the never-ending, simpering crying. I sought death but was too weak and afraid to pick up the gun and shoot myself. But perhaps, there was somewhere that faint spark of a will to live, a will not to die.

"Pull yourself together," the people said. "Get a grip. You have responsibilities!"

I tried and found myself sitting in front of innumerable psychologists, psychiatrists, marriage-guidance counsellors and other such professionals. To a man, or a woman, they all prescribed some sort of drug—either Prozac, valium and a variety of other tranquillizers and sleeping pills, and I lapped them up. To a man, or a woman, they all vociferously said I was not an alcoholic—in fact it was normal for a young man, particularly after a war situation, to drink a bit too much. But alcoholic? Nah, not possible, I wasn't in the gutter.

I hungrily accepted their counsel. It was okay to drink, to get blasted.

I sent the family up to Harare and followed a few days later in the 1959 Morris Minor station wagon. I'd forgotten what it was like without a company car. Of course, the car broke down several times on the road. What should have been a four-hour trip turned in to a fifteen-hour odyssey, most of it spent in a dusty workshop in Chivu.

We spent a couple of weeks with friends, before finding a small, rustic cottage to rent in Chisipite. The rental was horrendous, something like $900 a month. But property prices were shooting up, encouraged by an emerging, newly affluent black middle class, but more so by the hordes of 'foreigners' invading the country. Diplomats, aid workers, foreign businessmen—they were all climbing in. Scandinavians, Brits, French, Australians, Americans—they all came, with their Amex cards and buckets of hard currency. We couldn't compete. A residential property (estate-agent-speak for a house) worth $15,000 in 1982 was now selling for $400,000 and upwards.

My Shell pension and leave pay, which I'd cashed in, began to dwindle. I had to find a job. Carol, heavily pregnant again, couldn't work. I considered an agricultural repping job, but the thought of plunging back in to the world of corporate politics was an unsavoury proposition.

That's it ... I would 'free-lance' and be my own boss. Use my talents. Get creative!

So I did, or at least tried to. I took up music again and landed a gig at The Usual Place, the public bar at the Jameson Hotel. A coloured bassman called Henry attached himself to me and for a while we had a nice little duo going. He was very good, particularly at the 'slap and thump' style of bass guitar, which was all the rage at the time, having been popularized by Paul Simon's black South African bass player during the *Gracelands* tour. We also travelled to various country clubs, where we were reasonably well received. It paid the rent.

I asked Henry one day whether we should give ourselves a name, after all we needed to call ourselves *something*, particularly when the clubs wanted to advertise and publicize a gig.

"Ag, I dunno, *ek sê*," quipped Henry. "Not really a hassle. What about 'Chris and the Goffle'?"

'Goffle' is a derogartory term for people of mixed race, or 'coloureds' as they are known in southern Africa. I laughed and actually thought about it but in the end decided against it. The Usual Place had a predominantly coloured clientele and to offend them might have incurred the wrath of Arcadia, the sometimes violent coloured suburb. Definitely not on—I valued my throat. So we stayed nameless. In fact, none of the bands I played with ever had a name.

At this time, Fraser (my old 'muso' mate) and I formed an advertising company, in which we might jointly take advantage of our creative talents. Being very 'in' in the muso world, Fraser was able to organize free studio time through one of his connections. We had one client before we both got bored and threw in the towel. Perhaps the company name was a touch avant-garde for Zimbabwe—The Very Very Good Advertising Company. We secured for the client a prime spot on TV, just before the main eight o'clock evening news. The client wanted us to promote her new boutique, so with a dreadful reproduction of the client's logo and some corny lines such as "the dramatic fusion of art and high fashion" we booked a few weeks' advertising space with ZTV.

The client wanted to know to whom to make out the cheque.

"Oh, just make it out to TVVGAC," I said flippantly, the acronym rolling off my tongue as if I'd been doing it for years and we were RAL Merchant Bank's main client. As the company was as yet unregistered and did not have a bank account, I hadn't considered the problems of trying to bank the cheque. I gave it to Fraser, ever resourceful, who told me to "leave it with me". In a short while, he'd somehow cashed it and handed over my share. Fraser was like that—outrageous, flamboyant and individualistic. He'd walk into a bar and order three hundred brandies and Coke. He'd buy six hundred copies of the *Sunday Times* from the newspaper vendor on the street outside a nightclub on a late-night Saturday.

So that was advertising. What next? Journalism? Why not? Well, I was a writer, wasn't I? I'd become friendly with the editor of a suburban newspaper, a monthly as I recall, known as the *Northern Suburbs News.* Trevor Keeling, newspaperman par excellence and doyen of the stage, and I clicked immediately. I became the paper's sports reporter and found myself interviewing national cricket stars, rugby heroes (there were still one or two around) and various other 'sporting personalities'. I had my own column, 'At the wicket' and felt I had the world at my feet. The down side was covering the less glamorous events, such as the Under 13 schools' rugby festival at Oriel Boys High School.

Trevor asked me to do something on women's hockey. So I went scuttling off in my about-to-die, faded blue VW Beetle with the holes in the floorboards, that I'd bought from a once-close friend at Shell, to a pharmacy in the avenues to meet the national whatever-she-was of Zimbabwe Women's Hockey. I sauntered in to the shop, my slung gook medic's pack now carrying a camera and notepad.

An elderly bat squinted at me suspiciously over cats-eye spectacles, her purple rinse about faded to the same colour as my Beetle.

"Yeeees?" she asked warily. "How may I help you?"

"I'm here from the *Northern Suburbs News*. I wonder if I can have a few minutes of your time to chat about the state of women's hockey in the country?"

The old bat stiffened. "From the press, hey?"

"Yes," I nodded, eager to please. If I'd had a forelock I would have tugged it a lot.

She braced up haughtily, peering over her glasses, down at me. "Well, I don't give interviews to the press." She finished with a sort of 'so-there!' flourish.

"Why not?"

"Because you people distort and twist everything. I'm not discussing it further." Another 'so-there'.

I cringed momentarily at the 'you people'. It sounded so like Ian Smith. I was almost waiting for a 'reiterate'. Like Ian Smith, she also had the same irritating habit of saying 'een' at the end of her intransitive verbs—'discusseen' instead of 'discussing'. I wanted to ask her if she was at all related.

I was stunned. Me? Distort the truth? I really was at a total loss and added to her power play by slumping my shoulders and looking thoroughly dejected.

"Why don't you go'n talk to the softball people? They're always lookeen for free publicity."

"Why not indeed," I finished lamely. I wanted to tell her that I was a good guy, that I had also suffered at the hands of the press (the *Sunday Times* in South Africa) and I'd never say anything untoward about her. Promise. But instead I asked if she had any valium, on the offchance she wouldn't ask for a prescription. A flyer, because she looked at me with utter contempt, confirming her worst fears that I was in fact one of those Commie, *munt*-loving drug addicts that most reporters were. (Even a casual consumer of marijuana is a depraved drug addict to most Rhodies.)

I reported back to Trevor, who muttered some obscenity about hermaphrodites in sport and suggested I go back to the rugger-buggers who were only too keen to talk.

The *Northern News* was good while it lasted, but it was very much part-time work and I needed a regular income. The natural progression into the wonderful world of the media was radio. I decided I wanted to be a cricket commentator, so I phoned up ZBC and asked for the sports editor. I'd always liked his style on ZBC's Saturday afternoon sports programme and felt I could relate. I went round to the Pocket's Hill studios in Borrowdale and met him—a very pleasant black fellow with a wonky eye. He was a delightful man and agreed that yes, the standard of sports commentary in Zimbabwe was woeful and that they were always looking out for new talent. I wanted cricket because I love the sport and knew what I was talking about. But it appeared ZBC had enough cricket commentators for the moment, albeit most of the players couldn't abide them, considering them pompous old farts (that's what had prompted me in the first place). He would put me 'on call' and, if he needed me, would surely contact me, more than likely as a last-minute fill-in.

He asked if I'd be prepared to do football or rugby. Rugby maybe, football no! So I left, sure I'd never hear from him again. No mention had been made of any remuneration though I understood I'd be 'tried out' before any formal arrangement was set in place.

The following Saturday morning the phone rang. It was the wonky-eyed black man from the ZBC. They were desperate for a rugby commentator at a club match at Old Hararians that afternoon. Could I do it? I grabbed the opportunity with both hands and said I'd be there. Maybe this was the foot in the door I was looking for.

Only after I'd put the phone down did I realize the enormity of the task ahead. I'd never spoken on radio, I'd never sat in a commentary box (would I have to wear headphones?) and worse, I was not at all current with Zimbabwean rugby—although I loved the game and had been a passable player in my youth before 'hanging up my boots' in my mid-twenties due to a series of broken ankles and torn ligaments. But, what the hell! I'd handle it. No sweat. Just get stoned on a big, fat joint before the game and the words would flow. After all, I was an entertainer. It was right up my street.

At three oclock that afternoon I presented myself at Old Hararians rugby club and, finishing my big, fat joint in the blue VW in the car park, I swanned off to look for the commentary box. A curtain raiser was in progress with perhaps a total of fifty diehard supporters braving it out in the bitterly cold, winter afternoon wind. I found the commentary box and looked skyward with some trepidation. There, about a hundred feet up a vertical ladder, perched precariously on top of a fragile-looking mast, was an open platform. Not a commentary box, but a commentary platform—a bit like a crow's nest on a man o' war.

I braced myself, zipping up my denim jacket, and began the climb … to stardom. I got to the top and dragged myself onto a hard-back chair, surrounded by all sorts of radio transmission things. A black technician, headphones hanging round his neck, his back turned away from the howling gale, crouched low under various electronic machines and gadgets.

At the commentary table (types trestle) next to me was a big, fat, bearded white man in his late twenties, gorging himself on a revolting hamburger. Tomato sauce had dribbled onto his ginger beard. He put out a greasy hand and introduced himself. Something like Wayne or Zane, or Brett or Rhett. He wasn't overly friendly and asked me whether I'd done any commentating before. When I said no he lost all further interest in what he clearly considered a total greenhorn wanker. He did, however, in between whines about how he'd far rather 'do' soccer, condescendingly toss me a list of the players for the main game. He added I would be handling the running commentary and he would do the analysis bits, coming in with some pearl after a try had been scored or someone had been sent off—or at any other breakdown in play.

Five minutes to go and I frantically started scrutinizing the players' names. I knew none of them. Panic! What if the dope kicked in badly and messed with my mind?

The referee blew the whistle for the start of the game and the dope kicked in and messed with my mind—very badly. It was an unmitigated disaster and within minutes this greenhorn commentator fell apart.

There were long pregnant silences as I frantically scanned the list, trying hopelessly to identify a player. At any one time I was good fifty yards behind the run of play and on one occasion I was still talking about an incident that had happened on the one try-line, while some Carl Lewis-type winger had run the length of the field and scored a try at the other end.

Oh dear! I wanted to crawl into a hole and die but, before I could, the studio quickly switched over to Rufaro Stadium where a more articulate football commentator was doing a proper job. The studio put us back on air and thankfully the fat man took over, without asking. He clearly despised me and wanted nothing more to do with me.

The game came to a close and with it my embryonic commentating career. Fat Man lumbered over the edge of the platform, no doubt bending the rungs of the ladder, and was gone, with a parting shot that he was off to commentate on a basketball game and that I would have to handle the post-match summary.

I swished the tomato-sauce-stained, grease-proofed hamburger packet from the table and calmed down. I would be on air in a few minutes, little realizing that most of ZBC's listeners had long since switched off in disgust. The black technician emerged from his tangle of electronic gear and asked me if we could go home, bro'. I said no, not just yet, my china, and he disappeared back into his hole.

My post-match commentary, unaffected by the hallucinogenic effects of the marijuana that had worn off, was actually not that bad. In fact, it was quite good and I later received a few positive comments to that effect. But the damage was done. Never again would ZBC call me.

My self-esteem plunged to an all-time low, made worse by Fraser's reaction. He thought it the funniest thing he'd heard in years, funnier than the visits to his grandmother in the old Ward 12 mental institution.

I decided that the media was not for me. Fraser was right. I'd screwed up—big time!

So, stone-broke in terms of money and self-respect, I applied for a job as a salesman with a fertilizer company. Back to corporate back-stabbing. Carol successfully gave birth to the third child—a boy—and a fortnight later the landlady of our Chisipite cottage served us notice. Apparently, her daughter was coming back to the country and needed the house.

We found a small house to rent on a farm just outside Harare. It was convenient in terms of my repping job, as I had been given the Enterprise/Arcturus area to service. It was also within reasonable distance of the schools as the two older children were now at primary school. In spite of my reticence the fertilizer company was good to us. Again, there was a measure of security, and with great delight I was able to sell the VW Beetle (at a significant loss). The salary wasn't brilliant but the company assisted with school fees, medical aid and pension. And I was able to continue doing the odd gig—this time for pleasure and pocket money rather than as a living.

I borrowed some money from my mother-in-law and, with what I'd saved from my singing revenues, was able to buy a small plot in the not too untrendy suburb of Glen Lorne. Property prices were still soaring but plot values were reasonably static, the 'blerry foreigners' preferring to buy completed houses. I scanned the newspapers and after a week or two had a short-list of three plots that fitted my price range. I phoned the estate agent, Merv or Johnny or some such—a 'trust-me-I've-been-in-the-business-for-thirty-years'-type and he gave me the address of the plot I was interested in. The address given was "the plot on the corner of Glen Lorne Drive and Water End Close".

With the family piled in to the company Peugeot 504, we sped off to Glen Lorne. We found the plot easily enough. It was beautiful, relatively well treed with attractive *msasas*, but more importantly, relatively level which was unusual for Glen Lorne. The property did eventually slope down towards the boundary on the Mubvinzi River. Paradise!

We made up our minds and the following day I rushed in to town and sought out Merv or Johnny to sign an agreement of sale, which was produced with alacrity. I gave the greaseball a cash deposit and dashed back out to Glen Lorne, busting with landowner pride, to inspect more closely and admire the new property. It was exciting— now the fun bit of deciding where to build the house and what shape it would be and so on.

But along the way, some killjoy had said we should be careful and thoroughly scrutinize the sale agreement. I arrived at the plot and, on the killjoy's advice, began to search for the plot registration number, apparently marked on one of the corners of the property by a small cement cairn. After much searching and beating around the long grass, I eventually found it. Sure enough, the plot number on the cement cairn didn't match that on the sale agreement. I checked and double-checked. Something was wrong. Had I bought the wrong plot?

In short, the answer was yes. I'd actually bought the plot next door, an almost vertical cliff-face. I couldn't believe it and, almost weeping with frustration and anger, I got on the phone to greaseball Merv (or Johnny). I told him the story and that I was cancelling the sale agreement as I had been misled. I didn't say 'deliberately', but it was clear it hadn't happened purely by accident. I was going to go directly to the bank to stop payment on the cheque.

Greaseball was immediately on the defensive, having initially tried to bully his way out of it. He was typical of that white, post-war carpetbagger who thrived on the naïve business climate of a newly independent African country—and fools like me. After much spluttering and an overkill of 'there's been a huge mistake here'-type comments he finally asked if we could come to 'an arrangement'. I eventually calmed down and said I'd go back to the 'real' plot and have another look. I had another look and after much pacing and measuring, decided that, with a bit of levelling and chopping away in to the mountain, I could perhaps make it work. The 'arrangement' was agreed upon—extended terms for the balance, and I let it rest.

A few months later, I made an application to a building society for a mortgage, using the title deeds of the plot as collateral. The application was successful and we were given enough money to build a small, two-bedroomed house, which I did.

It all worked out okay and nine months later we moved in and set about a garden, a series of cunningly engineered terraces that fell away to the Mubvinzi River. It was home, but not for long.

The marriage was fast disintegrating as the new year of 1990 was ushered in.

Again Africa reminded me of her intrinsic capacity for violence and cruelty. We had a break-in and our TV was stolen. We'd had other attempts before, for example, our daughter woken up in the middle of the night by a black hand yanking her duvet off the bed through the open window.

I woke one morning to notice that the front door to the verandah was ajar. And where the TV had sat was now a void. Disbelieving at first, I inspected the scene and outside the front door found a large broken-off *msasa* branch that I assumed had been used as some sort of club to pulverize and prise open the door. I noticed Tex, the Labrador, lying on the lawn, apparently sunning himself and silently chided him for not having kept the intruders out. We didn't have a telephone (I'd applied for one in 1989 and here, ten years later, still hadn't been notified that I'd be getting one), so I climbed in my car and drove to Highlands police station where I made a report, more for insurance purposes than out of any hope the police would actually catch the thieves. Stolen TVs were low on the priority list.

There was little more I could do so I went to work as usual. I got home from work that evening and saw that Tex was still lying in the same position on the lawn. Strange! I went to him and he feebly wagged his tail at me. Bending down, I saw something was wrong. He was lying with his legs outstretched, as stiff as a board, almost as if paralyzed. I patted his back and he winced in pain. Then it dawned on me what had happened—the thieves had smashed his spine with the log and had broken his back.

I called my mother-in-law from her room, as no one else was at home, and together we made a stretcher out of a blanket and as gently as possible carried the poor creature to the car. The vet was very kind, horrified at the senseless brutality, and told us to leave the dog overnight.

After a final night of what must have been sheer agony for Tex, the following morning the vet asked our permission to put him down. So died Tex, our faithful, lovable companion of eight years.

The images of Ish and Jasper came back to haunt me and I sobbed for hours.

A bizarre postscript to this story is that a few years later, when I was recovering from an alcohol-induced suicide attempt in the Michael Gelfand Clinic, I noticed that one of the patients, Celia, had a fourteen-inch Matsui TV in her room. It was my TV. I recognized it from the homemade UHF/VHF switch that a local electrician had inserted when I'd brought the TV back from England a few years before. I surreptitiously studied the TV. There was no doubt. I broached the subject with Celia and asked her where she'd got the TV. She didn't know—apparently her husband had bought it somewhere. I didn't tell her the story and left it at that. I wasn't in a fit state to pursue the matter.

An old school friend visited me from South Africa. He was looking for someone to act as his agent in Zimbabwe for his import/export business, dealing in agricultural commodities and industrial chemicals. He was prepared to grubstake me and I grasped the opportunity. With a flourish I registered a trading company that went by the impressive title of International Promotion and Trading (Zimbabwe) (Private) Limited.

All companies of any stature had logos, did they not? I'd recently done a gig at the Japanese Embassy in Harare and had got chatting to the ambassador, a charming man. We were talking about business and I'd expressed my concern and nervousness at starting up a new venture. He was very encouraging and told me, "Old Japanese saying—'If you want to catch the baby tiger, first you must enter the mother's lair'."

This had a profound impact on me and consequently a baby tiger became the company's logo.

For the first year, more or less as a one-man operation, the business struggled. It was a hand-to-mouth existence, wondering where the rent was going to come from and when the next order might come in. But in the second year, the business took off. I hired staff—sales people, secretaries, a security guard, a tea lady. The orders began to flow and so did the profits. Annual turnover went from $250,000 in the first year to $17 million in the third. My ego increased proportionately as I slid effortlessly into the carpetbagger mode.

*

I walked out of the marriage. It was a painful thing to do and I still remember the day when I mechanically plonked a suitcase of my things into the car. My daughter, aged ten, was wailing in despair, pleading, begging me not to go. Kneeling by the car door, on the tarmac driveway, she clutched at my legs, her face streaked with tears.

Her words still haunt me: "Please don't go, daddy. Please, please. I love you daddy. Don't go."

Guy, a gangly thirteen year old, was silent, his face a mask of desolation and emptiness.

But I went.

I moved into a flat in Avondale and got stuck in to the real business of making money. It continued to pour in and with it a stream of people who wanted a piece of the action—some good, some bad, a few downright evil and many simply incompetent. But they made me feel good. I felt expansive—here I was 'making a difference', but to other people's lives … not mine.

I employed two old army buddies, Trevor Schoultz and Paul Abbott. Trevor had been shot in the head in a contact in 1977, standing at my side. He was still a cripple, mentally and physically. Like Paul, he was still fighting his own demons and it just didn't work out. Paul's demons one day went berserk and, encouraged by several triple vodkas, with baseball bat in hand, he demolished his house and nearly his wife. Every window was smashed, every door torn from its hinges and the next day, Paul's wife came to see me, afraid for her life.

I was the magnanimous tycoon and patronizingly said I'd see what I could do. But there was nothing I could do. I couldn't fight Paul's demons for him. I couldn't even fight my own. So, with heavy heart and fortified by half a bottle of brandy, I fired him. Sometime later I fired Trevor Schoultz. In fact, I ruthlessly fired a lot of people, many of whom were actually 'the good guys'. I conspired and consorted with the evil ones, the insidious carpetbaggers with their separate agendas. Even our office landlord—when he wasn't out loitering on the street picking up black hookers—weasled in to the fray, like a vulture sniffing around a kill. Several cases, varying from unfair and illegal dismissal, to allegations of racism, to financial claims were being heard in the high court at any one time. These coincided with a sudden downturn in the business.

It became a massive juggling act to keep all the balls in the air.

I didn't know how to deal with the mountain of problems facing me. So, instead of confronting them, I decided I'd escape—to Mozambique. There was plenty of new business just waiting to be had by anyone brave enough to hazard the roads and the roaming bandits. The office could take care of itself. Let the others fight things out on their own. Why was I always needed to fix things? I was very resentful.

Thus began my love affair with Mozmbique.

It was an ideal country for a geographical withdrawal from the hurly-burly of office politics and domestic upheaval. Maybe there I'd find my true persona. Mozambique was unlike Zimbabwe in every way imaginable. Not there the insidious ranks of white carpetbaggers, not there the ravages of lawyers and high-court suits, not there looking over your shoulder, waiting for the CIO to pounce. It was a wild frontier of opportunity.

I loved everything about Mozambique—the people, the lawlessness, the Portuguese legacy of siestas, good wine, good prawns and peri-peri chicken. In spite of the bitter wars that the country had endured for the past thirty years, there was still an excitement, an enchantment about the place. In spite of the bloodshed it was truly a multicultural and multiracial society.

Being in the agricultural commodities business, I believed that I was perfectly cut out to do business in Mozambique. I wasn't proved wrong and in short time I'd established strong, working relationships with several multinational estates, supplying them a variety of agricultural inputs.

It was an accepted thing that wine and marijuana were an integral and necessary part of life. I thrived.

I mixed with the ex-pats and I mixed with the locals—black, white and mulatto. I loved them all, rogues apart. People listened, people talked and they sang and danced. I travelled the country in turbo-jet aeroplanes, living the high life.

Once, with a fairly high-powered delegation of Zimbabwean and South African businessmen, we flew down to Vilanculos to investigate the possibilities of setting up a prawn-farming operation. Little did we know that the town had 'closed' for the day, awaiting an official state visit from the president, Joachim Chissano. With virtually the entire population waiting obediently at the little airport to greet the venerable leader, we staggered off the KingAir jet. There were no taxies to be had, so we collared the driver of a battered lorry and paid him a few million meticais to take us to the local hotel.

The hotel was deserted, save a lone barman. There was nothing to be done but drink and await the president's arrival, when hopefully the town would kick back into business mode. And drink we did, interspersed with short visits to the quayside to buy crayfish and prawns from the local fisherman who presumably had been at sea when the rest of the townsfolk was being press-ganged to wait at the airport. We wandered around the hotel, admiring the delightful Portuguese architecture, viewing the derelict fishing craft drawn up on the beach and chatting to the occasional local blithely unaware of Chissano's visit and therefore liable to severe punishment. And then back to the bar.

Evening was drawing near when we decided that not much was going to happen. There would be no business today—we might as well return to Beira. We clambered onto the waiting lorry and weaved our way back to the airport, the KingAir the only aircraft on the apron. The crowds were still there, perhaps two thousand people behind the taped-off barrier, waiting patiently for their leader, who clearly wasn't going to make it today. I assume the barrier had been put in place to prevent the adoring masses from mobbing their venerated president.

As the rest of the businessmen made their way to the aircraft, I approached the barrier and started engaging some of the schoolchildren in conversation with my pidgin mix of Portuguese, English, Afrikaans, French, Shona and red wine. They thought I was funny and giggled delightedly. I warmed to the subject and raised a fist in the air.

"Viva Mozambique!" I said drunkenly.

To my astonishment, the children responded with a "Viva!" Obviously it was ingrained in them.

So I continued, "Viva President Chissano!"

"Viva!" came a more enthusiastic reply.

This was fun, I thought. The children were clearly bored and welcomed the distraction from this silly, drunken white man.

"Viva Chris!" I cried out, passionately.

"Viva Chrees!" echoed the crowd.

"Viva Chris, who should be the president of Mozambique!" I shouted again.

"Viva *Presidente* Chrees!" bellowed two thousand people, fists aloft.

One of the businessmen collared me and dragged me off to the aircraft as two thousand people waved their goodbyes, chanting "Viva Chrees!" and laughing hysterically. I was shoved into a seat and promptly fell asleep, a half-finished bottle of wine dribbling on my jeans.

I met Afonso Dhlakama, the leader of Renamo. He was a very approachable fellow and we laughed a lot together. I presented him with a plan to develop the entire Zambezi Valley from Cahora Bassa down to the coast. I would rehabilitate all the derelict Portuguese sugar estates. He signed and stamped a piece of paper that gave me permission to do so. I lost the document on the way back to Zimbabwe during a drunken spree at the *Piscina* bar in Vila de Manica.

In 1994, I vaguely appreciated that I was losing control—of my business, my life and my sanity. Creditors were closing in and I was forced to start selling off assets. I got involved with a slimy Australian carpetbagger who was importing fish. I put my Glen Lorne house down as collateral with a merchant bank, unbeknown to my estranged family. The Australian didn't pay and the deal went sour. The bank took my house and, literally overnight, my family found themselves out on the street. At the same time, my financial director did a moonlight flit, pursued by Interpol.

I was sinking fast, kept alive by the spliff I'd have every morning in the car on my way in to work—and by the bottle of brandy I kept in my desk at the office. I'd sneak off work around midday on the pretext of a business meeting at Sandro's, the trendy club at the time. And there, I'd talk to anybody who cared to listen, until late in the afternoon, when I'd weave my way back to the office to close up.

There were car accidents and I wrote off my brand-new Toyota Sprinter, doing 160kph over the Samora Machel/Glenara Avenue intersection (witnessed by two ZRP traffic officers). There were breathalyzers, drunken-driving court cases, visits from the CIO and the Drug Squad, bribes, blackmail, threats …

Connelly killed himself on his Suzuki. He was set to accompany me on a trip to Johannesburg. I arrived one Saturday midday to pick him up and was met by a couple of people I didn't know. Hadn't I heard? John had creamed himself on the corner a couple of hours before. Almost had to scrape him up with a shovel.

The bastard! Now I'd have to pay for all the petrol myself. The selfish bastard! I bet he'd done it deliberately.

My life had become one squalid mess. The baby tiger had turned and was now devouring my soul.

There was only one way out.

Amor fati

This book has not been written out of any nihilistic, masochistic blackness. It has not been written as a eulogy to the dead—my dead comrades of the war—Hugh McCall, Mike Chance, Joe Byrne, Brad Little, Pete Garnett, Matt Lamb, Guy Mackenzie, Keith Locke, Tom Small and the dozens of others. Nor has it been written as any kind of tribute to my comrades who have died since the war—Frank Neave, Carl Oosterhuizen, John Coleman, Colin Bruchhausen, Bob Smith, Neville Harding, Malcolm Nicholson, John Connelly ... and the rest. It has been written for me and for my comrades who are still alive. For it is we who still live. Words mean nothing to the dead.

My friends from the war are now scattered over the globe. We have walked divergent but strikingly similar paths during the last twenty years. But there will be forever that special bond between us onetime comrades in arms. Surely that counts for something? Surely that bond is stronger than death? Surely it is something so special that very few people experience?

In 1995, I started the long, hard road out of my own personal hell. It has been an intensely spiritual, and painful, journey and four years later I can now dare look back with a measure of satisfaction, humility and gratitude. I am not well off, but neither am I poor. I am not fit and strong, but neither am I unhealthy. I have people who love me. I have no doubt that I shall face daunting obstacles ahead and I have no doubt that I shall attempt to face them clean and sober. My attitudes are changing—particularly about myself. I am learning that it's okay to love myself a bit. I cannot change the past, but I have a choice whether to live in it or not. I will never forget the past but instead of trying to re-live it, I am attempting to learn from it. A friend in New York, Steve Farrelly-Jackson, recently sent me an email, which I'd like to share:

> I sympathize with your difficulties in writing the new book. Twenty years is a long time, and I would imagine your feelings about the war and the country have, to say the least, become very complex. And it can't be easy looking back into and writing in detail about the darker times of one's life. (I try to forget them!) I wish I could believe that everything does indeed happen for a reason. I'm inclined though to the view that things just happen—either for good or ill—but there's nothing more to it than that. From within our own outlook our lives have a sense of permanence and inviolability that makes us think that when they are breached there must be a reason. But as you yourself will only know too well, having seen lives cut down in the random lottery of war, that sense of permanence is a grand illusion, and in reality life is fragile and all too easily swept aside.
>
> Saying that, though, when you manage to come through bad or wasted times, or overcome personal problems or tragedy, these can themselves come to constitute reasons of a sort— reasons to live your life one way rather than another, reasons for holding some things valuable rather than other things, and—in an important way—reasons for holding one's own life to be uniquely valuable. (Nietzsche was onto something I think with his idea of *amor fati*—learning to love one's fate, instead of bemoaning it, or denying it, or wishing it could be otherwise.) That way you can see that no part of your life is really wasted or valueless. Look at the unique value of what you've been doing in recent years and are doing now, and what it means to other people.

My story is not unique and at times I question its relevance. Perhaps there is none. But perhaps, in it, there might be one small grain of truth in a more universal context that is applicable. If there is, then I have written this for a purpose. I am nothing special—we all have our own demons, our own sinister alter egos, a capacity for murder. There are others still near the bottom of that vortex, there are others who have, still are and undoubtedly will, experience trauma and heartbreak infinitely worse than my humbling experiences. This is the nature of humanity.

I now strive for a small piece of that humanity and I am grateful for what little I have won.

So, just for today, I am alive and I live.

Afterword

It's almost ten years since I wrote this book. It has been an equally painful and humbling experience to revisit the text after such a long time—to actually stand back with an element of detachment and ask myself "Was that me? Did I really do those horrific things?" It's almost like going to the movies and watching a film, but this time it's not a matter of swishing aside the empty popcorn box and shuffling up the aisle into the glare of the outside world.

The past decade has not been an easy time for me, or for those closest to me, I must add. There are many lessons I did not fully comprehend, or learn, first time round. I again lost everything—in my second bankruptcy, this time in South Africa—with the difference being that I am more cognizant of the pain and suffering caused to those around me.

This time round, I would like to believe it's perhaps not so much about 'me'. I can say sorry, but 'sorry' is only a word, at times meaningless—especially to the dead. All I can do is pick myself up, using those inimitable words of Tim Allen in the wonderful movie *Galaxy Quest*, a *Star Trek* spoof —"Never give up; never surrender." It's clichéd, but it has become my mantra. And if I live by this, if I strive to become a better person, then there's a slight chance that in some way I might just be able to make amends.

I still recall the words of my marriage-guidance counsellor in 1988 when I was living in Chiredzi, in the Lowveld of Zimbabwe, when my first marriage was falling apart: "Chris, you're not a very nice person." Of course, at the time I blustered and cursed ("Just who does she bloody well think she is!"), but twenty years down the road, those words are still with me. They have become my challenge and, if I perhaps meet her again one day, I shall know I have succeeded when she might say: "Chris, you're actually okay."

It is easy to blame our leaders, 'the elders', for everything. After all, Ian Smith, P. K. van der Byl, Robert Mugabe, Joshua Nkomo et al— the architects of our little war—are either still alive, or have lived to a ripe old age, in comfort and financial security. The same cannot be said of their foot soldiers. Dead or alive, these are the victims of their policies.

But bitterness, self-pity and blame do not solve anything—they merely negate any positive choices one might have. What Steve Farrelly-Jackson is saying in his discussion on *amor fati*, or learning to live with one's fate, crudely paraphrased by me, is essentially: "Shit happens … so deal with it." Or not.

I moved to South Africa in 1996 to start a new life. This country has been good to me, in spite of the fact that it was here I experienced my second bankruptcy, where all I owned—house, car, everything—was seized by the liquidators.

Starting afresh with nothing but a suitcase of clothes and a positive state of mind can in some ways be refreshing. The past does not disappear but the slate is clean, a mite smudged perhaps, but cleaner. I rationalize that this is all part of my personal journey and that if I do not learn from these experiences then they will surely happen again.

The 'me' I talk about is in fact the ego. For me, this is the true enemy—not Mugabe, Smith or any of their cronies. Smith is dead and Mugabe will die soon. Their passing does not, and will not, make one iota of difference to my quest for personal peace.

Today, I am blessed. I have a most wonderful wife who loves me for what I am—warts and all; I have four delightful children; and I have a job that I love.

A man cannot, and should not, ask for more. I sometimes have to pinch myself and ask myself if this is all for real; why did I get to be so lucky. I don't know the answers or the reasons—I can only thank my god.

Chris Cocks
Johannesburg, 2008

finis

Glossary of terms

AD: accidental discharge (of a weapon)
AFA: African Female Adult
AFJ: African Female Juvenile
AMA: African Male Adult
AMJ: African Male Juvenile
APA: African Purchase Area (Rhodesian Land Tenure Act)
APL: African Purchase Land (Rhodesian Land Tenure Act)
AWOL: absent without leave

baas: boss, master (Afrikaans)
bakkie: pick-up truck (Afrikaans)
bivvy: bivouc, e.g. bivvy up—to set up camp
Blue Job: airman (slang)
bomb-shell: to flee or scatter in all directions (guerrilla dispersal tactic on contact)
braai: barbecue (Afrikaans)
Brown Job: soldier (slang)
BSAP: British South Africa Police (the Rhodesian Police Force)

cadre: guerrilla rank and file
casevac: casualty evacuation
Charlie Tango: Radio-speak for Communist terrorist
Chimurenga: Shona term for the Rhodesian bush/civil war. ZANLA's 'Second War of Liberation', first used in the Mashona Rebellion of 1896, or 'The First War of Liberation'

chopper: helicopter
CO: commanding officer
COIN: counter-insurgency
ComOps: Combined Operations Headquarters
CT: Communist terrorist

dagga: mud (Shona) e.g. pole and *dagga* hut
dagga: marijuana (Afrikaans)
dominee: priest (Afrikaans)
donga: ditch (Afrikaans)
doppie: expended cartridge case (slang)
doro: alcohol, drink (Shona)

ek sê: I say (Afrikaans)

Fireforce: airborne assault group
frag: fragmentation grenade

gandanga: terrorist (Rhodesian slang from the Shona colloquialism)
GC: Ground Coverage (grassroots intelligence-gathering arm of the
   BSAP)
gomo: hill or kopje (Shona)
gook: guerrilla (American military slang from Vietnam)
gwaza: piecework, task (Shona)

HE: high-explosive
hondo: war, conflict (Shona)

int: intelligence
Intaf: Ministry of Internal Affairs (abbreviation)

jesse: thick thorn scrub
JOC: Joint Operations Centre

kak: shit (Afrikaans)

KIA: killed in action

kopje: hill (Afrikaans—pronounced 'copy', also *koppie*)

kraal: African village (South African corruption of the Portuguese *curral* meaning a cattle pen or enclosure)

lemon: term for an aborted or botched call-out/operation (Rhodesian Security Force slang)

loc: location or position

locstat: positional co-ordinates

MAG: *matireurs à gas*—gas-operated, belt-fed section machine gun, manufactured by Fabrique Nationale (FN, Belgium) and used by Rhodesian Security Forces

mapolisa: police (Shona)

meneer: mister (Afrikaans)

mielies: maize cobs (Afrikaans, also mealies)

mombe: cow (Shona)

mtagati: 'bad medicine' (Shona)

mujiba: young civilian guerrilla supporter, the guerrillas' 'eyes and ears' (Shona)

munt, muntu: a black person (Rhodesian slang, from the Shona for 'a man')

murungu: white man (Shona)

NCO: non-commissioned officer

NS: national serviceman

OC: officer commanding

oke: lad, guy (from the Afrikaans *ouen*)

OP: observation post

ops: operations

PATU: Police Anti-Terrorist Unit (BSAP para-military specialist unit)

PF: Patriotic Front (ZANU/ZAPU alliance)

povo: people (Portuguese, and now commonly Shona)

poephol: anus (Afrikaans—lit: poophole)

poes: cunt (Afrikaans)

PRAW: Police Reserve Air Wing

pungwe: a large meeting, a political rally (Shona)

PV: protected village

R&R: Rest & Recreation

RAR Rhodesian African Rifles

RBC: Rhodesian Broadcasting Corporation

RF: Rhodesian Front, white political party headed by Ian Smith

RIC: Rhodesian Intelligence Corps

RLI: Rhodesian Light Infantry

RPG: rocket-propelled grenade

RR: Rhodesia Regiment (white Territorial battalions numbered 1 to 10)

RV: rendezvous

SABC: South African Broadcasting Corporation

SAP: South African Police

SAS: Special Air Service

SB: Special Branch (of the BSAP)

SF: (Rhodesian) Security Forces

sitrep: situation report

SLA: Sabi-Limpopo Authority

stick: four- to six-man unit or battle group (originally from a 'stick' of paratroopers)

take the gap: Rhodesian Security Force expression used to denote a rapid exit from a location

terr: terrorist

TF: Territorial Force

TTL: Tribal Trust Land/s (Rhodesian Land Tenure Act).

UANC: United African National Council, headed by Bishop Abel Muzorewa

UDI: Unilateral Declaration of Independence

veldskoene: rough suede bush shoes (Afrikaans)

vlei: swampy, open grassland (Afrikaans)

WP: white phosphorus

ZANLA: Zimbabwe African National Liberation Army, ZANU's military wing

ZANU: Zimbabwe African National Union, headed by Robert Mugabe

ZAPU: Zimbabwe African People's Union, headed by Joshua Nkomo

ZBC: Zimbabwe Broadcasting Corporation

ZIPRA: Zimbabwe People's Revolutionary Army, ZAPU's military wing

ZNA: Zimbabwe National Army

ZRP: Zimbabwe Republic Police